Praise for

ELECTROBOY

"*Electroboy* is as surreal as life can get, proving that truth is stranger than fiction. Andy Behrman's nightmare anecdotes are addicting."

—Eric Bogosian, author of *Mall*

"The compulsively readable *Electroboy* . . . is the genre's version of an action-thriller. . . . You can almost hear the frantic, thunderous scrape of [Behrman's] pen."

—W

"Without ever sounding self-serving or apologetic, Behrman tells the story of a man utterly at the mercy of his impulses. It's sometimes funny, sometimes horrifying, always fascinating."

—John Taylor,
author of *The Count and the Confession*

"This stark and unsettling memoir mimics the patterns of the manic mind. An astonishing story of uncontrolled desire told by one of the most endearing madmen you'll ever encounter."

—Katie Roiphe,
author of *Still She Haunts Me*

D0851790

ANDY BEHRMAN is a manic depressive who has undergone nineteen electroshock treatments. He has worked as a PR agent and an art dealer. His writing has been featured most recently in *The New York Times Magazine*. A graduate of Wesleyan University, he knows most of the all-night diners and after-hours bars in the major cities across the country. He currently lives mania-free on the Upper West Side of Manhattan. You can reach him at www.electroboy.com.

ELECTROBOY

ELECTROBOY

A Memoir of Mania

Andy Behrman

Random House
Trade Paperbacks
New York

BOCA RATON PUBLIC LIBRARY
BOCA RATON, FLORIDA

2003 Random House Trade Paperback Edition
Copyright © 2002 by Andy Behrman

All rights reserved under International and Pan-American
Copyright Conventions. Published in the United States by
Random House Trade Paperbacks, an imprint of The
Random House Publishing Group, a division of Random
House, Inc., New York, and simultaneously in Canada by
Random House of Canada Limited, Toronto.

RANDOM HOUSE TRADE PAPERBACKS and colophon
are trademarks of Random House, Inc.

This work was originally published in hardcover by
Random House, Inc., in 2002.

Grateful acknowledgment is made to Wixen Music
Publishing, Inc., as agent for Druidcrest Music Ltd. for
permission to reprint an excerpt from "Rose Tint My World"
from *The Rocky Horror Picture Show,* words and music by
Richard O'Brien. Published by Druidcrest Music Ltd. Used by
permission of Wixen Music Publishing, Inc.

Library of Congress Cataloging-in Publication Data
Behrman, Andy.
Electroboy : a memoir of mania / Andy Behrman.
p.   cm.
ISBN 0-8129-6708-9
1. Behrman, Andy—Mental health.   2. Manic-depressive
illness—Patients—Biography.   3. Electroconvulsive therapy.
4. Depression, Mental—Patients—Biography.   I. Title.

RC516.B395 2001
616.89'5'9982—dc21
[B]   2001019282

Random House website address: www.atrandom.com

Printed in the United States of America

4   6   8   9   7   5

Book design by Mercedes Everett

For my mother and father, with love and gratitude

I've got to be strong
And try to hang on
Or else my mind may well snap
And my life will be lived for the thrills

—Dr. Everett Scott
The Rocky Horror Picture Show

Electroboy is a memoir. However, certain names and identifying details have been changed to protect the privacy of individuals whose paths crossed mine at a time in their lives from which they have since moved on.

January 6, 1991.

1. Bleach bathtub, toilet, and sink
2. Make Holocaust documentary
3. Start tofu/tuna diet
4. Work out five days/week
5. Buy new scale
6. Confirm $35,000 wire transfer from Art Collection House
7. Open Munich bank account
8. Open escrow account for rent
9. Mail $20,000 to American Express
10. Bring $2,700 to Dr. Kleinman
11. Submit claims to Blue Cross/Blue Shield
12. Go to Metpath lab for lithium level
13. Pick up lithium and Prozac
14. Buy more Kiehl's Extra Strength Styling Gel
15. Get Lara's psychiatrist's phone #
16. Get Pamela's astrologist's phone #
17. Tanning salon
18. Visit Auschwitz
19. South Beach or Bahamas?
20. Book trip with Dad to Galápagos
21. Make reservations at Chanterelle
22. Write novel and screenplay
23. Read *7 Habits of Highly Effective People*
24. Pick up Liquid-Plumr
25. Buy a dog

Preface

Flying High

In Manhattan, even at 5:00 A.M., it's easy to find someone to talk to if you can't sleep. There's an entire network of actors, writers, bartenders, prostitutes, and drug dealers hanging out in after-hours bars and clubs across the city, waiting to transition from vodka and cocaine to orange juice, pancakes, and eggs. Somewhere in the East Village, guys with names like Edgardo and León sell coke to kids who snort it in unisex bathrooms. In a theater in Times Square, hustlers called Cody and Shane rush into cabs and limos and back to bedrooms and hotel rooms for $150 private shows. At a bar on the Upper East Side, two women laugh loudly—or is the one adjusting her skirt a man? An off-duty bartender, a guy in his late twenties with a healthy tan and curly blond hair, vividly describes to the bartender and a few customers his most recent group-sex scene, a private party where he and his buddies all banged one of the other guys' girlfriends. "We worked her over for more than three hours," he says. He does a shot of tequila and grins. A very thin thirty-five-year-old woman, with long chestnut brown hair, tan skin, and shiny pink lipstick, wearing a tight-fitting dress and strappy high heels, brags about the professional hockey player she fucked the night before. "He's a very well known athlete—he went down on me for more than an hour and then fucked me like I've never been fucked before," she says. I happen to be an art dealer, which someone once told me at a Soho opening was a notch above drug dealer on the career ladder. But tonight I might as well be a prostitute. After quite a few lines of cocaine and more than ten shots of vodka, I find myself trying to sell a Kostabi painting for $3,000 to a minor-league porn star (he tells me he's only done a handful of films). Chad is in his midthirties, big and muscular, with huge hands that envelop the shot glass. The more coke we do, the closer he seems to meeting my asking price. He's in New York hustling for the month and wiring money back to his wife and two kids in Las Vegas. I'm telling him that he can flip the painting for $5,000 in a day because I'm giving him a price that's even lower than wholesale, or he can wait to take it to Christie's and maybe get even more money at auction. He actually seems interested and takes my card. I stash my to-do list in my pocket and buy a kamikaze for each of us and a round of drinks for a group of faceless people across the bar speaking what sounds like a Slavic language, although the bartender, Mike, tells me it's Turkish. But it's nearly dawn and I'm drunk and wired, so my linguistic skills aren't quite there. It's too late to start talking to them about Turkey. Actually, I don't know much about Turkey except what the capital is. But I really want to talk to them and be a part of their group and its momentum, even if it's just to tell them I've heard about Ankara. Time is kind of frozen, and I feel like I'm going to live forever. I fear I'm going to be awake all night and can't imagine my head resting on my pillow. Will I ever sleep again? I don't sleep much—maybe two or three hours a night, sometimes not at all for a day or two at a time—so I end up killing a fair amount of my time hanging out downtown, drinking and doing drugs with my insomniac friends. I like the night. I'm scared that it's going to get light out soon, so I leave these people and journey back to the Upper West Side, which seems as far away as Poughkeepsie. In the cab, I throw my head back. I'm going to force myself to get some sleep and hide from the impending brightness—it's only minutes away.

6:35 A.M.

I'm lying between my chocolate brown, maroon, and hunter green paisley Ralph Lauren sheets wearing Calvin Klein briefs and feeling very un-Lauren, and frantic and guilty for wearing Calvin Klein briefs. I start worrying about whether or not it's acceptable to wear Calvin Klein briefs and sleep with a Ralph Lauren comforter. At last I decide that it's perfectly okay to mix and match. The elastic is irritating me, so I push the briefs down and they get lost in the sheets for a few days. Now I'm totally naked and relieved. Is it okay to sleep alone naked? I won't tell anyone. These sheets are supposed to be comfortable. That's what the saleswoman told me—something about the high thread count. Six hundred. She should recommend sleeping naked to her customers. But the dramatic swirling pattern agitates me. $100,000 split between Dave and me isn't fair. I'm in the mood for French toast. I can't get comfortable, so I get up and put on Abba's "Waterloo," turn on the lights, and start counting $100 bills from a shoe box I keep underneath my bed. Fifteen minutes later I've got $85,000. I double-check it. This time it comes to $83,000. Shit. I'm not going to count it again. I put three 3-inch-thick piles of cash back into the navy blue shoe box with "Ralph Lauren" embossed in gold on it. There's also 25,000 deutsche marks in the box—about $10,000. This is my German reserve, my strudel money. I put it back under the bed. I rubber-band $50,000, bring it into the kitchen, and stack it neatly in the freezer next to some Perdue chicken breasts, an old pint of Ben & Jerry's Chunky Monkey, a frosty bottle of Absolut, some half-empty ice-cube trays, and a bottle of amyl nitrate. It'll be safe here. I'll probably go through it quickly anyhow.

I get back into bed. Dave is a fucking cheat. He doesn't even deserve a dime on this deal. I'd love a bagel. The trucks outside sound like rockets being launched. They carry milk, soda, fruit, and beer. All of this will end up in supermarkets today. I walk back into the kitchen, take an Amstel Light from the refrigerator, and swallow three blue Klonopin and two plain white Ambien to try to knock myself out. I look in the mirror. Five more pounds to go. Legs look good. Big deal. That's a genetic thing. From my balcony, I see a man walking his cocker spaniel. I open the sliding glass door and drop the beer bottle four floors down onto the street. Just see him as a moving target and feel the urge. It doesn't hit him, or his dog, but he looks up and curses. Asshole. I give him a slight nod. Go through the mail. Pay some bills. After twenty minutes I realize that the pills aren't working. I can't get myself to fall asleep. This stuff is crap. Thank God the fucking insurance company foots the bill for this shit and not me. I get into bed and try jerking off to a video, but that doesn't work either. Probably because I'm so fucked-up and exhausted. I'm not in the mood for phone sex either. I throw on a pair of jeans (no briefs) and a black cashmere turtleneck. I've got to get out of my apartment and go somewhere. A diner, another after-hours bar, or for a walk up Madison Avenue. Early-morning window shopping. Fuck it. I pack my passport and prescriptions, a suit, and a dozen rolled-up canvases, then reach into the freezer and grab a rubber-banded wad of money. I feel like I should wear a matching black cashmere mask over my face. I'm stealing from my own freezer. An inside job. I've got an appointment with Dr. Kleinman at 8:30 A.M. Fuck him. He'll get his cash either way. Press for the elevator. Beer in hand. Good morning to the doorman. I'm not worried what he thinks. I hail a taxi. Where to? Kennedy Airport, I guess. I open the window and let the breeze blow on my face as we cross the park. We're picking up speed. Thank God.

9:30 A.M.

There's a flight to Tokyo stopping in Los Angeles, so I buy a ticket with cash. $8,600. Grab a hot dog with ketchup and onions. $3. The plane smells like Dove soap. Everyone in first class was probably showering at the same time this morning. It's a nice smell. Still, something tells me that this is going to be a painfully long flight. Usually it's fourteen hours. Time for "life-jacket follies." I already feel restless, and we haven't been in the air for more than two hours. That must be Ohio down below. The plane is filled with Japanese tourists. On my way to the bathroom I notice a few Madonna look-alikes with bleached blond hair sitting in coach. I squeeze a pimple on the side of my nose, and some pus squirts on the mirror. I leave it. I hate this flight. I really prefer to keep moving, and the layover makes me anxious. I stay on the plane. It's like coming down from a good cocaine high and waiting for the next "crew" to arrive with a supply of new "provisions." But it was the first available flight, and I'm in a rush. Got to get to Tokyo to sell art and make some deals. I've done it tens of times before, but this time I feel strange. Too energetic. I haven't slept in two nights. And none of the medications are calming me down. We're flying near clouds that seem like they're in arm's reach. If I could just stick my tongue out the window and suck one of those amorphous nimbus or cumulus or whatever-Mrs.-Robinson-called-them-in-fourth-grade clouds deeply into my lungs, maybe I could get rid of this feeling. I turn toward the young Japanese woman sitting next to me. *Eigo-o hanashi masu ku?* Yes, I speak English. In fact, she speaks perfect English. Her name is Emiko. Emiko Kawaguchi. River-Mouth. That's a silly name. At least in English. She could be an Indian maybe. Little River-Mouth. That sounds normal. She's wearing a Jewish star around her neck. She could be Jewish, too. I ask. She giggles. She tells me that a Jewish friend gave it to her for Christmas. I tell her I'm Jewish. She gets excited. Don't get so excited, Emiko. She asks me about the skateboard with a skull and crossbones dangling from my left earlobe. I tell her that I'm not in a religious cult or anything and that I recently had it pierced in Milan. I'm an art dealer, I tell her. That sounds strange. She loves Haring. Basquiat? Yes, but not as much. The conversation is painfully staccato. I can't keep this up for eight more hours with Miss Emiko. I want to bail out. I ask the stewardess for a vodka to wash down a Klonopin. There's turbulence. I could do a much better job flying this jet plane than our pilot. I should walk into the cockpit and demand to take control. Ask nicely like my parents taught me. How hard could it be? Don't you just switch on the automatic pilot? But I wouldn't want to go to jail. Emiko looks at the yellow pills in the palm of my hand and giggles with her hand over her mouth.

We're flying at 35,000 feet, and the sun beats down on me through the window. I've slipped into the Land of Stiff Neck and Drool, a warm and sunny place. I'm just about to start kissing and sucking on my ex-girlfriend Allison's breasts when the stewardess bumps into my left shoulder and I abruptly straighten up in my seat. Dream ruined. Is it a dream? Is it day or night? My contact lenses are dry and I'm thirsty. I take two Prozac, two more Klonopin, one lithium, and one Anafranil. I try to squeeze my feet back into my boots, but I think I've gained some weight on this flight. I flip through *Vanity Fair* for the eleventh time. I do not care for Demi Moore. I sample all the scent tabs. Descent. Seat backs in their upright position. I walk off the plane with my carry-on bag and canvases and wait for my luggage at the baggage claim. Then I make my way through customs after my long and rehearsed explanation that I am carrying my own paintings and that I'm an artist. I am. I take a cab to the Akasaka Prince Hotel. I don't know if I'm exhausted or wide awake or hungry or horny. I phone the concierge and ask them to send up extra towels. I take a half-hour shower. I check out the view from the thirty-eighth floor onto Akasaka—tons of bright neon and Tokyo Tower. For a minute I think I can see H&H Bagels in the distance. That must mean I need to get something in my stomach. The last thing I really ate was a hot dog at the airport. God, Manhattan is fourteen hours away. By plane.

Oz

Manic depression is about buying a dozen bottles of Heinz ketchup and all eight bottles of Windex in stock at the Food Emporium on Broadway at 4:00 A.M., flying from Zurich to the Bahamas and back to Zurich in three days to balance the hot and cold weather (my "sweet and sour" theory of bipolar disorder), carrying $20,000 in $100 bills in your shoes into the country on your way back from Tokyo, and picking out the person sitting six seats away at the bar to have sex with only because he or she happens to be sitting there. It's about blips and burps of madness, moments of absolute delusion, bliss, and irrational and dangerous choices made in order to heighten pleasure and excitement and to ensure a sense of control. The symptoms of manic depression come in different strengths and sizes. Most days I need to be as manic as possible to come as close as I can to destruction, to get a real good high—a $25,000 shopping spree, a four-day drug binge, or a trip around the world. Other days a simple high from a shoplifting excursion at Duane Reade for a toothbrush or a bottle of Tylenol is enough. I'll admit it: there's a great deal of pleasure to mental illness, especially to the mania associated with manic depression. It's an emotional state similar to Oz, full of excitement, color, noise, and speed—an overload of sensory stimulation—whereas the sane state of Kansas is plain and simple, black and white, boring and flat. Mania has such a dreamlike quality that often I confuse my manic episodes with dreams I've had. On a spree in San Francisco I shop for French contemporary paintings, which I absolutely love, and have to have on my walls. I spend the next two days in the gallery obsessing over the possible choices. I am a madman negotiating prices with the dealer. I'm in a state of euphoria and panicked about the prices, but I go ahead and buy them anyway, figuring I'll be able to afford them somehow. Two weeks later the paintings arrive, in huge crates, at my apartment in New York. I'm shocked. I really did buy them. I own them now. I could have sworn that weekend was a dream.

Mania is about desperately seeking to live life at a more passionate level, taking second and sometimes third helpings on food, alcohol, drugs, sex, and money, trying to live a whole life in one day. Pure mania is as close to death as I think I have ever come. The euphoria is both pleasurable and frightening. My manic mind teems with rapidly changing ideas and needs; my head is cluttered with vibrant colors, wild images, bizarre thoughts, sharp details, secret codes, symbols, and foreign languages. I want to devour everything—parties, people, magazines, books, music, art, movies, and television. In my most psychotic stages, I imagine myself chewing on sidewalks and buildings, swallowing sunlight and clouds. I want to go to Machu Picchu, Madagascar, Manitoba. Burundi, Berlin, and Boise (Berlin wins—I absolutely need to watch the Wall come down—CNN coverage isn't good enough for me). When things quiet down in the slightest, it's hard to lie in bed knowing that someone is drinking a margarita poolside at a hotel in Miami, driving 100 miles per hour down the Pacific Coast Highway, or fucking at the Royalton Hotel. I have to get out and consume. Those are the nights I might end up hailing a cab to Kennedy Airport and boarding a random flight. Once I found myself in St. Louis, once in Vienna. (It's better to end up in Vienna.) I want to be a chef, a model, an architect, a surgeon, and an astronaut. My mind consumes information at an incredible rate, and I organize this overflow using an intricate system, printing images in my head as I take in the data, laying it out visually in my mind, and later transcribing the images to notes. For example, I can visualize an image of letters, memos, calendars—even portions of dialogue. It's like having a photographic memory, except I am consciously aware of processing the information.

Manic depression, or bipolar disorder, is a disease that crippled me and finally brought me to a halt, a relatively invisible disease that nobody even noticed. Its symptoms are so elusive and easy to misread that seven psychotherapists and psychiatrists misdiagnosed me. Often the manic phase is mild or pleasant and the doctor sees the patient during a down cycle, misdiagnosing the illness and prescribing the wrong medication. One doctor treated me for severe depression with antidepressant medication that drastically increased my mania, turning me into a high-speed action figure. Another believed that I was just under too much pressure and needed to find myself a less stressful work environment. Yet another suggested group therapy as a way to improve my interpersonal skills and to draw me out of my depression. I was so entrenched in the manic-depressive behavior (or was it my personality?) that I was certainly in no place to make a judgment about my own condition. Today I can diagnose my moods and behavior, differentiating between extreme happiness, too much caffeine, and mania.

More than two million Americans suffer from manic depression, usually beginning in adolescence and early adulthood; millions more go undiagnosed. It runs in families and is inherited in many cases, although so far no specific genetic defect associated with the disease has been found. Manic depression is not simply flip-flopping between up and down moods. It's not a creative spirit, and it's certainly not joie de vivre. It's not about being wild and crazy. It's not an advantage. It's not schizophrenia. My euphoric highs were often as frightening as the crashes from them—out-of-control episodes that put my life in jeopardy. Contrary to what most psychiatrists believe, the depression in manic depression is not the same as what unipolar depressives report. My experience with manic depression allowed me very few moments of typical depression, the blues or melancholy. My depressions were tornadolike –fast-paced episodes that brought me into dark rages of terror.

Manic depression for me is like having the most perfect prescription eyeglasses with which to see the world. Everything is precisely outlined. Colors are cartoonlike, and, for that matter, people are cartoon characters. Sounds are crystal clear, and life appears in front of you on an oversized movie screen. I suppose that would make me the director of my own insanity, but I can only wish for that kind of control. In truth, I am removed from reality and have no direct way to connect to it. My actions are random—based on delusional thinking, warped intuition, and animal instinct. When I'm manic, my senses are so heightened, I'm so awake and alert, that my eyelashes fluttering on the pillow sound like thunder.

ELECTROBOY

Chapter 1

Aboard My Spaceship

I could tell you that I had the most unhappy childhood of anyone I know, but that wouldn't be true. I know someone whose mother's boyfriend, in daily alcohol-induced rages, forced him to eat his dinner from a dog-food bowl underneath the kitchen table. True story. Although the torment of my childhood pales dramatically in comparison, there was still a curious misery, one I haven't yet totally deciphered. But the subject of childhood angst is so tedious and commonplace, I'll spare you the specifics and just share the highlights with you.

Actually, I was presented with a rather enviable deal: the Deluxe Male Progeny package. This included an intact set of two relatively sane Jewish parents, a pretty older sister, Nancy, a comfortable split-level house, orthodontics (I removed the braces myself with a pair of pliers after two torturous and humiliating years of hiding my metallic smile), a bright orange ten-speed Schwinn Varsity bicycle, Little League baseball, tennis and indoor swimming (at the local Boys Club), tutoring, Hebrew school, summer camp, a visit to Washington, D.C., and Disneyland, skiing trips, winter breaks to see the grandparents in Florida, a summer in France, and a high school exchange program in Japan. A manicured lawn and well-landscaped property (for which upkeep I was luckily not responsible) skirted our house in Oradell, New Jersey, a picture-perfect suburban town with pretty street names like Laurel Drive and Amaryllis Avenue (and, later, streets named after local boys killed in Vietnam). Oradell was a staunchly Republican and predominantly Christian town (did it matter that we

were Jewish?) eleven miles from the George Washington Bridge—
11.6 miles if you were watching over your dad's shoulder on the
odometer. I pretended our house on Spring Valley Road was my
spaceship and that I, of course, was the commanding astronaut.
At night, when I was about seven or eight, I would press my nose
against the cold glass window and watch the snow falling, feeling
incredibly safe inside our split-level Apollo spaceship. It was warm
and we had plenty of supplies in the kitchen for our mission,
enough milk and Mallomars to last at least through high school.

Curiously, my parents had planned to name me after John
Glenn, the first American astronaut to orbit the earth and whose
Mercury space mission was delayed on January 27, 1962, the day I
was born. My parents figured that naming me after an astronaut
whose mission had been postponed and could have ended in disaster would probably not be the most auspicious decision. Growing up, I naturally assumed they had great expectations for me. I
identified with John Glenn and fantasized about orbiting the earth
or traveling to some distant planet. I remember looking at an old
copy of *Life* magazine that my father had saved, with black-and-
white photographs of Glenn inside the *Friendship 7,* wrapped in a
bulky spacesuit, his eyes just peeking through the glass of the hel-
met covering his crewcut. Here was Glenn, orbiting the earth
three times solo—it echoed how it was to grow up inside my own
suburban spaceship, for eighteen years, isolated and alone.

Life spun very fast on my spaceship. When I was about eight
years old, I sat on my bed at night in the control room, my *National Geographic* map hanging on the wall, monitoring the imaginary controls and counting the cars whizzing by while my parents
and sister slept soundly in their cabins. I would promise myself to
go to bed when fifty cars had passed in either direction. Police cars
counted double. The rare ambulance counted triple. Then I
changed it to one hundred. One hundred fifty. I would keep myself
up all night. This was the beginning of what I began calling the
crazies.

I spent hours imagining what was hidden beneath the striped
carpeting of my control-room floor—great treasures, tons of

money, and classified documents—but I never actually investigated. Instead I vacuumed the carpeting endlessly and opened up the vacuum bag to see how much dust, hair, and junk I could collect, sifting through it for the odd paper clip or coin. I hoarded change, counting and wrapping it methodically in coin wrappers, storing the rolls in a secret box in my desk. I washed my hands at least a dozen times a day. My parents once brought me into the backyard and rubbed my hands in dirt to try to break my obsessive habits. I used to sit by the washing machine and dishwasher and watch them while they were running, opening the lids at different stages to check their progress. Digging huge holes in the backyard and burying things fascinated me; I buried books, food, garbage. My parents encouraged me to play with other children, but mostly I kept to myself. When I did consort with neighborhood kids, I charged them a nickel to visit my house. I was more interested in geography than football and wanted to travel to every country on my *National Geographic* map (I also had a globe with an atlas), swim in every ocean and major body of water, climb every mountain range, and try every native food. I devoured information, obsessed with numbers and statistics, comparing and memorizing them—state and world capitals, population figures, election returns, and stock quotes. Most significant, I cleaned, organized, and polished the control room daily, so that every item was in place and every surface glistened. There were days when I was about thirteen or fourteen when I would be home alone, and I would remove everything from my bedroom, even emptying out the closet, the bookshelves, and the desk drawers, and put it in the hallway. Then I would vacuum and immediately put everything back into place. I remember feeling tremendously cleansed after this ritual. Clearly, I wasn't an ordinary kid. I was obsessive-compulsive and neurotic from the start. Often I was frightened, lonely, and exhausted. From the time I was seven, I felt different, uncomfortable, out of place. Yet there was never a doubt in my mind that I was a special child. I had a heightened sense of self-importance—I felt larger than life, too creative, too smart. My grandiose thinking was reinforced when I was separated from the rest of my class for special instruction in creative writing, reading, and art.

I was fascinated by Mrs. de Lime, my first-grade teacher, a two-hundred-pound woman who wore a tight houndstooth dress that hugged her stomach and rear end, and she was even more curious about me, her "gifted child." I was reading at a fifth-grade level, was extremely verbal, and was interested in exploring the world. I needed the answers, was more interested in what lay underneath and behind things. Thoughts raced through my head, which was crammed with wild ideas and colorful images. I was obsessed with keeping it all in order. One afternoon Mrs. de Lime took me to lunch downtown, which was only a block from school. I had a piece of pizza and a Coke (she had two pieces, maybe three), and I remember other kids from my class looking at us and my feeling ashamed to be seen eating with her. After we ate, she took me to the hardware store and bought all kinds of flower seeds for us to plant on the windowsill of the classroom, our own little project. Over the year she devised other special projects; we explored weights and pulleys, we visited a bank, and she bought me an ant farm. She had me read to the kindergartners. As the first male child, I also filled a unique place in my family. Everybody—my parents, my grandparents, my aunts and uncles—made a huge fuss over me. Somehow I completed the family. With all of this attention came the pressure to achieve and succeed.

When I was in second grade, I was standing on line at the bottom of the stairs waiting for the school bell to ring. A girl named Allison stood at the top of the stairs, her skinny legs clad in a pair of wrinkled white tights, her feet stuffed into a pair of black Mary Janes. I was tremendously curious about her. That night I told my father that I had seen a girl's legs at school that morning. I know now that this was my first certifiable crush, and I held on to this image for quite a while.

My parents met as camp counselors in the Berkshires in 1958. They married soon afterward and had my sister, Nancy, followed by me two years later. My father was a professor of physical education at the City College of New York and later director of athletics. He became the director of Camp Mah-Kee-Nac, a beautiful boys' summer camp on Stockbridge Bowl in Lenox, Massachusetts. This is where I spent my summers. His father, who had died of pneumonia when my father was a teenager, had been an attorney who kept odd work hours and was known to have mood swings and quite a temper. My father worked long days, and I always waited up at night for the headlights of his car to project a pattern on my walls and ceiling as he pulled into the driveway. He had an extraordinary sense of humor and was a pro at crossword puzzles (he used a pen), cleaning, folding laundry, paying bills (I used to watch in amazement as he wrote out each check, marked it off as paid in a special notebook, and did the calculations in his checkbook in pen), doing odd jobs around the house, smoking Chesterfields, and drinking Scotch. As I recall, we were the best of friends and did everything together. My mother thought I should have friends my own age, but other kids didn't interest me. My father played all kinds of games with me—word games, quiz games (I knew the capitals of all fifty states by the time I was six). We went on outings to the hardware store, made repairs around the house together, and invented our own language, which was more of a tonal dialogue, emanating from the throat. My sister spoke it, too. When I was ten he let me drive around parking lots in his VW bug.

My father is also one of the most neurotic and obsessive-compulsive people I've ever met. Each night, before bedtime, he would coach me through hundreds of sit-ups and push-ups in a narrow hallway outside my room. He would hold my ankles and count each time I pulled my elbows to my knees, urging me on to do another. I think my record was once in the four hundreds. He was proud of these physical accomplishments. He was, after all, a professor of physical education. He kept the house spotless. Sometimes he'd get particularly revved up, racing around with the vacuum cleaner in one hand and a trash can in the other. "This place is a disaster," he'd announce, removing vases, ashtrays, and knickknacks from the coffee table so that he could polish it. He'd massage the wood vigorously with Lemon Pledge. When the surface was shining, he'd replace the items exactly where they'd been—he has a photographic memory. He'd move into the kitchen and load the dishwasher, clean the counters and table, scrub the sink, and polish the hardware. Then he'd clean out the refrigerator. I would watch in amazement and feel helpless, cringing as he put the Sunday *New York Times* back together, section by section, making sharp creases at the folds. He relentlessly organized piles of bills and mail. As soon as something dirtied, he was there to clean it. He taught me the "proper way" to fold clothes, shine shoes, wash a car. Watching him shine a pair of shoes was thrilling. He would brush them off, hold them under the light, spit into the polish and rub the cloth into it in circles until he had the perfect amount on it. Then he'd massage the shoe with the polish until it was perfectly covered and lay it on a piece of newspaper to bake. After twenty minutes he would inspect the shoe and buff it with the brush until it shined perfectly.

My mother was the epitome of the suburban housewife, but with a touch of the obsessiveness that marked all in my family. I used to watch her kneeling on the kitchen linoleum, happily scraping out the wax between the tiles. This comforted me because it relaxed her. So did watching her smoke her Winston cigarettes and drinking her coffee-flavored No-Cal soda. She always made certain that my sister and I had everything that we wanted—pulling things off even when times were lean. The product of a broken marriage, she grew up with a single mother whose parents helped support the family. Her father was a liquor salesman who passed on his competitive qualities to her. She went back to complete her college degree in her thirties, as she had dropped out early to marry my father. She passed on her sense of competition to both my sister and me and taught us both to "be tough." It wasn't until she was in her forties that she had the chance to apply her natural skills in business, becoming extremely successful in the field of executive recruitment. My mother didn't give me much space for being different from other kids. I just wanted the freedom to do whatever crazy things I felt like doing—taking apart a telephone and trying to put it back together, connecting a Matchbox car to a wire and plugging it in and getting shocked, baking a frog in the kitchen oven. She was always encouraging me to do what the other kids were doing. One spring night after dinner, when I was about twelve, my father and I were in the backyard throwing a baseball around. It was an instructional session as opposed to a recreational one. "Don't throw it like that," my mother's voice barked. I looked up and saw her head sticking out her bedroom window. Now I had the additional pressure of having two coaches. I held in my rage and kept throwing the ball back to my father as he threw it to me, but not as she wanted me to. She wanted her son to be like everybody else; she wanted him to be a baseball player, not a mad scientist.

But even with their shortcomings, I thought my mother and father were the ideal parents, full of life, witty, attractive, and stylish, and I wanted to be just like them. I didn't envy any of my other friends' parents like I did my own parents. We were a close-knit and a relatively happy family. Nancy and I watched television together at the foot of my parents' bed, and we had spirited political debates at dinnertime. Of course, there was some screaming, fighting, and hair pulling in our house, too, but no more, I imagined, than in the average American home. I often ended up serving as the mediator, the buffer, and the referee. My sister was often the target of my parents' outbursts. My father even kicked her bedroom door in once, which was rather out of character for him. She was dating a boy from "the other side of the tracks," a punk who had no plans to go on to college, and getting C's in all her classes. The more my parents tried to control her, the more she resisted. One evening at dinner she told my parents that she was going to see her boyfriend that night. My mother forbade her to leave the house, and a huge fight ensued. My mother began screaming about what a "lowlife" the boyfriend was as my sister tried to escape the kitchen and climb the stairs to her room. I tried to keep the two apart, but my mother's hostility was so intense, she looked like a heavyweight fighter getting ready to take a swing. Luckily, Nancy escaped to her bedroom. In general, Nancy seemed to run into more of the normal adolescent problems than

I did and screwed up quite a bit. I was the one who followed the rules by the book and entertained and made jokes for my parents and their friends. I developed these defense mechanisms against conflict and gradually took on more responsibility in order to keep things running smoothly within the family.

Growing up in the Jersey suburbs was like playing Color-forms. We all had the requisite vinyl pieces—the house, the yard, the trees, the fence, the lawnmower, the patio, the picnic table, the grill, the mother, the father, the son, the daughter, the golden retriever, the martinis, the hamburgers—you could put them together any way you wanted and make a suburban dream life or fuck everything up by putting the mother on the grill and the golden retriever underneath the lawnmower.

New Jersey is a strange place. It never seemed like we were near the center of anything or were extraordinary in any way, and I longed to be extraordinary. I wanted to do things differently from everybody else, better than anyone else. And I wanted to be famous. Even though we lived eleven miles from the city, it might as well have been Omaha. I longed for the big city, more opportunity and excitement and adventure. Sometimes I'd wonder what it would be like to have to live on the opposite side of my map, in a mud hut in some Third World African nation, and eat grain that had been drop-shipped on the village by the Red Cross. Maybe I was spending too much time reading back issues of *National Geographic* at 4:00 A.M. when I couldn't sleep. Visions of women nursing starving babies, men with bones through their noses, and children with distended bellies filled my mind and kept me up devising plans to save the world. I imagined rescuing all of the starving and homeless people, building enormous feeding centers and shelters for multitudes.

Politically, my family always seemed to be on the wrong side of popular opinion. My parents were liberals who took my sister and me to protests against the Vietnam War and to a McGovern rally in 1972. Toward the end of the war, on a cold and snowy night in December 1974, my mother took my uncle and me to huddle around a bonfire on the lawn of the Episcopal church in town. We held candles and sang Christmas carols with the minister, his wife, and some other people from the church. I was holding my mother's hand, and I remember her tears and the warmth of the fire.

Although my parents encouraged me to get involved in all kinds of after-school activities, school was the main focus of our lives, and in the truest sense of the Jewish tradition, a tremendous emphasis was placed on our academic achievement. In addition to being "the smart one," I felt even more important because I had a slight speech impediment, difficulty with my S's, that got me separated from the rest of the class for one-on-one instruction. I had very little self-control and was loud and liked to incite trouble. My competitive drive forced me into the limelight by the time I reached junior high school, when I became both student council president and yearbook editor, a rare feat for a thirteen-year-old. I worked compulsively and around the clock, a perfectionist who was very accomplished academically and extremely popular. I walked around the halls of River Dell Junior High School with meticulous notebooks and clean book covers. My locker was orderly, supplied with extra notebooks, pencils, and pens. I was the master of rewriting notes into new notebooks and retyping term papers when I found the slightest error. My student council campaign posters featured my superb graphics, painstakingly executed in my basement headquarters. I spent hours drawing my simple election message, "Elect Andy Behrman President," making sure each letter was the same size and perfectly aligned with the next. I went through sheets of colored oak tag and numerous Magic Markers, and ended up with magnificent-looking posters that put my opponent—who had just scrawled her name on some white cardboard—to shame. But inside I was suffering from a combination of anxiety and depression, dogged by uncontrolled obsessive behavior, relentlessly, repetitively cleaning, organizing and aligning objects so that they were symmetrical, constantly washing my hands, counting and checking. Filled with doubt, I needed to touch things repeatedly to count them or check them— pennies in a coin wrapper, a light switch, or the knob on my door. Nobody noticed. It was my secret. When I was sixteen I started pulling out my hair. I have always had a very full head of hair, and one day I noticed, as I was twirling it with my fingers and around a pencil, that I was actually yanking it out by the root, one strand at a time. Sitting in my classroom, listening to my sopho-more English teacher lecture, I would pull hairs off the side of my head, over my right ear; then I'd examine the root and scrape it onto a piece of white paper to study the stain it left. Each time I plucked a hair from my scalp, I would put myself into a deep trance; the excitement was intense, like an orgasm. I often looked around to see if anybody noticed what I was doing. Over a period of a couple of months, during school and late at night when I couldn't sleep, I pulled hair until a four-inch patch of my scalp was bald. Unlike a girl in my class with the same condition, who had to wear a bandanna to cover her baldness, I had enough hair on top to cover the bald patch. The smooth, hairless spot felt pleasurable to touch. My parents thought the bald spot was a dermatological problem, and so did the doctor they took me to see, a top-notch dermatologist at Columbia Presbyterian Hospital, a man nearly in his eighties. I remember driving across the George Washington Bridge thinking how silly this whole thing was because I knew why I was losing hair. The elderly doctor in his white lab coat and white hair examined the naked skin on my head and stared blankly at me. "Son, I don't know what this is," he said. "But I'll give this a try." He swabbed the patch with a solution that burned for hours. It was supposed to promote regrowth. It felt like I was being punished for ever pulling a single hair from my head. I was so frightened by the severity of the treatment that I never touched my hair again and probably replaced this habit with squeezing blackheads. Fifteen years later I learned that I had trichotillo-mania, a disorder in which one pulls hair from the scalp, eyelashes, or eyebrows and often plays with the root, to relieve tension. The act results in tremendous gratification and humiliation.

My weirdness took many forms. I was obsessed with the scuffed soles of celebrity guests' shoes on talk shows and riddled with fantasies of a half brother in Japan (my father had been stationed in Kyoto for two years). To test how long I could with-stand extreme heat, I'd sit inside a car with the windows shut. On beautiful sunny days, I was in the dark basement mixing chemi-cals and powders from my Mr. Wizard chemistry set, hoping that by not following the directions I could create a disaster. My moods swung from happiness and pleasure to sadness and tor-ment, and none of it was predictable. When I was about seven, my father caught me frantically cleaning my record collection with turpentine, and when I was about ten, he watched as I put lightbulbs in the dishwasher. He never yelled. I had no explanation for either act.

Then, when I was about twelve, there was the special kind of crazies. Late one night, I accidentally discovered a huge burst of energy that I could access through my penis. It was tremendous. At first I was sure it was somehow connected to bedwetting. As a young child I had found the sensation of lying in a puddle of my own warm urine, feeling it on my genitals and thighs, to be very stimulating. Later I found out about pornography, coming across a stack of *Penthouse* and *Club* magazines atop my father's closet. *Penthouse* was tame compared with *Club,* which featured pale Brit-ish women, slutty Jackie Collins types, with bright cherry lipstick, big boobs, and garter belts, splayed out on deep velvet couches. I spent many afternoons and evenings studying these images, fil-ing them in my memory and masturbating. I always returned them quickly to his closet when I was done with them, and re-placed them exactly as I had found them. Soon I discovered that I was turned on by just about anything—I guess you could say that I was omnisexual from the very beginning. I was fascinated by looking at my own body in the mirror, at women's bodies, men's bodies, and particularly men's and women's bodies together. I had a recurring fantasy of a young woman in a sunny white bedroom undressing in front of a mirror, admiring her own body, with a stranger, sometimes a cowboy, watching from behind a half-open door. The woman touches her breasts, and finally he walks in and presses his body against her. She takes off his clothes and they lie naked in bed together. I imagine every possible position they can arrange themselves in, and they ultimately have sex. I enjoyed creating fantasies about friends, people I saw in magazines, on television or in the movies, or just strangers in the street. I was obsessed with this private little sex world I could create and keep secret.

Toward the second semester of my senior year I was feeling miserable. On weekends I would sleep into the early afternoons, and I was eating more than usual. I desperately wanted to graduate from high school and get out of the house. My obsessive-compulsive thinking was exhausting me, and I wanted some relief. It distressed me that I couldn't overcome it on my own. I was planning on going to college in the fall, and I suppose I thought a psychologist could provide me with a crash course and whip me into shape before college started. So after dinner one night, sitting around the table, my parents were drinking coffee and I was folding a napkin into the shape of a fan. I told them I had something important to discuss with them. They both perked up. Was I okay? Well, I was fine, but would it be possible for me to make an appointment to see a psychologist? They didn't seem shocked—my mother had seen a psychologist, as did many of my parents' friends—but they were very curious as to why. Is it something that you want to talk about first? I told them I just needed to talk to somebody about some private problems. My mother agreed to get a referral through her psychologist. But they wanted to know more. What was going on? I just said that "I felt weird"—which was a perfect description for how I felt at that moment. And that was enough for me to explain to them for now. My mother drove me to see Dr. Paul Goldman after school one warm spring afternoon. We were both quiet in the car. She adjusted the radio to a Top 40 station, dropped me off, and told me she'd be waiting outside when I was finished. I think she thought I was independent enough to go inside on my own and let me handle the meeting myself. Dr. Goldman was in his thirties, with a big forehead and oily skin. He sat in a big brown leather highback chair. I sat across from him on a smaller version of the chair and tried to compress eighteen years of obsessions, compulsions, anxiety, and depres-

sion into fifty minutes and get $75 worth of answers on the first
visit. He listened intently and said little. Sharing tremendous se-
crets with this man with the big forehead gave me a great sense of
relief. He told me that my behavior was highly neurotic, but he
never diagnosed me or referred me to a psychiatrist, and I never
knew to ask about seeing one. I didn't know about medications.
Drugs like Prozac weren't even available yet. I saw him for six
months, until I went away to college, and we just talked ad nau-
seam about every detail and event of my childhood. I made no
concrete progress in my therapy with him, except that I did start
to trust somebody with my most intimate feelings. My parents
never attended the sessions with me or asked me directly about
what transpired, and they told me that they hoped my visits to Dr.
Goldman were helping me with my problems. I think they saw
him more as a coach, in a positive way, who was going to work out
the kinks and get me in shape for college. And when our sessions
ended in late July, college was only a month away.

Suburban Refugee

The summer after I graduated from high school, I worked as a lifeguard at a nearby pool club. It wasn't the most demanding position; the club was on the Palisades overlooking the Hudson River,
so at least I had an incredible view of Manhattan. I sat high up in
the lifeguard chair in the hot sun, staring at the Empire State
Building, counting down the hours until the big day when my parents would drive me to college and I would finally be emancipated
from suburbia. One day, about halfway through the summer, after
a long shift up in the lifeguard chair, I announced to my twenty-
year-old boss that I was quitting. I had made a snap decision a few
days earlier to have some plastic surgery. I had always been inse-
cure about the size of my misaligned nose (I had broken it when I
slipped on a marble coffee table when I was five) and kids had
often teased me about it. It seemed like a good idea to get it fixed
before I went away to college—to make a clean start with a new
nose and a whole new me. Early diagnosis: narcissistic personality

disorder. But I had the classic deviated-septum alibi. I did some quick research on several doctors at Columbia Presbyterian Hospital and made an appointment for a consultation to see one who had been highly recommended by a family friend. With my parents' hesitant permission, I was admitted to the hospital about a week later. I had taped to my chest a picture from *People* magazine of the nose that I wanted to have superimposed on my face. It belonged to the not very well known actor Hart Bochner, who made his debut in a major role as the macho frat boy in 1979's *Breaking Away*, and was perfectly straight and narrow, coming to a very fine tip. I'm not sure if the doctor thought I was kidding, but he told me that he "understood generally what I was looking for." I spent only two days in the hospital and the actual procedure was painless, but the bruising was a disaster—I looked like I had been beaten up by a street gang. For days I sat inside the house with ice packs on my face and cotton swabs shoved up my nostrils, spitting up blood clots, checking my progress in the mirror, and vowing I'd never do anything this stupid again. But the new and improved nose was an incredible work of art that looked pretty similar to the Hart Bochner model. I no longer saw my nose right in front of my eyes, and it seemed to be in perfect proportion to my face. I didn't have to be obsessed with it anymore. After it was healed, I drove to my friend Allison's house—the same Allison I'd fallen in love with in second grade. She had always been critical of my nose and fantasized about my face with a perfect nose. She was shocked and thought I looked incredibly handsome. Mission accomplished. Now all I had left to do in preparation for college was to pick up some khakis and button-down shirts.

At the end of August, complete with updated nose, I left the tranquil suburbs for the frantic pace of college life in placid Middletown, Connecticut. I ended up at Wesleyan because I didn't get into Harvard, Yale, or Princeton. Of course, I was crushed when I was rejected, but relieved that Wesleyan wanted me. Middletown is on the Connecticut River smack in the middle of nowhere in Connecticut, which is only the most happening part of the country if you happen to be Martha Stewart. The campus was exactly what I imagined a small liberal arts university to look like—old stone buildings covered with ivy, rolling grassy hills, and, of course, a row of fraternity houses. I had been waiting for this for years.

Clark Hall is the oldest dormitory on campus, and during my freshman year I lived there in a single room, attached to a room shared by two grinds who studied around the clock. I was never there—I spent hours in the freshman dining hall or the library meeting people, obsessively learning names and matching them with faces. I saw myself as conducting a political campaign, the year as a chance to prove that my popularity wasn't just a fluke. I was exposed to all types of new stimulants, and I quickly came to crave more and more of them: alcohol, drugs, sex, and staying up all night. After a two-month energy binge in which I met hundreds of people, went to parties, drank, and experimented with drugs, I lapsed into my first real depression. One morning I had a Japanese exam for which I had spent the night studying, but when my alarm clock rang at 8:00 A.M., I went back to sleep and slept through the exam. I couldn't move from my bed. I was paralyzed, exhausted. I stayed there all day. When friends from my hall stopped in to see if everything was okay, I just said that I was feeling under the weather. I had lost my appetite and just wanted to be under the covers. In the morning I was well enough to get some breakfast, but then I returned to bed. This became my new pattern for a month. I missed all of my classes and summoned friends to my bedside by shouting out their names or by telephoning them to come visit me and to bring me food and drink. Getting myself to class was impossible, and I joked with my friends that I could take notes from bed and arrange for take-home exams. I finally decided to seek help from the university's mental health services department.

Dr. Andrea Logan welcomed me into her office and offered me a seat opposite her desk. She was in her thirties, blond, WASPy, and neatly dressed. Her manner was very straightforward. "How can I help you?" she asked. "Well, I'm not exactly sure," I said. I told her that I had seen a therapist before coming to Wesleyan but

I wasn't sure what kind of progress we made. She wanted to take a chronological approach to my history, to learn about my background and family dynamics. But I didn't feel like that was heading in the right direction. "I have current and pressing issues to deal with," I told her, "issues that are interfering with my day-to-day functioning as a college student. I lie in bed for days at a time and can't move." I told her about my drug and alcohol abuse, sleepless nights, poor class attendance, my inability to focus, reckless driving, starving myself, and hyperactivity. She took notes and looked up at me while I spoke. "Well, that's quite a bit you've got going on," she said. "I guess we've got to get you functioning. Are you willing to work with me?" I was struck by her sincerity. "Yeah, I am," I told her. That began our four-year therapist/client relationship.

———

It was a perfectly clear day in October, and Wesleyan was playing Williams at home. I was sitting with a bunch of friends, a few girls and a couple of guys who could really drink, on the grassy hill behind Olin Library watching the game. We were passing around a bottle of vodka and drinking beer from a keg and getting pretty drunk. It was the first time I ever saw anyone with a Walkman. I wanted to have one of my own at that moment. Wesleyan easily defeated Williams, and we celebrated by going out to Peking House, the local Chinese restaurant that was a favorite haunt of ours. After dinner we went to a party at the DKE frat house. At about 1:30 A.M. Stephanie, one of the girls I'd been with all day, invited me to her room to do some coke. When we got there, two other friends, a guy and a girl I knew from a film class, were already sitting on the edge of the bed leaning over a pile of white powder on a mirror on the coffee table, snorting it up into their noses through a straw. We joined them and were up until about 5:00 A.M., spending half our time talking about how great we felt and the other half discussing our chances of finding more coke, since ours was almost gone. I was dripping water into each nostril with my pinky so that the coke would drip down my throat. I loved that numbing feeling. I drove to my bank machine with Stephanie, took out $200, and started cruising around campus in my red Kharmann Ghia looking for someone I knew at a frat house who had told me that night he had some coke to sell. We looked all over, and at 6:00 A.M. we gave up. I dropped Stephanie off, then I headed back to the bank to take out another $300, and drove over to Route 66 and into Manhattan because I needed to keep moving. I was still feeling pretty high, enjoying the drive and listening to the radio. I parked my car near the Port Authority and walked down 42nd Street looking for action, but it wasn't even 8:30 A.M. yet, so I ended up at a diner on Eighth Avenue, drinking cups of coffee to try to keep myself awake and maintain a high. "Do you want something for breakfast?" asked the waitress, a woman in her late sixties with dyed black hair piled atop her head. "Yeah, I'll have two sunny-side-up eggs, hash browns, and rye toast," I told her. I ordered something because I was convinced she thought I was a drug addict who needed to eat because I looked so terrible. I went to the bathroom and pissed out a whole night's worth of beer and cocaine and felt relieved. The coffee did its job; so did the eggs. I was alert and ready to go. I wandered frantically around Times Square, looking in porn shops, electronics stores, and jewelry stores. I didn't know if I was looking for something for myself or a gift for Allison, who was now my girlfriend, or someone else; I was just on a shopping expedition. What did I come here for? But I found a combination pen and light that I liked for $20 so I bought that. I had a hamburger and fries at the same diner where I'd had breakfast in the morning, and the waitress recognized me. "How you feeling this afternoon?" she asked. "Just fine," I answered. After lunch, I had about twenty minutes to kill before the start of a live sex show, which I had seen once before when I was in high school. I picked up a cup of coffee at a deli and walked over toward the theater, where I paid my $8 admission, walked through the turnstile, and found a seat in the first row. The fifty or so seats were plush but worn and shaky, and they surrounded the stage, which was raised a few feet from the floor. By 1:30 P.M., there were about twenty men in the audience. A few were young guys like me, but most were in their fifties and sixties, all carefully spaced apart from one another. I watched a man and woman have sex onstage on a mattress covered with a sheet for thirty minutes. It wasn't a very erotic experience. Probably because they weren't very attractive. He looked a lot like Charles Manson, and she was pale and overweight and in her forties. Afterward I drove uptown to Charivari, where I bought a pair of pants for $250. I decided it was time to drive back to school.

My academic career was particularly uneventful, with the exception of my film classes and filmmaking experiences. I had a particular fondness for one of my film professors, a woman with a keen sense of humor and an astonishing knowledge of film history. My other courses I usually missed, thanks to my altered sleep schedule and inability to remain awake. I relied on the notes of friends and any materials that were handed out in class. Sometimes it felt like I was attending a correspondence school. I knew that I was sabotaging myself and even discussed my problem with the dean, who'd had complaints from my Japanese professor during my sophomore year—the dean warned me to "pull it together." I tried to focus on the course material, but my mind wasn't there, and I eventually dropped the course. The dean encouraged me to keep seeing Dr. Logan.

But the mania was helpful, too. It propelled me forward and (along with NoDoz and caffeine) kept me up for hours on end cramming for exams that I was absolutely unprepared for. It was easy for me to catch up the night before because I had an excellent memory. I wrote term papers the morning before they were due. I was on overdrive and got things done. My grades were mediocre, but I graduated with high honors on the merits of my senior thesis project, a sixteen-minute black-and-white documentary film about filmmaking called *Screentest*, which won the Frank Capra Prize for best film.

The mania also transformed me into an extremely outgoing and sociable character. Fueled by drugs and alcohol, I constantly socialized and partied, avoiding the possibility of sliding into a dreaded depression.

My weekly sessions with Dr. Logan were the one appointment that I never missed, even if I was otherwise glued to my sheets. I became addicted to them. I spent hours with her, free-associating, exploring my dreams, making stick-figure drawings of my family, and sharing anything I could think of in the hopes of coming up with answers to the crazies. But the therapy never actually helped relieve my depression or control my mania. In fact, it was the mania that relieved the depressive states, and I continued to function at a ridiculously manic pace for four years. I don't believe Dr. Logan ever got me to function the way that, in our first session together, she had suggested I could. I've always suspected that she didn't have any understanding of what I later learned was my illness.

June 3, 1984.
The day after the bright blur that was graduation I returned my red satin cap and gown and started the impossible task of packing up four years' worth of accumulated junk: textbooks, tapes, boxes of index cards with brilliant observations about life and my existence, copious notes from my four years of therapy sessions, journals of unanalyzed dreams, and senseless notes I made on scraps of paper when I was stoned. The thought of leaving paradise behind was frightening. Not that I wasn't curious and excited about the next stage. Fame and fortune lay ahead, didn't they? I replayed my dead grandfather's "youth is wasted on the young" lecture in my head all the way home on the Merritt Parkway and cried. A little melodrama to pass the time. I told myself the trip home was only a temporary layover.

Chapter 2

Manhattan Transfer

Driving across the George Washington Bridge into New Jersey—the wrong side of the river again—feels like a visit to the dentist. Mom and Dad greet you as if you've just returned from another galaxy. Our son, the college graduate. Back home to recuperate from four years of intensive orbiting and scientific research. Within an hour, you realize you are living in a mental hospital. Only here, the walls are wallpapered. Frightening floral pattern from another decade. All of it presses down on you. The *National Geographic* map over your bed. The globe on your desk. The stamp album. The *Penthouse* magazines in the exact same place you left them in the closet. Not much goes on in the suburbs when you have no schedule and you've just graduated from college. The next day, you make sunny-side-up eggs and toast at noon, read the obituaries in the *Times* (a disproportionate number of German architects and Hollywood makeup artists from the 1930s), maybe watch some television, and wait until the mailman comes. You get the feeling that your parents wouldn't mind if you stayed home for another twenty-two years. You don't do too much else during your monthlong hiatus except for watching Letterman with your door closed and sleeping late. Each morning you're awakened by phone calls from your parents' friends, congratulating you on your graduation and in the next breath asking you what you're going to do next. Easy answer. Find an apartment in the city.

The funny thing is that I have it all planned out. My life, that is. I am moving to New York to live off my inheritance and make independent films. Actually, it's only about $25,000 my grandfather left me when he died my sophomore year in college. But in June of 1984 it seems like a huge amount of money to me, and somehow I can't imagine it will ever run out. And since it will never run out and nobody is telling me how to spend it, the first order of business, of course, is to buy some cocaine.

In keeping with my "cash shall always flow like water" credo, I start apartment hunting on the Upper West Side. I don't worry about finding a job first. It seems like the right neighborhood for a future yuppie. I don't put much effort into seeing what's out there. After looking at four apartments within a five-block radius with one broker, I take the most dramatic, a large studio at 84th and Broadway. Let there be no pretense of poverty—it's a $1,200-a-month luxury rental, a great space with high ceilings, brick walls, and shiny hardwood floors on which I can do my *Risky Business* routine in my briefs if I am so moved. And I think I am. The building is in a gentrified neighborhood—Columbus Avenue is already a suburban mall choked by bars and restaurants. It doesn't have much of a view—it overlooks a Sony movieplex next door—but at least I can fantasize about a movie of mine opening there one day. It's only four blocks from the notorious Zabar's and H&H Bagels, and across the street from Charivari, where I quickly drop $1,000 on a few pair of pants and a couple of shirts before I even move in, unconcerned that this represents 4 percent of my inheritance. There is so much available to me twenty-four hours a day in my new little neighborhood—and I haven't even ventured below 79th Street or above 86th Street yet. I'm living on my own for the first time, and my parents are keeping their distance; they're not asking too many questions.

I always knew that I would live in New York. After four years at Wesleyan, I was whirling—an adrenaline junkie, used to sleepless nights, drug and alcohol binges, and wandering around campus looking for fun. There was no doubt in my grandiose thinking that this surge of energy would sweep me here, where I'd choose something incredibly risky to do and soon find fame and fortune. Since my film thesis project at Wesleyan had been very successful, winning an award, I have the confidence to undertake making an independent film.

The second order of business is to create the ultimate bachelor pad, due to my need to perpetuate the myth that I am a rich kid and exude a sense of success. I like the idea of spending this chunk of money I have, and I take the project quite seriously, consulting a few magazines and a friend's mother who is a decorator. I envision a "modern country farmhouse on Broadway," replete with pine furniture and such uncountryish details as a sectional couch, a glass-and-metal table, a platform bed, halogen lighting, and the most up-to-the-minute stereo, TV, and VCR— a place where a gentleman farmer will be just as comfortable as an investment banker. I go straight to the seventh floor of Bloomingdale's and within an hour and a half choose a few pieces from one room and mix them with a few from another room, making the salesman very happy. I also pick up a few electronic toys—television, VCR, stereo, answering machine—and pay for everything with cash. Later in the afternoon I buy a set of Stendig chairs and a halogen lamp from George Kovacs, then make a brief stop at the Whitney Museum to pick up a Fairfield Porter mountain-landscape poster. Now all the apartment needs is a wine rack, a case of wine from the liquor store across the street, and some final decorating touches—a couple of baskets and a few pieces of tumbleweed. Maybe I can find tumbleweed downtown or just have a friend pick up some when he passes through Santa Fe.

Determined that the apartment be painted precisely the perfect color, I become involved in an obsessive search for an earth-tone paint I've seen in a magazine layout. I remember that it is called something like Country Paté. Or is it Country Plate? I go crazy trying to track it down. I have visions of having to smear the walls with paté from Zabar's to get a sense of what country paté will look like. Finally I find something close enough, called Mushroom Mountain. I decide not to attempt the job myself and hire Calvin, a professional painter and, I learn later, a professional drinker. Calvin gives me a long list of supplies to get: rollers, brushes, pans, turpentine, and beer. He reeks of alcohol when he greets me at 9:00 A.M. I leave Calvin alone for the whole day and head across the street to the hardware store, where I buy every conceivable houseware object and tool: lightbulbs, extension cords, screwdrivers, a wrench, a power drill, hangers, coat hooks, screws and nails, a tape measure, and vacuum bags, although I don't even have a vacuum cleaner yet. Total cost: $500. Then on to Zabar's, where I spend $1,500 on dishware, glasses, cutlery, knives, pots and pans, pot holders, measuring cups, a Cuisinart, a blender, the wine rack, and other odds and ends for the bachelor gourmet. I am making sure not only that the apartment is well stocked for entertaining but that it has all the accoutrements necessary to be the model apartment. The gratification from my shopping comes from the ability to spend money and actually get something that I find valuable in return, transaction after transaction. The more transactions I can make, the better I feel about myself. When I return to the apartment at the end of the day, Calvin is gone, along with a dozen beers and a pint of gin.

My first night in Manhattan. I can't stay in the apartment because the paint fumes are so bad. My friend Lindley Boegehold, whom I met during a summer job at Macmillan Publishing a few years earlier, and who is a few years older and wiser, takes me out to Teachers Too, a neighborhood restaurant, for my Upper West Side indoctrination. I have the Thai chicken with peanut sauce. We talk about my plans for my film, which I imagine as a comedy set in the suburbs. I tell her I think I'll ride the trend in filmmaking and raise the money independently and make a teenage movie. She is encouraging and believes that I can pull it off. After dinner I walk Lindley home and go back to my apartment. When I walk in and turn on the lights, it feels like a hotel. And it still reeks of paint fumes. There is no blinking red light on my new answering machine. Not a good sign for such a popular guy like me. It feels like the world is crashing down on me because I have no messages. Fuck it. It's only 10:30 P.M., so I decide to take a walk down Broadway and see what's going on. It's a Sunday, so it's pretty quiet on the street. I stop in at Shakespeare's and look at some photography books. I don't know anyone in this store. I feel like I'm in a foreign country. I leave and walk farther down Broadway. It's extremely humid. At 79th Street, a light breeze provides me with some relief, coming up from the Hudson River.

I take the subway four stops and surface at Times Square. It's like a fucking desert. Just with a few thousand more people, and without cactus and sand. The digital thermometer flashes 94 in bright red, but it feels like someone has turned the heat up to 118 degrees. The streets are swarming with pastel-clad tourists from Warrendale, Pennsylvania, and Mansfield, Ohio, wearing baseball caps, eating hot dogs, drinking canned Nestea Iced Tea, and smiling up at all of the neon. Everyone is soaking wet. Flashbulbs bounce off the sweaty, pale faces of fat couples and their chubby progeny, pretzels shoved in their mouths like pacifiers. I could be at a county fair in Kentucky. The number of people on the sidewalks overwhelms me; I feel terribly turned-on and lonely. No messages on the machine, not even a call from Allison. And where were my parents tonight?

In Times Square, beneath the veneer of neon lights, billboards, and theater marquees, is an entire supermarket of sex—porno theaters, live-sex shows, massage parlors, adult video and magazine stores, any kind of sex that money can buy. I've spent my share of time here, and it always feels like I'm on another planet. Planet Fuck. My model apartment is light-years away. I check out the row of porno shops on 42nd Street. I thumb through some magazines—old issues of *Penthouse* and *Oui*, shrink-wrapped packages with three or four hard-core fuck magazines in them for $7.99. Frustrating when they're wrapped up. You never know what you're going to get. It's usually raunchy and kinky stuff. Women putting their triple-D tits in their mouths. Scrawny men spanking fat women wearing leather. Not a turn-on to me, but apparently to someone jerking off out there. The soft-core magazines are more my speed. Guys fucking gorgeous models from behind. All kinds of videos. Straight. Gay. Bi. Gang bang. Oriental. Amateur. Maybe I should raise money to make adult films, forget the avant-garde. I browse glass showcases of dildos, vibrators, vacuum pumps, blow-up dolls, lotions and creams. Maybe what I need tonight is a blow-up doll. I could bring her to my aunt and uncle's house in Connecticut for Thanksgiving. I shuffle around the video section and am overcome by the logical thought that everyone in this store is horny like everyone in a restaurant is hungry. I walk out with my discreet brown paper bag, which screams "porn," and go into Howard Johnson's at 46th and Broadway. I sit at a booth and order a clam roll and a chocolate shake. I spot two guys in their early twenties, definitely male strippers, sitting down in the booth behind me. Obviously waiting for their next show at the Gaiety. I'm trying to listen to their conversation, but I can't hear them too well. It sounds like some weird language. It's like being in a hotel room and knowing the people next door are fucking and not being able to see and just hearing some muffled sounds. Except now I can see but can't hear. What's better? To be able to see or to hear? They are laughing hysterically about something. I think they're speaking Portuguese. I follow them out after they pay their bill, and they walk up the stairs into the Gaiety. Perfect butts. I was right. Strippers. Hustlers. I walk down the block to McHale's, sit down at the bar, and order an Amstel Light. I bum a cigarette from a blond girl who, if she isn't a hooker, is badly trying to look like one. She tells me that her name is Tina and that she is from Ohio. I decide that at any given time there are more people from Ohio in New York than there are in Ohio. Tina tells me that her brother is the bartender and that she is waiting for him to get off work. The beer is on her. I thank her. She asks me what I do. I tell her I'm starting at Columbia in the fall. The school, not the country. Little giggle. Her skirt and heels, the beer and the smoke make me nervous. I am anxious for what might happen next. Tina stands up, picks up her purse, and walks into the bathroom. The bartender nicely tells me that he is, in fact, not Tina's brother. I promptly pay for my beer and leave.

I'm not looking for a whore tonight. But I also feel scared about sleeping alone in my apartment. And maybe I'll die from the paint fumes. I'll be the first to die in my graduating class. But

I really just want to get off. I think that'll make things better. At about midnight I walk over to Show World on Eighth Avenue to see what's going on. I'm surprised that there are still lots of semi-clad women hanging out in booths waiting to take dollars from horny guys like me looking to jerk off at this hour. Just walking around topless in heels. Big boobs. Small boobs. Pert ones. Firm ones. Real ones. Fake ones. The place smells like disinfectant, and there is an old Pakistani man mopping cum off the floor. There are some pretty young women with nice bodies and some older, less attractive ones who look like they've been working there for years making money for cigarettes, groceries, and lottery tickets. People's mothers, sisters, and girlfriends. I follow a petite redhead inside a booth, and for $20 she lets me play with her tits for a few minutes. They feel nice. She tells me they're real and smiles. I jerk off and for some reason kiss her forehead gently after I come on the floor. I walk up to Columbus Circle and hail a cab. I make it home in time to see the sun rise over the East River. There are still no messages on the machine.

Smash

Summer in Manhattan. It feels like I am waiting for the next se-mester at Wesleyan to start again. I explore Columbus Avenue, Amsterdam Avenue, and Broadway and make it my business to get to know my bank manager and all of the tellers, the dry cleaner, the owner of the liquor store, the owner of the hardware store (he actually knows me well from my spree—all of the loot still unused), the owner of the stationery store, and the guy at the newsstand. I want to be the mayor of my little five-block neigh-borhood as I had been at the campus of Wesleyan. But this is going to be a tough feat, just from a numbers point of view. I waste hours wandering the streets, talking to neighbors, and walk-ing in the park. I often forget that I have come to New York with the intention of starting an independent film company, which I have decided to call Smash, suggesting not only a huge hit but also a sense of being "out of control." It also has a kind of hip British sound to it, which I like. The type for the stationery and announcements, which I work on for weeks with a graphic designer at his studio in Chelsea, is bold—copperplate—and printed in bright red ink—it really leaps off the page. I'm obsessed with packaging this project and haven't given much thought to exactly what it is I'm about to plunge into. My plan is to raise $250,000 for my first project, a zany comedy in which a family moves to a New Jersey suburb and meets a bunch of wild neighbors. With Jill, a good friend from college who is a film fanatic and an editor at a cable-television magazine, I sit down and start working on a full-length script. We put it together in less than four months. I intend to raise the money from family members, friends, and colleagues of my parents, mostly a group of dentists, doctors, and businessmen. With the help of an attorney who is an alumnus of Wesleyan, I set up a corporation and a limited partnership by the middle of the summer. Then I start lining up people who will talk to me and read the script and listen to my fifteen-minute pitch, stressing the huge teenage audience for the film and the fact that we can shoot it for less than $250,000 and probably make back a few million dollars.

I arrive at the Park Avenue apartment at exactly 7:30 P.M., dressed in pleated khakis and a navy blue polo shirt, carrying a handsome black Porsche briefcase my parents bought me in Italy. I am here to meet the parents of a college friend to discuss the possibility of their investing in my film project. The doorman announces that I have arrived, and the elevator man brings me up to their apartment. I am greeted warmly with hugs and kisses by Mr. and Mrs. Lehman, whom I haven't seen since graduation day at Wesleyan. "You both look healthy and tan," I tell them. They've just returned from Spain. Their son, my friend Todd, is off in Europe on vacation. Their apartment is exquisitely decorated with lots of floral patterns: floral everything. In fact, since I walked in, the Lehmans are becoming floral themselves. I take a seat on the floral couch and pull out a video of my thesis film, an investor's packet, and a press kit, with the name Smash Films emblazoned on it. Mr. and Mrs. Lehman are sitting opposite me on the other couch. "So, what exactly are you up to, Andy?" Mr. Lehman asks me. "I'm making a low-budget film for $250,000, which I expect to return several million dollars," I tell him. "Damn, you've gone out on your own," he says. He seems impressed. "I looked over the limited-partnership agreement you sent me, and everything in it seems fine. I'm just not sure if I'm sold on the idea." "Come- dies targeted at teenagers are the newest trend, and teenagers represent the greatest part of the filmgoing audience," I tell him. "Why not?" says Mrs. Lehman. I explain to Mr. Lehman that the producer is a Wesleyan alum and that once he assembles our crew and we've cast the film, we can probably start shooting in three months. "Will there be any well-known actors in the film?" he asks. "No, but there will after it's released," I respond. They both laugh. There's a pause. "Maybe you need more time to think about it," I tell them. "No, no," Mr. Lehman says. "I've always had a good feeling about you. I'm good for $5,000." Mrs. Lehman walks into another room and returns with a checkbook. She hands it to her husband, who writes the check and signs the forms. "Don't let us down," Mr. Lehman says. "We want an Oscar." I am selling the deal based solely on the success of my college film project—but that simply isn't enough. In time I realize that my ex- pectations are slightly delusional. My investors are only willing to part with small amounts of money, and it seems highly improba- ble that I'll be able to come up with all of the budget in time. After four months my inheritance is gone and I'm dipping into the in- vestors' money to finance my lifestyle. I'm spending it faster than I can raise it. As time passes, I am losing control and feeling more and more paralyzed.

But I go through the motions of working on the project every day—doing related chores and errands, making telephone calls, following up with prospective investors. Somehow I think the money will magically materialize, so I pretend that I'm working twelve- to fourteen-hour days circulating dupes of my college video and the synopsis and prospectus, working with my lawyer and a prospective producer, and hoping to find my angel. Though I'm on the verge of financial disaster, with almost no money in my bank account, I keep courting prospective investors, going to the movies—*Repo Man* and *Star 80*—and out to dinner with friends at the Odeon and Ruelles. In the morning I work out at the Vertical Club, trying to forget about my fear and focusing on creating the perfect body—I become addicted to a neurotic routine of cardio-vascular training and lifting that is purely narcissistic. My week-ends are taken up with brunches at Barney Greengrass or Ernie's, or hanging out at places like the Dublin House on 79th Street and Broadway, a scruffy, dimly lit Irish pub with a long dark wooden bar, paneling, and a jukebox. But I'm starting to panic. My mother had always told me that I took all the shortcuts. Maybe I should have gone straight to film school. Or business school. Or law school. Like most of my Wesleyan friends.

Slave to Fashion

My lucky way out comes in September 1984, when I think about going back to work at Giorgio Armani, where I had a temporary job recently over school break. They are rushing to open their first United States boutique and they desperately need help. They hire me to start the day after I call them. Good timing. I need the money, and I can work on my film project at the same time. In the back of my mind I'm just putting the film on the back burner, con-fident that eventually I will make it and pay back my investors. But I'm curious as to where my next experience might take me. The next day I begin working in the public relations and marketing de-partment, on a staff of only six or seven. My experience at Armani proves to be a crash course in ridding myself of any leftover naïveté.

The film *American Gigolo* has provided Armani with tre-mendous exposure in the United States, since Richard Gere wore exclusively Armani in his starring role. Suddenly, Armani is syn-onymous with "minimalist chic," and everybody wants to wear him. The large specialty and department stores are buying up his clothing, plans for freestanding boutiques are in the works, and the Armani image is being carefully groomed and disseminated through magazines and billboards.

With the flagship store on Madison Avenue still under construction, the opening has been delayed several months, so there is plenty of pressure to speed things up and open in time for Christmas. There is a tremendous amount of tension between the boss and her underlings. The Armani empire is run out of Milan, but the United States fiefdom is directed by a dynamic woman named Martina Bartolini, who comes just about up to my waist and barks orders in Italian (to those who speak it and those who don't) or in her bastardized English. Intent on creating a huge splash for Armani in the United States, she supervises an army of construction workers, lighting experts, display and visual artists, and floral designers working around the clock to ensure that her austere boutique at 815 Madison will be the jewel in the crown. She runs Armani like a mini-Mussolini, and many around her find her laughable.

I serve as her gofer, secretary, assistant, and jester, trying to lighten the mood of an extremely tense group of people who take fashion a bit too seriously, as if it is a science and we are an emergency medical unit, rescuing the world from bad taste. I work ridiculously long hours, sometimes up to sixteen a day. Whatever Martina demands, I do, from writing press releases about the next season's line, working with media people consigning clothing for fashion shoots, and assisting in publicity to picking up meals from hot spots like Mezzaluna or espresso from Gardenia. For the first time, I get an up-close look at a slick world I had only seen in the movies and magazines. I remember one shoot we do for *Amica,* an Italian magazine, featuring Matt Dillon in a bathtub surrounded by beautiful underage female models.

From my first day at Armani, I start consigning clothing to myself—suits, jackets, sweaters, leather jackets, anything lying around the office that I consider to be a sample and that looks great on me. I'm thrilled each time I leave the office at the end of the night with new clothes, and I become addicted to acquiring more. I'm always wondering if anybody else is doing the same thing.

October 3, 1984.
I'm on the crosstown bus headed to work, frantic that I'll be late. The day begins at 8:00 A.M. and I make it with just enough time to pick up some coffee and settle at my desk, which is stacked high with fashion magazines and covered with yellow lined legal paper on which Martina has illegibly scrawled memos and letters to be typed, unalphabetized files, and pink message slips from yesterday, which was technically only seven hours ago. My coworkers arrive in the office, dressed magnificently but looking tired and drained from working into the early hours. Martina is in her office with the door closed, but you can hear muffled Italian seeping out through the walls. Ellen, the receptionist, who is the only employee dressed in a wrinkled navy blue skirt with an unpressed white blouse sticking out, sits out in front of the elevators typing, organizing files, and shuffling papers. The understated waiting room, in which the only decoration is a white orchid on a single black table, fits the Armani mantra: minimal, minimal, minimal. Inside the office, Rafael, a public relations assistant, argues on the phone in Italian; his hair is perfectly in place, and he is dressed impeccably in his navy blue blazer and gray flannel pants. Olivia, the accountant, is busy with her calculator, her head buried in a pile of checkbooks and ledgers. Tina, the office manager, is running around from floor to floor, trying to keep everything under control, nervous that we're not going to meet our deadline. And Clare, the office public relations consultant/stylist/gossip, walks in at around 10:30 A.M., because she's been out at a party until 4:00 A.M. She entertains us with the names and details of the celebrities she was with. "Quasi celebrities," I say. I start typing Martina's memos when Tina asks me to help her organize the back storage area because I'm tall enough to reach the top shelves. Martina comes out of her office with a snarl on her face and asks if I can type two letters and have them messengered as quickly as possible. I crank them out right away, she signs them, and I call a

messenger and bring them downstairs. Samples are delivered to our floor, and we need to check that everything on the inventory list has come in. I'm addicted to the frenetic pace of this place, and it fuels my mania. Martina could spit out ten more chores, and I could handle them all. In the meantime, I still haven't gotten to her memos, and she needs them right away. But she sends me out to pick up her lunch, and when I come back she tells me that she wants me to go downtown and meet a photographer and to bring a duffel bag of clothing to a shoot. I get into a cab, find the studio on Greene Street in Soho, and deliver the clothes. When I return, Rafael is half laughing at me because it's almost 4:00 P.M. and I've been running around and haven't sat down all day or had lunch. He orders a sandwich for me. Clare has taken a break, so I end up answering the phone for the next hour and start working on a press release for the opening. She comes back two hours later. "Where were you? You're late, I'm pissed," I tell her. "Sorry," she says. Martina comes over to me and squeezes my cheeks and says something sweet in Italian. I guess I'm doing something right. It's already dark outside, but we're just getting ready to put together new press kits. I'm sitting on the floor in stocking feet, collating hundreds of photocopies and stuffing them into folders. Then I'm attaching labels to photographs and inserting them into the folders; this goes on into the night. Everybody else is slaving away, at their desks, while Martina is out to dinner entertaining clients. Soon people start leaving. At midnight I finally decide to call it quits. I've done my sixteen hours. At home I stay up for a few more hours watching television until I can fall asleep and start the cycle again in the morning.

The Pill

I'm visiting Allison at Yale, the fall after my graduation, and we come back to her dorm room slightly drunk after dinner one evening. There's a message from her mother on the answering machine about some unpaid bill. Slight intrusion. I take off my pants and T-shirt and lie down in bed and watch as she strips in front of me. She's laughing like this is a game. It's kind of charming. We haven't seen each other all week, and I'm pretty aroused. I light a joint. She asks me about places I'd like to travel to, and I tell her Iceland, China, Africa, and Australia. She thinks those places are so far away—maybe too far away, I think. The pot is making me crazy and a little paranoid. Her hair smells like smoke now, and I feel like a voyeur, like I'm watching this couple kissing, about to make love. Afterward, we go out for scrambled eggs and bacon and ice cream sundaes and start laughing hysterically when we see a napkin stuck to the waiter's shoe as he's passing by. It's not really very funny at all. We finally get so tired that we go back to her room and sleep until noon.

My relationship with Allison becomes more serious, and we start spending more time together. She is finishing her final year at Yale and she spends the weekends with me in Manhattan. There are so many notations in my datebook about our incredible sex ("great night of sex," "up all night," "hot sex"). It seems like the perfect relationship, but it clearly isn't. I don't know how to communicate with her. I take on a very controlling role in the relationship, minding her day-to-day activities and taking care of her errands and appointments. I try to make her life as simple as possible, and she becomes accustomed to my omnipresence. When we first started sleeping together, she used a diaphragm, and I would do the prep work. I thought it was fun, real teamwork. But she tired of this nightly ritual, and her doctor recommended that she go on the pill. Now each night I remind her to take her pill, and if she's too lazy, I pop one of the little peach tablets out of the case and give it to her with water. I also keep track of her menstrual cycle in my date book, so we know when to expect her next period. When it's late, we are thrown into a panic. We're not talking to each other; she's crying and telling me that this time she's sure she's pregnant. Each time I assure her that she isn't and show her the calculations. I suggest that we go out to dinner. It'll happen by tomorrow morning. She's only two days late. We go out to Nishi for sushi. She comes home and gets her period. It's the wasabi. I make a red star in my date book and I'll know when she had her period so I can remind her for next time.

Years earlier, the loss of Allison's virginity to someone else left me crushed. She was dating a guy a year younger, and I was constantly jealous. One day she called me, sounding scared and on the verge of tears. "Andy, what am I going to do?" she asked. "I think I might be pregnant." I assured her, for some reason, that she probably wasn't pregnant but that I would make an appointment for her to see my mother's gynecologist, Dr. Strauss, a man in his early seventies. It was to be our secret. "Please, don't even tell your mother," she pleaded. "Have you told Tim?" I asked. "Not yet," she said. The appointed day came, and we drove in my red Kharmann Ghia to Dr. Strauss's office, which was located in his house in a very nice neighborhood in Englewood, New Jersey. I waited in the car listening to the radio for about forty-five minutes wondering what was going on inside. She walked down the steps and toward the car, got in, and looked like she was about to cry. "So, what happened?" I asked. "He examined me and took some blood and urine and I'll know in a day or so," she said. She reached over and gave me a big hug. "Thanks. Thanks a lot for this," she said. The next day she called and told me she wasn't pregnant. I was relieved, but I really didn't want to talk to her. I was still angry that she had lost her virginity.

The Pimp

Several weeks after I start working at Armani, some of the Milan-based executives come to New York to check on the progress of the U.S. empire. They are busy in daily meetings with Martina, in photo sessions, and with the press, and I am at their beck and call. I order cars and limousines for them, fetch their lunch, make reservations, and pick up tickets for Broadway shows. They are staying at the Carlyle Hotel, and some of them want videos of foreign films—Jacques Tati, Luis Buñuel, Jean Renoir, Fritz Lang, and Jean Cocteau—as well as gay porn. I am sent in search of the

newest releases, with titles like *Sizing Up* and *Like a Horse,* or anything else of my choosing. I don't question any of the requests,
just take the cash and do the errands, never return the change, and
always forget the receipts. I am sent on all kinds of what I call
"homo missions": picking up macho military clothing at Kauf-
man's Army & Navy Store on 42nd Street, camouflage shorts and
nylon vests and all kinds of undergear, jocks, bikinis, and thongs
at stores on Christopher Street. This logically proceeds to being
asked to track down and assemble "young men." One of the executives is interested in meeting a model we had used on a recent
shoot, and I'm asked to arrange it with his agency. I am naïve, but
I know this isn't a legitimate go-see. One of the executives asks me
if I will find other "types" of models for them, and I take this to
mean nonlegit types—escorts and hustlers. I find these guys in all
different places, mostly through advertisements in the *New York
Native* and in the theaters. I meet Scott, a tall, well-built, muscular
guy with short black hair and green eyes, at the Gaiety Theater in
Times Square, after his performance. He's impressive. Handsome,
with a great jawline and a hard body. They'll like him. I tell him
that there are a couple of business executives in town looking for
escorts after his last show at 10:30 P.M. and that they'll pay him
$200 an hour. I also tell him they have tons of money and plenty
of time. It sounds good to him. I give him one of the executives'
names and the address and phone number of his room at the
hotel. He thanks me. I can barely imagine what's going on at 76th
and Madison, but it is very busy, and the reports are never too
alarming. Nothing wilder than a lot of exhibitionism, posing, and
jerking off. I make arrangements to pay these boys between $200
and $500 each; sometimes they head up there a few at a time (as
many as nine or ten for orgies). Most of them want to be models
or actors, some lawyers and doctors, but settle for being escorts,
strippers, or the most coveted position—porn stars. These boys of
the adult-film business, hard to find in New York, command
higher fees. One of the best known is Brent Cummings, a huge
blond bisexual with enormous shoulders and a powerful chest and
arms, who is handsome in a dim-witted sort of way. Brent is

twenty-five and brand-new to the big city. He performs at the Follies, a triple-X all-male theater on Seventh Avenue that features live shows and adult male films. He becomes a favorite of the Armani group.

Soon I become friendly with these working boys. Most of our contact is on the phone, but sometimes we'll meet for a drink just to talk. Jason is a twenty-three-year-old med student at NYU, strong-looking and healthy, with blond hair, bright blue eyes, and a great smile. Once as we're standing outside the Oak Bar at the Plaza Hotel a middle-aged man dressed in a beautifully tailored suit approaches us and asks if we'd like to join him for drinks in the bar. Jason nods at me. "Sure, we'd love to," he says, and we follow the man into the smoky bar. We find a table, and he introduces himself as Henry Alton. He shakes Jason's hand and then mine. "Andy," I say. When the waiter comes, Henry orders three shots of Jack Daniel's for the group. He leans back and takes a deep breath. "So, boys, tell me a little about your lives in New York, won't you?" Jason tells him he's a medical student, and I tell him I work for a well-known fashion house. He seems equally impressed by both, which I find amusing. The waiter returns with our shots, and at the count of three we down the awful-tasting whiskey. "It's good medicine," says Henry. "I'll get us another." He signals the waiter. "Now tell us a little about yourself," Jason says. "I'm just a real estate investor from St. Louis and I get to New York as often as I can to enjoy the finer things: the museums, the theaters, the restaurants, the shopping, and the men." "Yeah, there's some good shopping here," Jason says. I try to hold back my laughter. We all drink our second shot of whiskey. "Boys, would you be interested in coming back to my hotel room at the Waldorf for a little romp?" he asks. "The both of us?" I ask. He nods. "$350 for two hours, plus a tip," he says. "I think that's a bit low. How about $500?" asks Jason. Henry excuses himself to go to the bathroom. We order another round of drinks and are really getting drunk. It seems like the bar is closing, and Henry hasn't come back yet. "I have a strong feeling that Henry isn't coming back," says Jason; "I don't think he liked that we turned down his offer." The waiter comes to the table and hands us the check. It's for $85.

On the Couch

Around the beginning of December, a strange combination of extreme anxiety and depression takes over me. My moods are unpredictable from day to day. Sometimes I feel fantastic for weeks, then I take a dive. Allison urges me to get professional help, and I start seeing Dr. Myron Levitt, a psychiatrist on the Upper East Side. He has paternal qualities that I like—he's gentle and caring—but he speaks in a monotone that practically hypnotizes me. I am under extreme stress, because of the failure of the film project and my financial situation. I have tremendous amounts of energy, which I don't know how to channel or control. I create compulsive lists of errands, possible job leads, people to call, things to buy, and doctor's appointments. I get nothing done. There is too much swirling around in my head—I can't contain it all in my brain.

December 16, 1984. 8:45 A.M. Upper East Side.
As usual, I'm early for my 9:00 A.M. appointment with Dr. Levitt, so I stop to pick up a bagel and chocolate milk at the corner deli. I'm sitting in his waiting room staring at a horrifying piece of art hanging on the wall—a black-and-white abstract image that looks like an anorexic's severed arms, folded. The print is slipping down into the mat. I want to mention it to him, but I keep it to myself. The waiting room is furnished with "contemporary" pieces from the seventies: a brown knotty couch, a chrome arched lamp, glass-and-chrome end tables, and two wooden chairs with cushions. Nothing matches. I'm not comfortable here. It isn't clean enough for me. I have to work out my issues in a clean environment. I don't understand what's causing how I feel every day I wake up, whether it's anxiety or depression, and I feel like they need to operate on me. I don't want to open myself up and get infected by his psychoanalysis in this shabby office and die on his fake Oriental rug. I'd prefer to be lying naked, covered by just a sheet, on a

steel table in a big white room with a white ceramic floor and bright lights, talking to my psychiatrist. The door to his office opens. "Come in," says Dr. Levitt. I sit in my assigned seat, the tan leather-and-chrome couch, in my customary position—my legs spread-eagle, leaning backward. I'm still drinking my chocolate milk. Dr. Levitt sits about five feet away from me, notebook in hand. He smiles, remains silent, and looks at me to begin the session. It's a contest between psychiatrist and patient. I stare blankly at him, but after about thirty seconds I start laughing. Patient loses. Dr. Levitt doesn't laugh. He doesn't laugh because he doesn't know what's so funny and because he has no sense of humor. There is another silence. To ease the tension, I give in quickly and tell him that I have nothing new to talk about and that I'm just as anxious and depressed as I was the week before. His therapy obviously isn't working. Or *I'm* not working at my therapy. As I speak, he looks down at his pad, takes notes, and mumbles, which annoys me because I'm not sure that he's really listening or that what he's writing on that pad is even about me. Then he looks up, leans forward, and asks me, "Andy, how do you feel today?" I pull my legs together, sit up straight, clasp my hands, and think about this one. I'm insulted because he knows the answer, but I give him a response anyway. "Like the fucking pressure in my head is building up and is going to explode any minute," I tell him. He presses me further. "And what exactly does that feel like?" he asks. I refuse to answer and slump back into my original spread-eagle position. He takes a sip of his coffee and waits for my response. This session is never going to end. He attempts to bring our focus back to the issues we've been discussing over the last few weeks. "Is your relationship with Allison in any way like your relationship with your mother or sister?" he asks me. "Sometimes," I say. "But I don't feel like talking about that now." He wants me to update him on my financial problems and career plans. But to me this is missing the point; I'm not seeing him to problem-solve. I'm suffering and I'm withholding information and am not very open about the derailment that is really going on in my daily life. I've lost my golden-boy self-image, and I'm not about to admit it with this simpleton. And more important, I'm not able to articulate the intensity of what's going on inside my brain anyway. So I just sit on the tan couch staring at the ugly brown and blue rug hoping he will magically help me understand the pressure I'm feeling. I take a tissue from the table in front of me and pretend to blow my nose; I try to throw it in the garbage can but miss, so I have to go pick it up. I look at my watch. "You have more time," Dr. Levitt says. The next thing I know he's talking to me about narcissistic personality disorder. "Can we save that for next week?" I ask him. "Fine, it's your time," he responds in an easy manner, which makes me feel rather guilty. I stand up and walk out of his office, passing by his next patient, a frightened-looking girl in her midtwenties, and a woman I take to be her mother, anxiously awaiting their appointment.

Triple-XXX Live Acts

The third week in December, Brent Cummings is appearing at the Follies, and he wants me to come see him there. I stand at the top of the steps leading down to the entrance and, as usual when I'm at a porn show, I look around nervously before I descend. I take one step down. It's like I'm putting my foot into an icy-cold swimming pool. It's too late to stop—anybody might be watching. Like friends of my parents or an old high school English teacher going to see a Broadway show. The walls going down the steps are covered with photographs of bare-chested boys and men, and I wonder if they're the same guys inside getting ready to go onstage. Sitting in the ticket booth is a man I can barely make out but who looks like Mr. Wizard from my chemistry set. Superimposed on the glass over his forehead is a sign that reads ADMISSION $6. I smile and give him my most masculine "Hey."

"You here for an audition?" he asks. "Yeah," I respond without the slightest hesitation.

He signals me to walk through the turnstile. I am in a dark vestibule.

"What's your name?" he asks.

"Eric. Eric Colter," I say. Not a bit of thought. Where did that name come from? He shakes my hand and I smile. His name is Jerry. My name is Eric. Inside the dark theater I can see about fifteen men bathed in light from the screen on which two skinny young blond kids are in a sixty-nine position. There's no way either could be older than sixteen. This is not a turn-on for me. I'm a little nervous now, a bit afraid. Something about this place repulses me. It's musty and smoky and not very clean. Jerry asks me if I've danced before, and I tell him that I have, just not in New York. San Francisco. And Montreal. He calls over a well-built young guy and introduces him to me as Justin. Justin is an all-American hunk. Tall, broad-shouldered, dark complexion, bright green eyes, not quite good-looking enough to be a model, and he's just wearing a towel wrapped around his waist.

"My real name is Joe, but they like Justin better. It sounds more porn-star-like," he says. This leads me to believe Jerry's name might not be Jerry either. But what does Jerry have to hide? Justin is posing in front of a mirror. It's funny I chose a first and last name. Almost as if I intend to have a serious career in porn. Justin tells me he's from West Virginia. He leads me back to the locker room, a dingy gray-painted space with exposed wires, bad overhead lighting, and a few benches. He sits down on a bench, his abs not moving an inch.

"Have you ever done this before?" he asks.

"Does it look like I haven't?" I say. I take off my sweater. I'm just wearing a T-shirt underneath. Justin kind of looks me over.

"There are six shows each day. The lineup switches every Monday. It's a much better place to work than the Gaiety. The clientele is more upscale and has a lot more cash to burn." He starts oiling up his chest and arms. "Better tips and better private shows," he explains.

I'm not sure what Justin's talking about. He tells me it's really easy. "They announce your name, put on some music, you walk onstage fully dressed and then strip down to your underwear or jock, dance around the audience a little, and then come offstage and get a hard-on." He makes it sound like such a normal thing to do. "Then the music starts up again and you go back and work the crowd. Guys in the audience will fondle you and tip you and put dollar bills in your socks. You've got to work the crowd to get the privates. At the end there's a grand finale, and all seven guys come out hard for the audience. Kind of like a chorus line. There's always lots of applause."

"Sounds easy enough. $10 a show plus tips and privates," I say. "And you can really get up to $50 for a private on the premises?" I ask.

"Yeah, a jerk-off thing. There's a narrow hallway in the back for that. Or you can do something outside for whatever you can negotiate," he tells me.

"I like to negotiate."

Justin tells me there's a star of the show, a guy named Brent Cummings, who has just appeared in a new porn film. I pretend I don't know him.

"And he's bi, too. Are you bi?" he asks.

"I guess so," I say.

"Well, are you into pussy?"

"Yeah, totally. I've got a girlfriend uptown," I tell him.

"You should bring her down here one night. Maybe we could all bang her." He throws his head back and laughs.

The show starts at 8:30 P.M. and the rest of the guys are coming into the locker room, most of them eating their dinner. Something is making me nauseous. Maybe it's the sight of those two skanky teenagers outside on the screen combined with the smell of fried chicken in the locker room. Those boys could never dance at a place like this—they'd be heckled and booed. In walks the star of the show, Brent Cummings. He's a strapping Adonis with a handshake like none I've ever felt. (The only person I've met with a handshake that even comes close is Bill Clinton, as I discovered years later when I met him at a fund-raiser.)

"So, you came down to see me? Gonna audition tonight?" Brent asks me. He speaks in a dull monotone voice like Dr. Levitt and seems bored with having to perform tonight. Jerry pops his head in and tells me I go on last, which gives me a chance to watch

the show from backstage and get a feel for it. Brent is fixing his
streaked-blond hair in the broken mirror on the wall. He's wearing a pair of jeans and a T-shirt. I watch the whole group of guys
do their routine before Brent is announced. I'm fascinated by what
they'll do onstage—how far they'll go and what they think turns
the audience on. Some of them will satisfy a customer's ass fetish
by bending over and touching their toes; others will thrust their
cocks right into a customer's mouth for a few dollar bills. Others
will even jack off the customer, right there in the audience, if he is
willing. There are no boundaries in the basement of the Follies.

Brent takes the stage, and the audience cheers. The theater is
filled with his fans. They've all seen his movies: the one where he
fucks a cheerleader on a bench press and the one where three guys
on a diving board take turns sucking his cock. He struts his stuff
awkwardly, with a kind of Vegas-style stride, taking off his shirt
first and then stepping out of his jeans to reveal a pair of white
briefs. He turns his back to the audience, spreads his legs, and pulls
his briefs down a bit in the back, revealing a tan line. Then he turns
around and shows a little bit of blond pubic hair. He really doesn't
dance, he just touches himself and tugs at himself a little. But it
doesn't matter. He grabs his cock and makes a mock grimace, to
the audience's delight. I can do that. He comes backstage and gets
undressed, his cock already hard. He oils up his chest and his
thighs and asks me to do his back, butt, and legs. He strides back
onstage and the audience claps and whistles. He stands with his
back to them, then turns around, covering his cock with his hands.
From where I'm standing, I see the red spotlights bounce off his
chest. He walks into the audience and pulls his hands away, and
guys from both sides of the aisle start grabbing for his cock and his
ass as he moves from shadow to shadow to collect tips, all the time
stroking his big dick. This is going to be a hard act to follow.

The announcer introduces the final act: Eric Colter. I have no
connection to the name. I do kind of a silly jog out onto the stage.
The lights are practically blinding me, and I can't see the crowd.
I'm wondering how many people in the audience recognize me. I
dance to the music—Madonna's "Like a Virgin"—the best I can. I

must look like an idiot. I take off my shirt, then my jeans. This is the first time I've stripped except when I've done it alone in my studio in front of the mirror. It feels like a visit to the doctor. The air is cold from the air-conditioning, and it's smoky. Bad combination. Freezing smoke. Offstage. Dip three fingers into the communal lube. Start stroking my cock. Thinking about Allison's tits and Brent fucking her from behind, and all of a sudden I realize I have a huge hard-on. Easy. Next song. Madonna again. "Lucky Star." Clapping from the audience when I get back onstage. I'm walking around bare-assed in a basement in Times Square. Men are shoving dollar bills into my socks. I feel totally naked—I am totally naked—but pretend I'm just in the locker room at my gym and it's over pretty quickly. Now it's time for the grand finale. Backstage Brent and I stroke each other's cocks until they're fully hard and we're ready. He doesn't look at me or say anything. We all walk out together—seven guys with hard-ons—dancing poorly to the music on the bad sound system. We collect some more tips, get dressed, then mingle with the customers. A sweet-looking Chinese man offers me $50 to go in the back hallway and jerk me off. He smiles at me and flashes two gold teeth and some cash. I'm feeling totally pathetic for being in this darkened room. I pull my jeans down, and he starts jerking me off. I just want it to be over with quickly. He whispers words that I can't understand. I can just pick up "good." It takes about five minutes for me to come. Justin is walking out with two men, taking them back to his hotel room. Brent is already starting with a second customer. Slow night for privates. Jerry tells me I was fantastic and we'll talk after the next show about working me into the schedule. Brent and I go back to his room at the Fulton Hotel on West 46th Street. He tells me that I can borrow his room if I need to use it for a customer. It's $50 a night, and sparse. Bed, dresser, TV, ceiling fan. He's got the bathroom neatly organized: baby oil, hair gel, shaving cream. He tells me I can hang out with him until the last show. He's going to take a shower. I see him take off his shirt and jeans. I'm watching the news. He walks out of the shower dripping and dries himself off in front of me. I'm starstruck. And jealous. I want people to love

me the way they love and admire him. He flexes his thighs for me
and laughs. Says he's going to add it to his routine. Turns around
and tightens his smooth butt.

Private Dancer

The dichotomy of my smart yuppie lifestyle on the Upper West
Side and my career stripping and getting jerked off in a seedy
Times Square theater is surreal at times. When I take the subway
downtown, I stand next to passengers dressed just like me wondering where they're going and if they would believe me if I told
them where I was going. I think I can do anything and be anyone.
And being a stripper and hustler seems entirely logical. I have no
idea what is going to happen next in my life, but this feels right for
now.

   The risk of hustling gets me high. Most of the situations I get
myself into demand very little of me sexually. I try to be careful,
to simply function as an exhibitionist. It is my role to arouse these
men, and I don't mind showing off my body. Most of them ask
me to undress and masturbate for them while they jerk off; others
just sit and stare. But soon I realize that I am really the voyeur—
watching what's going on between the customer and myself.
Sometimes my mood changes and I get so depressed by what I'm
doing that I feel like I'll get stuck doing this forever. Fortunately,
it's only a few nights a week and a couple of times a night. One
night I head to the Edison Hotel with a customer, a guy in his
midthirties in town from Miami, and he seems friendly. I'm in a
pretty good mood, and we're just talking about living in New York
versus living in Miami, the pros and the cons. He wants to enter
the hotel separately and have me meet him at his room. Fine. He
opens the door as if we've never met. "C'mon in," he says. Soon
he's naked and playing with himself while I'm taking my clothes
off for him. The eleven o'clock news is on, this nice guy from
Miami is jerking off in this crummy hotel room with bad overhead lighting, and I'm undressing. I should have gone straight
home tonight and gone to bed.

A few regular customers just want to take me out to dinner or find out more about me, which feeds my narcissism. I never reveal anything about myself, and the dinners tend to be quite routine and boring—I end up doing more listening than talking. I am Dr. Myron Levitt.

One night after the last show I meet a man at the theater who seems to be what I term "a safe bet"—respectable, well-dressed, in his midforties, and Ivy League–educated (so he later tells me). He's a psychiatrist who lives on Fifth Avenue in the 70s. He asks me out and tells me not to worry about money. We can go out for a drink or to his apartment, my choice. As usual, I go for the bigger option. We take a cab to his apartment, walk into his stark lobby, past his doorman, who, I realize, is probably used to seeing him bring home guests. His wife and kids are on vacation in Nantucket. He proudly shows me around his apartment, which is filled with spectacular Asian art pieces. I don't remember if I tell him I'm in law school or an actor—I mix them up. I prefer the anonymity and enjoy the game. I am nervously awaiting his plan for me. And then he tells me that he is into what he calls breath control, which involves playing with gas masks and plastic bags, the Hefty lawn kind. He explains that he is fascinated by choking and strangling fantasies. I am a bit naïve, and scared to death. Are we going to be playing out these fantasies? Dressed or undressed? I must seem hesitant, because he tries to reassure me by telling me that I don't have to take my clothes off. Is that supposed to calm me? He leads me into the bedroom—there are photos of his wife and children on the night tables. I hesitate and tell him that I don't think I'm interested. But I do end up playing a little, because I'm somewhat curious and he's promising me money. When he goes into the closet and pulls out the gas mask—the World War II kind that looks like a horse's head—I must look shocked. I take my shirt off anyway and fold it neatly on the bed, then step out of my jeans and throw them across a chair. He puts the mask over my head, and I see myself standing—just in my briefs—in the mirror. The sight horrifies me. He asks me to take off my briefs, and I strip down. I find it frightening that the seemingly nice, healthy doctor with strangling fantasies is actually treating patients with mental illnesses. I tell him I can't go on with this anymore. I laugh nervously and he smiles. We both feel a little embarrassed and sorry for each other, and I get dressed. He offers to take me out to dinner, which I definitely don't want to do, so instead I make us scrambled eggs and toast and try to turn the experience into something normal—there's nothing more normal than some breakfast food for dinner. Wondering if I'll leave this apartment without being strangled or taken out in a Hefty bag with the garbage, I talk with him a little about his practice—he sees mostly schizophrenics and manic-depressives. He tells me that he feels overwhelmed by their mental illnesses and the burden of being responsible for their well-being twenty-four hours a day. He says the anxiety hardly allows him to function. I can't believe that he is so weak. Is Dr. Levitt this weak? But quite honestly I am more interested in his fascination with choking and strangulation and am curious to get him to talk. Was he aroused as a small child by a choking episode? Does it have something to do with losing his breath while having an orgasm? Does losing his breath get him high? He prefers complaining about his patients. I never see him again after this night. I also never look at a psychiatrist again without thinking of a gas mask.

There are others. Plenty of them. A rather obese man in his late forties approaches me after a show, introduces himself as Scott Zohn, and asks for a private session with me. Standard. He seems nice enough though not very attractive, and I tell him that I have a room down the street at the Fulton Hotel. He tells me that he wants me to come back to his office at *Time* magazine. He's a theater critic there. I've read some of his reviews before, and he strikes me as a little nervous after he discloses his identity. We take the elevator to his floor, and he leads me through a maze of desks and into his office, which overlooks the city. He leaves the door slightly ajar and instructs me to pull my jeans down to my knees, show off my ass, and then jerk off on his latest review. How I get myself excited I don't remember, but I come on the magazine pretty quickly while he plays with his cock. I am embarrassed and self-conscious imagining that everybody outside knows what I'm doing in his office—but obviously not too embarrassed to return a few more times to visit him to pick up a few $50 bills. I later learn from an editor at *New York* magazine that I am not the only boy asked to perform this ritual.

It didn't take much to get me onstage, and soon I feel as comfortable as Brent getting the crowd aroused, walking into an audience of horny and appreciative businessmen who applaud and have cash to burn. Brent teaches me how to hustle a client, and I am letting guys give me blow jobs and jerking them off for $50. This becomes a routine activity for me, a business deal, like fund-raising. I am making $500 a day (including hourlong private sessions) and have built up a decent clientele—doctors, lawyers, businessmen—most claiming to be heterosexual and liking me because I am, too. There is quite a bit of confusion here. I am drinking too much, taking amphetamines, and doing coke again. I love the idea of being good during the day and bad at night. The incongruity thrills me.

After the last show one Friday night, there are only a few guys hanging around looking to hook up, but none of them turn out to be serious customers. So a group of four dancers walks over to Howard Johnson's in Times Square for something to eat. I always get the same thing: a clam roll and a chocolate shake. I stare and count the hundreds of people as they pass by the big picture-frame window. When the check comes, Jason, the med student, picks it up, turns it over, and says, "Who made the most money today?" Everyone responds at the same time: "You did." So he ends up paying the tab. We walk out onto Broadway. "I'm not ready to call it a night, guys," says Jason. I'm not either. "Let's head downtown," I say. Corey takes his vial of Dexedrine from his jacket pocket and gives me a handful. He keeps promising me he'll get me a hundred. "I need something to wash these down with," I say. They just speed me up and make me feel on top of things. Donovan, the kid from Alberta with the weird-looking curved cock, is staying at a friend's apartment in the West Village, and he invites us back there to party. We stop at a Korean deli and pick up four six-packs. I make sure one is an Amstel Light. The apartment is a shabby one-bedroom on the fourth floor of a walk-up. The furniture is scarce and worn, old newspapers and maga-zines litter the floor, the ashtrays overflow with cigarette butts, there are empty beer bottles on tables and dishes stacked high in the sink. "Sorry, this place is kind of a dump," says Donovan. "Where's your friend?" asks Corey. "He's living with his girlfriend in the East Village," says Donovan. Jason is looking through the kitchen cabinets and then opens the freezer and finds a brand-new bottle of vodka. "I've struck gold," he announces. He pours four healthy shots, one for each of us, and we gulp them down. And a second. Donovan disappears into the bedroom. The three of us are sitting on the two couches drinking our beers when Corey comes up with an idea. "Should we bag this place and go to the titty bar my ex-girlfriend works at?" he asks. We don't feel like it. Donovan appears with his hands behind his back and a grin on his face. "I have a surprise for you," he announces. He pulls out a thick plastic bag of cocaine, enough to keep the party going for another three days. "Where'd you get all that from?" we ask him. He tells us a customer gave it to him for being "extra special," but he won't go into details. Who cares? Jason goes into the kitchen and cleans off a mirror that's on the table. I'm wasted from the vodka and beer. But I open another bottle. Jason dumps a pile of coke on the mirror that looks like a scoop of cottage cheese. High-quality rock. I start chopping it into a fine powder and separate out eight 3-inch lines. Donovan brings a straw from the kitchen. I snort the first line and am immediately anesthetized. I'm sens-ing that I'm going to be staying in this apartment overnight. Everyone else takes his turn. Feeling euphoric, I open another beer. "Let's really pace ourselves tonight," says Corey. "Why? We have enough to last a lifetime," I say. I just want to do more and more as fast as possible. I lean over the mirror and do two lines. I'm telling everyone how great I feel, while Donovan is just lying on the couch. I love this stuff. I convince Jason to do a line with me. "Slow down, buddy," Corey tells me. Wetting my fingers from a glass of water I put on the table, I pick up excess coke off the mirror and rub it on my gums. Donovan gets up, lowers the music, and heads to the bedroom. Then I show Jason and Corey my favorite trick. I take a tiny bit of coke on my index finger and drop it into my eye. It burns for a second, but it rushes straight to my brain and I get an instant high. "You know, you're an asshole," Corey says. Jason is lying down, ready to pass out. Corey is still doing lines with me but tells me this is his last one. But I don't see an end in sight. It's 8:00 A.M., almost eight hours after we started this party. Corey and I are finishing the last couple of lines. Jason is gone. Donovan is sleeping. I figure I should get in a cab soon and go home and come down from this high. This day is shot.

My first homecoming at Wesleyan—returning to campus for the first time since graduation, seeing old friends and friends who are still there—provides another bizarre contrast. We go to all the frat parties. Most of my friends are in law school, business school, or graduate school, or have entered the business world. Dressed in impeccable stolen Armani, I feed them all the bullshit line that I'm making an independent film while I am really pimping and prostituting and hanging out in dark porno theaters in Times Square. Very impressive.

One night, a husband-and-wife team from Philadelphia meets me at the Follies and escorts me back to the St. Regis Hotel. They are friendly, in their midforties, and they offer me a drink when we get upstairs to their deluxe suite. I have a glass of champagne with them, and we share a joint. He asks me to undress, and I quickly remove my clothes and lay them on the bed. She stands next to me and starts playing with my hair while he pulls me toward the bathroom door and ties my hands behind my back and explains that this is how they like to play. I'm too scared to try and get dressed and call this whole thing off and leave the room, and I'm too curious to protest. After I'm tied securely to the inside of the bathroom door with rope that she pulled out of a dresser drawer, they both, fully clothed, begin fondling me and kissing me. After about twenty minutes they tell me they'll be back soon, and they leave. After about an hour goes by, I realize that this is a disaster, that these people may never return and I may be in big trouble. I can't undo the knot. I don't know when to declare this an emergency. I don't want to scream. What am I going to tell the person who finds me in this condition? I promise myself that this is the last time I'll ever do this. At 3:30 A.M., three hours later, I hear a noise at the door of the suite and it's them, drunk and giggling and surprised to find me there. They untie me and give me $300 and hurry me out of the room. I rush to the elevator and through the lobby past the front desk, hoping that nobody notices me. This event instills in me a modicum of self-preservation, and I ease out of the exciting but dark world of prostitution.

Three's a Crowd

May 17, 1985. Upper West Side.
It's the last day of classes at Yale. Allison moves in tomorrow. We've been looking forward for months to living together and having all of our things in one place. I make lots of room for her things, clear out space in the closets. She has no idea about my other lives—and I'm almost glad that these identities will wither away.

I tell myself the crazies will most likely go away, and I won't stay out, or be allowed to stay out, until four or five in the morning, roaming the streets and dabbling in all kinds of lascivious behavior. Her presence will keep me under control. I'll be on her schedule. Of course, real mania is marked by delusional thinking.

Less than a week after Allison moves in, we realize that there is no way we can live together comfortably in a studio, no matter the ceiling height. We both hate living in one room. We're on top of each other. She's drying off after her shower in the "living room" and I'm trying to squeeze by to make breakfast. Having another person around all of the time without a break is driving me crazy. I'm used to going out at night, picking up *The New York Times,* and taking hourlong walks down Broadway to Columbus Circle and back without telling anyone else where I'm going.

I don't like the way Allison has organized the closets. She doesn't have a system. She doesn't think she needs one and doesn't think a closet needs to look good. First of all, I don't like keeping the hangers from the dry cleaners. They look awful. That's why I bought all the black plastic matching ones. "We've got plenty of them, let's use them," I tell her. She ignores me and mumbles under her breath, "Do what you want to do." One Sunday afternoon, while she's eating breakfast in front of the television, I clean out her closet, making sure all of her shirts and blouses are buttoned at the top button and facing in the same direction. Skirts and pants in the middle section, dresses to the left. I refold her sweaters and stack them neatly on top of the closet, and it looks like a housekeeper has come in and done the job. "What are you doing over there?" she asks. "You are sick," she says, smiling. "Anything else need to be done?" I ask her. "No," she says. "Just sit down with me and watch TV and relax. You're driving me crazy."

I start looking at ads in *The New York Times* for one-bedroom apartments on the Upper West Side. We'll have to increase our rent by about $500 per month at a time when I have very little money in the bank, but I won't let that minor detail get in my way. But when it comes to an apartment, for some reason I place no limit on what I will spend. I want Allison to have a nice place to live. The first place we look at is in a renovated landmark building at the Level Club on West 73rd Street, between Broadway and West End Avenue. The apartment is a simple one-bedroom for $1,650, which is extremely expensive, but I'm fully confident that I'll be able to pay the rent. I'm also counting on Allison to pitch in. I am sold on the marble lobby alone. I push for this apartment. I know it's out of my league at the time, but go ahead and sign a one-year lease, thinking that somehow I'll probably be able to buy an apartment in the building within the year anyway. I imagine I'll find some executive-level position soon and make a six-figure income and my financial problems will be solved. I know it is a choice that makes Allison nervous, but I do it anyhow. I like that it makes me feel a little stressed and edgy. It's a risk. Signing the lease creates the sense of danger and excitement that I thrive on. So what if we're evicted.

In the meantime, with the very little money that we do have saved, we spend a week relaxing on the beach at a resort off the coast of Venezuela. After we return, we are visited by Brad, a friend from college, and the three of us are sitting around our apartment watching television. Brad and Allison have always been a bit flirtatious with each other and are putting out some sexual energy sitting on the couch next to each other. It's exciting watching my friend and my girlfriend interacting like this, and I'm curious about what's going to happen next. Brad has always told me about his attraction to Allison, and she's told me about her interest in him. Now I'm aware of a strong sexual energy between all three of us. It's very quiet except for the television, which is reporting a big hurricane in the Caribbean. Brad leans toward Allison. "Is it okay?" he asks me. "Sure," I say. She reaches for him and looks at me for my approval. I nod. Now here I am, the voyeur boyfriend, and I'm watching in amazement as things unfold. But after he leaves, Allison is quiet and doesn't want to talk much about it. Somehow, I've crossed a boundary by allowing this to happen. I don't think she ever has the same kind of trust in me again. But we never speak about it.

To take my mind off things, a few days after we move into our new place I start snooping around the building looking at apartments and talking to the doormen, and soon I find out about an apartment in the building that's for sale. Buying an apartment would add an element of pressure to my life at this point that I want to add. Not only would it provide me with a tremendous challenge, it would increase the pressure to produce and create, and trigger the anxiety and fear that keep me functioning at a frantic pace, making my daily life exciting. More responsibilities and obligations give me an incredible sense of purpose and satisfaction and keep my ego high. So I go see a broker. Although in fact I barely have enough to pay the rent, I think I can easily write the owner a check for the entire amount. It's a one-bedroom, 719 square feet, for $195,000. Great southern exposure. Even before I see it I tell the broker I'm almost certain that I'll take it. Get me two. Break the wall down. Make one big apartment. I go see a bank officer at Marine Midland to talk about a mortgage. He's enthusiastic about working together and flashes me his biggest grin. He tells me he'll run a credit check on me and that I should get all of my financials in order. I don't know where I think I'm getting the money from, but I imagine armed guards walking into our apartment and filling it to the ceiling with stacks of cash. I'm obsessed with money and addicted to spending it—but I barely have any left, and it looks like Armani won't be needing me anymore, since their flagship store is open.

My one-year anniversary of trying to produce an independent film is coming up, and the fantasy is ending. Thank God. It's a big flop. I haven't come up with the money. Not even close. And what I have raised, I've spent on junk that I can't even account for. I don't know if I'm depressed or relieved that I'm throwing in the towel. I owe my investors a small fortune, about $50,000.

The Queen of Schmooze

My sister Nancy has a public relations firm that represents several doctors. She is twenty-four years old, beautiful, smart, and driven. And she has real chutzpah. She is the only person I know who can walk into Yves Saint-Laurent on Madison Avenue in the middle of the winter and ask if they have a pair of shorts in the stock room that she can try on. She had worked for a small PR firm for a year, quickly picking up the tricks of the trade and fine-tuning her schmoozing skills. She was unhappy and unappreciated at the agency, so one of her clients there, Dr. Stuart Berger, offered to set her up in her own business, which she now runs from her apartment on the East Side. She attacks the promotion of his book, *Dr. Berger's Immune Power Diet,* with everything she has, booking him for print interviews and on television and radio shows. Although he is a diet doctor to the stars—singer Roberta Flack and ballerina Leslie Browne were patients—Dr. Berger is a hulking six-foot-five, 365-pound man who sweats profusely, is known to ingest huge amounts of cocaine and alcohol, and has a horrible Percodan habit, not to mention his addiction to brisket, corned beef, and pastrami sandwiches. He doesn't look like the healthiest guy in the world. But ultimately Nancy is able to convince a producer at *Donahue* to do an entire show on his weight-loss program, and within days she has created an instant number-one best-seller.

I have always maintained that Nancy has the most finely developed schmoozing skills, no doubt one of the reasons for her success in public relations. She gets a call from Dr. Robert Giller, a well-known nutritionist and holistic practitioner with celebrity friends like Halston, Bianca Jagger, and Liza Minnelli, who wants to discuss the possibility of hiring her to promote his book, *Medical Makeover.* She meets the young doctor, who is as well known for his art collection as for his B_{12} shots, in his Park Avenue office. In his meticulous study, he is sitting behind a contemporary desk, wearing a white coat, waiting to hear her pitch. He doesn't appear to have much time, but Nancy's not quite ready to begin. She engages him in conversation about her success with Dr. Berger's first book and retells the story of booking him on *Donahue.* Giller seems impressed. She promises that she can deliver even more national exposure than Berger received and that his book can become a number-one best-seller in less than two months. "I know the producers of two of the biggest shows, and they'll use you for the full hour," she tells him. He just stares at her. "How do you know you can do it?" he asks. "Trust me," she says. Then she outlines a ten-city national book tour. "We'll hit all the best shows with the highest ratings," she says. Giller is liking this PR woman. "Is this going to stretch far into the summer?" he asks, beginning to worry about all of this interfering with his summer plans in the Hamptons. "That should be your biggest problem," she says. She warns him that his office will be flooded with new patients, and he seems to get nervous. "You'd better expect it, your phones will be ringing off the hook," she tells him. "You're a young, good-looking guy who's going to be great on television." She makes him feel good and gives him hope for a best-seller that he didn't have fifteen minutes ago. She tells him she wants to set him up with a media coach and have him meet with a few close friends who are magazine editors for a drink to start talking up the book. Who is this superwoman? Giller hires her.

Brother-and-Sister Act

I'm spending the weekend in the Hamptons at Nancy's summer share. Even though I'm the loser brother, for some reason I'm feeling a little high anyway. This weekend is supposed to cheer me up, give my pale complexion some color, help me to relax and give me a chance to think about plans for the fall. Allison and I sit around Nancy's pool one late afternoon drinking Amstel Lights and eating guacamole and chips with her friends. Nancy starts talking about the success of her business and brings up the issue of my coming to work for her full-time. Embarrassing. She loves to bring up the ridiculous. Is she serious? Sometimes I can't tell. I mean, I can't imagine anything crazier than my sister and me working together—we're siblings and we're much too competitive. And I couldn't think of any job worse than working *for* my sister. Part-time or freelance work would be fine—I need the income—but taking a full-time job with her would be beneath me. I can't bear the thought of her being my employer. I'd feel like a small child again, and she would be the rebellious teenager. I could just start my own PR business or launch another type of business or go back to Armani if I was desperate. But after a few more Amstel Lights, Nancy insists that we'll make a great brother-sister team and it's such a great opportunity and what else am I going to do? She has a point. She makes it sound great. She tells me she's already got three clients on retainer and several interested in meeting with her. She wants me to take care of all of the writing and proposals, work my old contacts, and structure the business. And it's a guaranteed weekly paycheck. It seems like she's acting genuinely. And she's always tried to protect me.

We have a barbecue, and somehow before we go to bed we're not only working together but we've become equal partners in a new venture called Behrman Communications. Monday I show up at her apartment at 9:00 A.M., and by the end of the day we have a brand-new bright red logo that uses the same type as my Smash logo. We're in business.

In the early fall, Nancy and I are referred to our first "celebrity" client—at least we think she is a celebrity—socialite Cornelia Guest, the "Debutante of the Decade" and the daughter of C. Z. and Winston Guest. Cornelia has developed quite a reputation as the youngest of the Studio 54 gang. Her business manager from the company that handles her trust fund calls us in, ostensibly to promote her new humor book, *The Debutante's Guide to Life*. But what we really do is keep her life calm and under control. We involve her in some charity work and get her some good press and try to keep her name out of the club scene. She lives high up in Olympic Tower, overlooking Fifth Avenue and Central Park, with her little West Highland terrier, Lyle, in a lavishly overdecorated one-bedroom apartment. As you walk into the apartment, an imposing square Warhol portrait of her stares out from the wall. It is an impressive home for a twenty-three-year-old, and Nancy and I simply pretend that we are just as successful and wealthy. We dress and act the part, the way we have always been taught by our parents. Nancy handles more of the day-to-day activities of the "Cornelia account," which she both enjoys and despises, while my relationship with Cornelia is more ironic. Neither of us takes any of this too seriously. She has unbelievable delivery and a fantastic, racy sense of humor. I ask her if she is interested in working on a project for a group involved in ending homelessness. "I'll do anything to end homelessness—anything," she says, Lyle curled up on her lap.

We continue to represent Dr. Berger, who drives around Manhattan from gala events to pseudoglamorous openings in the backseat of his navy blue Silver Cloud Rolls-Royce, snorting cocaine and drinking vodka. By this time, Allison is working for him as an assistant, so I am privy to all the inside stories about what is really going on in the office, wild stories of throwing away blood tests, charging patients for tests not done, and his alcohol and drug abuse on the job—doing lines of coke and drinking a mixture of milk and vodka at his desk.

I approach an energetic producer I know at *ABC World News Tonight* to pitch him a story idea on the dark side of Dr. Berger. This is not your usual pitch. I believe Dr. Berger has taken advantage of patients and also of my sister and me, financially. We are furious at him, but don't turn away his checks. The producer has heard some other gossip about Dr. Berger and thinks it's a great story. At around the same time, Dr. Berger makes an arbitrary decision to clean house, and he fires Nancy and me and several people on his staff, including Allison and a few of our friends. I quickly organize a group of ex-employees to go on camera and speak in disguise about his quackery. Of course, Dr. Berger is shocked when the piece airs, and it is the beginning of more investigations into his practice.

Meanwhile, Dr. Robert Giller is determined to have a number-one best-selling book and is willing to do whatever it takes to reach that spot. Nancy and I mastermind a publicity tour and handle it like a presidential political campaign. We are on the phones constantly, trying to get through to our contacts at the major national television shows. Once we finally make contact with the producer, we have to make a pitch in thirty seconds. We get only one shot. The pressure is enormous. We sell Dr. Giller's book as the most modern approach to changing overall health through diet, vitamins, exercise, and nutrition and link him to his successful celebrity clients. In the first two months we book him on *The Sally Jessy Raphael Show* and *The Oprah Winfrey Show,* turning his book into a number-one *New York Times* best-seller. We talk to producers and editors in the fifteen largest television markets in the country, booking him on local shows, setting up radio and print interviews. I become particularly passionate about this book because I enjoy watching the sales grow weekly, in proportion to the work we are doing. The high that I experience from turning this commonsense book into a best-seller is phenomenal. Then my behavior becomes obsessive—I don't want to see him fall from the best-seller lists and start sending him to small markets for any type of exposure. I convince him traveling to Portland, Oregon, is worth the trip. As his practice becomes busier, Allison comes to work for him as an office assistant. Eventually, after a few months, the book falls off the list, and I am the only one who is crushed. Staying at the top is what makes me feel good—the money is secondary.

High-Wire Act

At home Allison and I are like two little kids playing house. The only things holding the relationship together are sex and spending money. Our communication is increasingly limited. Many nights I smoke a little pot before going to bed. One night I lie naked waiting for her to join me, and when she walks into the bedroom her entire body is glistening with oil. It's the most erotic sight. We're making love and for a while everything is fine with us again. But then, just as quickly as it started, it's all over.

Allison and I make another move in 1986—an incredibly ridiculous one way above our heads, a $2,300 huge duplex on the second and third floors of the same building, overlooking the lobby. It has an enormous living room, one bedroom, two full bathrooms, a loft/den, and gloriously high ceilings. We hire a decorator and start working on it right away, even though Allison has stopped working for Dr. Giller and is spending her days playing housewife, taking care of our two cocker spaniels, and working out.

Soon I find myself just as addicted to the gym as Allison is. At the beginning of the new year, 1987, I start an intense exercise and diet regimen—cardiovascular workouts and lifting four times a week with Sean, my trainer, an actor in his midthirties who has no qualms about making me work hard, or about sharing the weekly dilemmas of his private life. I have an incredible amount of energy that isn't absorbed by work, and I've fallen for the "no pain, no gain" motto. I make notes in my date book—no dairy, no meat, no bread, no pasta, no sugar. I'm not eating much except for protein and vegetables, and I've lost weight and built muscle. I'm in the best shape I've been in since college, and I'm addicted to the two things in my life that I can control—diet and exercise. I have the strange desire for my body to become stronger than my mind.

It's January, and we're starting to have problems with our landlord because the apartment is freezing cold. We walk around bundled up in layers of clothes shivering, and our landlord does nothing. I decide to withhold rent, and we become involved in a bitter legal battle. Until he fixes the heat, I will not write another rent check. Defiant, I ignore all warnings from the court. We are finally evicted several months after we start withholding rent. This puts an incredible amount of stress on our relationship. Allison and I barely speak to each other, and she blames me for my poor handling of the situation, believing that I was too aggressive. Allison decides it's best that we move to separate apartments. We're both forced to quickly sign separate leases and start packing boxes of clothing and dividing up what we've accumulated together. This is Allison's idea, and I am opposed to it from the beginning because it's such a dramatic response, but I agree to continue the relationship with these living arrangements. We find a new home for our dogs with a family in Connecticut.

When we realize that the problems in the relationship are so serious that they might bring it to an end, we start seeing a therapist in New Jersey, Dr. Dworkin, whom we are referred to by Allison's parents, who think we're both a little bit crazy at this point. Our relationship has seemed headed toward marriage in the next few years, as our friends are getting married, and eventually we'd like to start a family, so we are extremely cautious in handling our problems. Yet neither one of us is in any particular rush to get married, and it's not even an issue that's discussed for a few years. Our parents are perfectly comfortable with our living arrangements and never question us about our plans. Allison seems somewhat jealous of my work and of Nancy and feels I don't pay as much attention to her as I used to, and she's angry that I am so work-obsessed. Seeing Dr. Dworkin is extremely inconvenient, since it's a half-hour bus ride each way, but we both like him and the fact that he can help us create some dialogue, and we have confidence that he can guide us through what we hope is a temporary crisis. We are learning to listen to each other, and that's the first major step.

At a dinner party at her apartment one night, my friend Lucy Lehrer from Wesleyan and her boyfriend, Dan, introduce Allison and me to her friends Lauren and Jonathan. Lauren works as a personal assistant to film director Jonathan Demme, and Jonathan, her boyfriend, works at *The New Yorker*. Allison and I are quite taken with them. Jonathan has angular features, intense green eyes, and light brown hair and looks like a character Norman Rockwell might have painted. Lauren has dark hair and dark eyes and looks like an Italian movie star. They met at college. They are sitting next to each other on a loveseat; Jonathan is drinking a beer and Lauren a glass of wine. When they stand up to say hello, we see that Jonathan must be six-feet-four. It's a pretty small apartment, and we're squeezed around a cocktail table. Jonathan and I make eye contact in reference to the spatial problem, and I realize that we share a similar sense of humor. Jonathan is fascinated by what I do. He can't get over the fact that every plastic surgeon has a PR agent. "Dentists, too," I tell him. That really makes him laugh. Lucy serves the quiche, which she proudly tells us she has made herself, and it looks delicious. We all start eating. "Lucy, you used a goddamn graham-cracker pie crust," screams Lauren. We all start laughing. It's a fun evening, and when we're leaving we realize that we live on the same block as Lauren and Jonathan. We make plans to get together with them soon.

The PR business often takes me to the West Coast, mostly to Los Angeles. Driving on the freeway there, listening to the radio, makes me feel carefree and euphoric. I'm staying at expensive hotels racking up huge bills, paid for by the company, entertaining prospective clients and just enjoying myself for the first time in a long time. I've never felt better. The freedom of being on my own leads me to believe that I need more independence when I return to New York and that my working conditions with my sister are much too tense. I try working on several client accounts on my own, but it appears that I'm trying to hide something. One day I'm sitting at my desk, which is right next to Nancy's, talking on the phone to a client while I hear her backtracking on work that I have already done, talking to someone about the same client I spoke to them about the day before. I quickly end my conversation, and an explosive argument ensues between us. I scream at her, "You're screwing everything up, you're fucking up everything!" I throw everything on top of her desk onto the floor, grab her by her throat, and push her against the wall. She is shocked by my aggressive behavior and screams back at me, "Let go! Stop, stop!" The entire staff is watching. The fight is over in a couple of minutes, and we both realize that our relationship must be severed immediately. I rush out of the office within five minutes, ashamed of my abusive behavior but relieved that the business relationship has finally come to an end. My father comes in to meet with us at the Westside Diner to calm us down and try to reach some type of settlement, but he is unsuccessful. The next morning I pick up a copy of the *New York Post* at the newsstand. Nancy has made the feud public by leaking a story to "Page Six," implying that she didn't like the way I was handling the company finances and insinuating that I was dipping into the funds. I make a settlement with her without an attorney. I'm enraged by the publicity and vow not to speak to her for the foreseeable future.

I leave the company with only a handful of loyal clients, taking as many as I can from my sister. The next day I start scrambling for more, going back to old clients, scraping new ones from any place I can find them, including the Yellow Pages. That night I see Allison, who is glad that I've finally stopped working with my sister and thinks that I've made a great decision to work independently. She's extremely encouraging and tells me I'll have my business off the ground in no time. It's exactly what I need to hear. A few days later she surprises me with the news that she's ready to move back in with me. I find it curious that this comes after I make a separation from Nancy. I've long been aware of Allison's antipathy toward Nancy and her jealousy of our work relationship, but I've always ignored it. Still, I'm glad that she's had a change of heart and am happy to have her live with me again.

But after a little while I get a strange sense that Allison doesn't know how much time and effort I'm going to have to put into my new PR agency to maintain my old income. I'm concerned that she'll resent the amount of time I devote to work. Already it's beginning to feel like the undoing of a bad marriage.

Chapter 3

Polka-Dotted Hair

July 15, 1988. New York.

It's so hot and humid outside that I'm tempted to call and cancel my 1:00 P.M. appointment—I can't deal with another day of this weather. I've already postponed my breakfast meeting with this big-shot fitness guru from L.A. because it was too hot out and I didn't feel like schlepping all the way down to Soho to meet with an overenthusiastic set of hard abs for an egg-white omelette and dry toast. He's going to meet me uptown for drinks later tonight. I have an appointment to interview the "nonartist" of the moment, a downtown artist named Mark Kostabi. I've already blown him off once, and I've got no excuse this time. Kostabi doesn't actually create work with his own hands—he pays artists minimum wage to paint for him, and he just signs the work. He's gaining lots of notoriety for this gimmick. It's not exactly the most original idea. Andy Warhol did it with his Factory in the sixties. I'm going to submit an article on Kostabi for a gossip column for *7 Days,* a magazine in its prepublication phase. He's already received some extremely negative publicity in the media for a comment he made about AIDS being a good thing for the art community. He's also well known for his outrageous insults aimed at his collectors. "Anyone who buys a Kostabi is a fool," he says. "Every time they buy a Kostabi, I spit in their faces." He should be a real character.

I've been toying with the idea of working for *7 Days* in addition to my PR business. At the least it could be an interesting side gig, and at best it could lead me out of this mindless career of public relations. It's just so routine—flipping through my Rolodex all day long and talking on the phone pitching clients to editors and producers. I don't know how much longer I can take it. It's not the most intelligent work that I can find—anyone with half a brain and a whole lot of charm can do it. But I can't complain about the money. Now all I can think about is getting to this interview on time. I hail a cab. The driver takes me down Broadway, and in my mind I start tallying my monthly client billing—$2,000, $4,000, $7,000, $9,000, $11,000, $13,000. Let's see if I can get everybody to pay me on time. Sounds great, but my expenses are much higher this month. I don't even know what I'm really spending so much money on: traveling (Los Angeles and San Francisco), restaurants (four or five nights a week), clothing (weekend trips to Barneys), artwork (just bought one more painting by Robert Combas in San Francisco). I can always use more clients—and more paintings. I'll represent anybody. I'm not very picky. Anybody who wants to write a check or pay me cash makes a great client. Doctors and dentists with big practices are usually good for double the fee. Spiritual healers and astrologers are good prey, as are exercise gurus and nutritionists. Even a veterinarian who was referred to me this morning by my friend's gynecologist will work. I'll think of something to do with him. I'll get him booked on *Sally Jessy* somehow. I can promote just about anybody. If these clients want exposure, I'll get it for them. And even though I hate it, I do enjoy the adrenaline rush of being extremely successful in a competitive business—and the cash.

1:00 P.M.

Kostabi's studio, down near the Lincoln Tunnel, is up a steep flight of steps in a pretty run-down three-story building. The floor and walls are painted a glossy white, and lime green sixties modular furniture is scattered throughout the space. A shiny black baby grand piano sits in the far corner. I'm dressed in my summer PR uniform—khakis, a white button-down shirt, and black loafers without socks—and I'm quick to notice that not one person in the entire place is dressed even remotely like me. I'm sweating. I feel ridiculously out of place. The receptionist greets me wearing an aqua plastic micromini with a matching vest and platform shoes. She's very pretty, with a slight bluish tint to her black hair, and she asks me my name with a strange accent. Kind of a cross between British and Long Island. A double isle accent. She tells me that Mark is on the telephone to Europe but will be with me shortly. There's an odd choice of seating—a chair in the shape of a hand and a hanging bubble seat. I decide to walk around the space. An assorted fun pack of people wanders around the studio. A haggard dyed-blond guy with a pale angular face and a roaming eye is carrying all kinds of camera equipment. Later I learn he is Mark's younger brother, Indrek. He gives me a strange stare, and already I don't trust him. A woman with dyed jet black hair and deep purple lipstick sporting a black lace dress and combat boots looks through racks of canvases against a wall. Three Japanese men in dark suits and white socks are huddled around a stack of lithographs with a guy who has flame red hair and motorcycle boots, whom they keep referring to as Dr. Fry (I later learn his name is Dr. Fly). I take a look around at paintings of faceless, high-contrast figures, many wearing pointed hats, that I'll come to know as "Kostabi figures." One is a simple portrait of a faceless man holding a globe. Another is a faceless naked woman looking in a mirror. Lots of black, red, and white. Strange stuff. Pretty awful. Not my taste at all. It all looks mass-produced. There must be at least five hundred paintings in this room. I feel like I'm at a factory-outlet sale of modern art. And there's too much of it crowded into one space, which is making me feel uptight and nervous. I hope I don't knock anything over. I'm not sure if this stuff is worth anything or not because I've never seen his work before. I ask the blue-tinted girl with the hybrid accent if I can use her phone to check my messages. I call, and my assistant, Lara, is holding down the fort. Nothing urgent. The blue-tinted girl offers me a piece of her pink bubble gum. No thanks.

I've been waiting around for about twenty minutes. About a half hour later, a gawkish young man in his late twenties with medium-length bleached blond strawlike hair with black polka dots scattered evenly throughout comes from an office in the back of the studio. This must be Kostabi. His face is gaunt and pale, and his skin is kind of bumpy, like the surface of the moon. I'm thinking he hasn't eaten in days or seen the sun in years. He has very Eastern European looks, with a long jaw, and he seems friendly and excited about meeting me. He's smiling and laughing the way you would if you were seeing an old friend after a few years. He's wearing a pair of tight black pants, a white blousy shirt, and black platform shoes—he kind of looks like a court jester. He runs toward me apologizing profusely in this singsongy voice for being so late. He extends his limp hand to greet me and shakes it awkwardly. I immediately get the sense that something is slightly off with this guy. I've heard people say he's mysterious; if you ask him a simple question, he responds sometimes as if he has no idea what you're talking about. Maybe it's an act. But I'm really curious to sit down with him and find out what he's all about.

He invites me into his office and sits behind his desk, contorting his hands and arms, with one knee up on the chair, almost blocking his face from my line of sight. He reminds me of Gumby. He plays with his pen. He proudly shows me a recent full-page ad for his work in *Flash Art* magazine and displays some of his line drawings. He offers me one, a man in the shape of a dollar sign, as a gift. I like it. He starts eating a salad and tells me that food is very important to him—he can't work without a good meal. The salad dressing drips down his chin and onto one of the drawings; he wipes it off with the napkin. I ask him if this drip increases the value of the drawing. He laughs nervously. He points to a sculpture of a man holding the earth in his hands; it's just been made for him and he still has to approve it. He asks me if I like it. My opinion seems important to him. Switching from subject to subject, he talks about everything from the current art scene to his plans for the new Kostabi World. The phone rings. It's a call from Tokyo—it'll just be a minute. As his conversation progresses, he raises his voice and enunciates each word carefully. It's obvious that the person at the other end hardly speaks English. He instructs the caller to wire $200,000 into his account immediately

and gives him wiring instructions from a card in his Rolodex, re-
peating the instructions slowly and loudly. When he hangs up he
explains to me that he's involved in all aspects of the business except the actual painting. He hasn't painted in years, he explains,
but he is at the center of every creative decision. Kostabi World
has a regimented production process, I learn. An idea is created by
an "idea person" in the "think tank," approved by a "committee,"
assigned to a painter, who projects it onto a canvas with a slide
projector, sketches it, and paints it. The painting is then approved
and titled by the committee and finally signed by him. I ask him
for a tour of his studio, and he brings me upstairs, where there are
about twenty painters working side by side on different Kostabi
images. They each turn to see who the guest is, make no effort to
smile or say hello, and abruptly turn back to their work. I get the
feeling that tours are a daily occurrence and that there is a clear
sense of disdain for Mark. It is dead quiet except for a radio in the
background. He keeps the tour brief. There is a sign on the wall:
PEOPLE WHO WORK FOR MINIMUM WAGE LIVE IN A CAGE. I ask him
about it. Some painters, he proudly tells me, make more than
minimum wage. He created the sign himself and seems almost
proud. He chuckles. I'm not sure if I like him or if I think he's a
jerk.

Back downstairs, I ask him about his adolescence, about
his years studying art in California, about his influences, about his
East Village art years, and finally about creating his "factory." He
breezes through his responses as if he's answered these questions
a hundred times just this week. He tells me it's his turn now—he
has more interest in asking me questions than he does in answering any of mine. I've been warned that he could make a big joke
of the interview, but he seems to be taking our meeting seriously
so far—maybe it's my khakis and loafers. He is curious about my
business, the type of clients I represent and the media people I
know, and what I think I could do for him to build his image. My
initial reaction is to keep the interview professional—my purpose
in meeting him today is to write an interview and find out something nobody knows about him and submit it to 7 Days—not to

sign him as a client. But it is clear he wants to be a client, or is at least interviewing me as a potential PR agent. So I switch gears and start talking to him as a prospective client. I tell him about the importance of doing national television and keeping his name in the gossip columns, about creating scandal and intrigue. He's giddy with excitement and has lots of questions. By the end of the hour, he's sold on me. We discuss working together, but he's not willing to pay a monthly retainer. He wants to work with me in exchange for artwork. "When can we start?" he asks. But I'm not so sure I really want this artwork because I'm not sure I would even store it in my closet. But he convinces me of its tremendous resale value, and I have these pathetic images of myself carting this stuff off in the back of a cab to Christie's. But I also know full well that in a month or so I'll be able to manipulate him into paying a hefty retainer anyway because he'll be impressed with what I'll be able to do. Mark wants more from me than an interview, and I want more from him—it's an ideal relationship. We leave with a perfect understanding, and I never write the article, abandoning the notion of becoming the gossip reporter at 7 Days.

Jack of All Trades

It is clear to me from my first conversation with Mark that none of the loose ends of his business—publicity, marketing, and sales—have been tied together. I want to get going on this before anybody else realizes the opportunity is wide open. Within days of our first meeting and without any type of written agreement, Mark and I start working. Soon we agree on a $1,000-a-month fee and an unspecified amount of artwork. I quickly rewrite all of his press material, making it more mainstream and less underground, and promoting him as the ultimate con artist. After a few days, I book him on the Morton Downey, Jr. Show, in a never-broadcast segment where he and Downey stage a fight that turns real. Downey ends up in a neck brace and with a thumb fracture. This creates a huge amount of spillover press for Mark, and he finally seems to understand how the media game really works. The incident is reported everywhere, sealing his reputation as a bad boy. Although my other clients demand more of my time, in the first two months I get Kostabi regular mentions in the gossip columns of the *New York Post,* the *Daily News,* and *New York* magazine. When I have extra time, I make a phone call to someone in the media on his behalf, although we do speak on a daily basis and I am looking to book him on national television shows. Kostabi is impressed, confident that I can pull off just about anything. I feel the same.

I'm sure that I can generate some major publicity for the opening of the new Kostabi World, an enormous three-story warehouse facility on West 37th Street near the Jacob Javits Convention Center, But I also want to get involved in selling Mark's work in the international market. Kostabi already has one Japanese dealer and a few foreign dealers, but for the most part the foreign potential seems untapped, and I realize that there is significant money to be made. I feel like all I need is a few good suits and a new briefcase, and I can talk my way through selling these paintings and prints to anyone, based on the press we're creating. Day one for me on the road feels like I've been doing this for years—I'm confident, organized, relaxed, and energized to make sales at a 10% commission. I look like I'm making the buyer a good deal; I don't get turned down. I'm still busy hustling other clients and a new one, a condom company called Rubber Ducky. (I mail thousands of condoms to media people across the country hailing this condom as the hottest new contraceptive available on the market, and there's nothing even special about it except for the graphic of the Rubber Ducky on the package.) I even have my hand in pornography, working for *Oui,* the men's adult magazine, to promote its editorial content (political, media, sex, health, and exercise) in other print media. It's not a successful project. At the other end of the spectrum I launch a fragrance and bath-product line for children, called William & Clarissa, at F.A.O. Schwarz. For two years I use my apartment as an assembly plant, devoting ten to twelve hours a day during holiday season to the project, managing promotions and sales. The number of clients I am promoting is out of hand, and they range all over the map. My apartment looks like a warehouse of condoms, bubble bath, and diet books stacked from floor to ceiling. I think seriously about scaling back on my clients so that I can focus on Kostabi, but the rush I get from all these simultaneous projects is too good to give up.

Cashmere and Caviar

I am obsessed with working ridiculously long hours, earning plenty of money, and spending it as quickly as I make it—on anything I can get my hands on: frequent weekend trips to Los Angeles and San Francisco to visit friends; shopping sprees at Barneys and Bergdorf Goodman; dinner dates at Petrossian and Le Bernardin. I believe that the more risk I take on in a business deal, the better the payoff will be. All of this gives me an amazing sense of power and control—and tremendous elation. When I get my salary or hefty commissions, I sometimes cash the large checks so I can have the money in my hands. I love paying the bills and the tabs—especially in cash, for the attention it gets me from salespeople, waiters, and even dinner partners. I'm crazy when it comes to the sight and touch of money. When I go to the bank, I withdraw $5,000 from my account in $20 and $50 bills; the look and feel of so much money give me a jolt and a great sense of security. I try not to worry about what the teller is thinking when she's counting out the cash. I like the power of being able to buy anything I see that I want and just shelling out the cash as if it's no big deal. Losing control during a shopping spree is probably the ultimate high for me now; it causes a strange sense of panic, a near blackout state. My heart races—I'm nervous, I'm frightened, I'm pressured, I'm stressed. My body becomes numb and tingly, and everything around me is spinning and I feel like I'm going to pass out, but there's a force inside driving me forward.

One Saturday I feel like spending money at Barneys. I find a good-looking and slightly hip young salesman, who looks like he probably came to New York from Indiana to model after college, to show me some casual jackets. We pick out about six or seven, and I'm trying on one after another, looking in the mirror, asking him for his opinion. "It's a great-looking jacket," he says. "And I've got the perfect turtleneck for it," he adds. I make a mental note: turtleneck with black-and-white checked jacket. I switch to the next one, a simple navy blue blazer. "Oh, this is a good one," I say. "I've got to have this one." The next one, gray, looks fantastic, too. He smiles at me and laughs. "Should we keep going?" he asks. I try on the others, a black one, a dark brown one, and a maroon one, and now I'm totally confused and tell him that I have to think about it for a while. I guess people do this to him all day, because he doesn't seem too upset. I go look at shoes and find a pair of black boots that is exactly what I've been meaning to buy. They're ankle-length and have a simple buckle on the side. The salesman tells me that he has another pair with a slightly different heel, and he brings both out. I tell him I'll take both. $650. Simple. My mind is focused on the jacket dilemma. I go back and I don't see Indiana man. I need to find him. I don't know his name. Finally, he appears from behind one of those mystery curtains that leads to nowhere, recognizes me, and smiles. "You're back. Have you made up your mind?" he asks. "Yes," I tell him. "I'm going to take the black-and-white checked one, the navy blue one, the gray one, and the black one." He looks surprised. I feel like I've redeemed myself. "Do you want to look at some pants and shirts?" he asks. "Sure," I tell him. "And the turtleneck for the black-and-white checked jacket you mentioned." He shows me around, we pick out some pants and shirts, and I go into the dressing room to try everything on. I'm sweating and my head starts pounding. The tailor comes and hems the pants and fixes the sleeves and it's a done deal. $6,200. Indiana guy shakes my hand and tells me the clothes will be delivered by the end of the week. "Thanks for your help," I say. I don't go more than one hundred yards when I see a black cashmere V-neck sweater that I love instantly. There's no reason for me to ask a salesman for assistance because there are no questions to be asked. Do you have the $500 or don't you? I'm feeling kind of torn and thinking about returning the boots because they were $650, but I've just spent over $6,000. The sweater is incredible, too. I can pay cash for it, and not feel as guilty. A saleswoman approaches me. "Do you need any help?" she asks. "No, I was just looking at this sweater," I tell her. "I can show you others, if you'd like?" she asks. Others? There are others to consider? My mind is racing. She shows me an entire counter filled with cashmere sweaters in all different styles. I take off my coat and start trying on sweaters and looking in the mirror. I'm sweating like crazy. The black cashmere V-neck sweater in the case is $800. I touch it and it feels luxurious. I'll take it. "You'll have these sweaters for years," she tells me. So I also buy a navy blue cashmere crewneck for $500. I'm getting the urge to buy another, but at this point I'm so hot, I just want to get some air. "How would you like to pay for this?" she asks me. "Cash," I tell her. I pull a wad of bills out of my wallet and pay her for the purchase. She seems surprised. I've spent more than $8,000 in three hours, and I'm only making $20,000 a month, so I'm feeling pretty guilty at the moment. On my way out of the store, I realize the only thing I've forgotten is some Kiehl's tea tree oil shampoo, so I run over to the counter and pick up the shampoo and a few other things: conditioner, scrub, soap, and toner. The saleswoman rings it up, and then I ask her if I can add something to it. She sighs deeply. I throw in a tube of shaving cream. I pay for the items, she wraps them up and puts them in a bag, and I find my way out the front door onto the street and into a cab, where I collapse. My three-hour high at Barneys is similar to what it feels like to prolong an orgasm for hours and hours. There's a brief moment of guilt overshadowed by euphoria, and part of me wants to return it all (and sometimes I do several days later), but usually I move on to the next store after a few deep breaths and do the same thing all over again. It's kind of like marathon masturbating.

In the Buff

Allison and I escape the city most weekends, flying to Martha's Vineyard and staying at bed-and-breakfasts. We spend our days at our favorite beach, a nude beach at Gay Head, and in the evenings we go out for dinner and a movie. It sounds like a relaxing way to spend the weekends, but I'm finding that I'm not that good at hav-

ing fun on these trips. The peace irks me; I need more stimulation.
I'm much better in the city, running from museums to stores to
bars to restaurants, than on the beach, lying around tanning my
butt. I notice for the first time ever that I can't sit still for more
than ten minutes. Sometimes we go with Allison's friends, which
for me the first time was somewhat awkward but for her seemed
perfectly natural. She appears to be perfectly comfortable walking
around naked, aware of both men and women looking at her as
she walks on the beach or just lies in the sand. I'm just totally
aroused by the entire situation. But otherwise, I can't understand
why people flock to the beach to do absolutely nothing but look at
the clouds and sky and the water and lie in the sun. I get hot. My
organs get edgy. I can feel them moving around inside. I remind
myself not to go to the beach ever again. My agitation causes a
great deal of uneasiness between Allison and me; she can't understand why I just can't naturally unwind the same way that she
does, and it drives her crazy. She feels like I'm purposely trying to
ruin her vacation. She thinks that I'm too involved in my career
and that I can't keep my mind off it. Actually, I'm more focused on
her being exposed and watching her interact with other people.
There's a group of young college guys, sitting about twenty-five
yards away, looking in our direction. One of them comes over to
us, his cock swinging out in front of him, and asks Allison if she
has an extra cigarette. I'm amazed that she handles this request
without any embarrassment and am kind of turned on. Later they
watch her wade into the ocean. I am in awe of her body: her firm,
round breasts, her small waist, her tight ass. She seems to get embarrassed when I stare at her. Our relationship feels like a bad marriage again, and we barely speak to each other. I'm holding on to
the relationship and trying to make it work out because I feel
terribly responsible for its success and for taking care of her. And
I *am* much too involved in my work and in building a career. But
my brain is moving too quickly for me to be lying naked in a
pile of sand and soaking up cancer-causing ultraviolet rays that
will prematurely age me and be the cause of my death in thirty
years.

The (Con) Artist and His Muse

Kostabi World begins to come together, and it's exciting to see Mark's ego and ambition (and therefore mine) take such physical shape. The first floor of the building is used as an exhibition space; the second floor houses my office, an outer office, and the "think tank" and serves as a storage space for paintings; and the third floor is the actual painting studio, where close to twenty paintings are churned out each week. I am constantly taking private clients and dealers from one floor to the next, showing them lithographs and paintings and giving them a sense of how a Kostabi is produced. Mark's office on the second floor is removed from most of the activity—it's in the rear of the building—so he's kind of out of the loop. Most of the time we're not even aware he's there.

Mark and I start spending a lot of time together socially, although we only talk about business. For dinner we go to Trattoria dell'Arte, one of his favorite restaurants. He delights me with clever sketches on a small pad as we wait for our meal to be served. He draws a faceless man carrying a dollar sign on his back. Another faceless image with a television as a head. Sometimes they're very good, even usable. I'll give them to his idea person, Lis Fields, when I go to work in the morning, and she'll throw them into a pile, to be turned into actual drawings and later, if approved, paintings. The food comes to the table, and Mark stops everything he's doing; he is very serious about eating. I talk about the possibility of getting him on *Letterman,* and he likes that—he loves to see himself on television or read about himself in the gossip columns. I tell him about an upcoming exhibition in Tokyo that he will have to attend that will be huge—maybe more than a hundred pieces of his work. I explain that it's a new client of mine, Art Collection House. "Wow!" he says, never getting too excited about anything. But he tells me that he's never seen sales look so good. It never feels like a real business—it just feels like we're playing around. Almost like the paintings aren't real either. It's like we're printing our own money. And we're just making it all up as we go along. One day I'm a publicist, the next day I'm an art dealer. The energy is so powerful that I feel like I could show up at a hospital operating room and perform arthroscopic surgery successfully and nobody would even notice that I had absolutely no training at all. Mark encourages me to continue my sales efforts and I'm happy because I'm still working with my other clients. His brother Indrek, who pitches in with a little bit of sales work and some photography, is not pleased with our financial arrangement and in general is not happy at all with my presence at Kostabi World. He keeps a close eye on me and literally looks over my shoulder, walking into my office to see what I'm doing, or following me around the studio.

Cookies and Milk

The grand opening of Kostabi World takes place in November, with a huge press party for about a thousand invited guests. The morning of the opening is a busy one for me—hanging paintings, setting up the physical space, the lighting and the music. Allison lures me to the East Side to help her to find something at agnès b. to wear that night. As much as I gripe that I don't have time, I relish the thought of adding one more thing to my to-do list. The tension of the last-minute deadline, finding the perfect thing at the last possible minute, thrills me. It's a silly sort of heroism. She never seems to have the confidence to shop on her own, and I like going with her to manage the situation. After a few hours we choose the perfect outfit—a low-cut black sweater and skirt that get her a lot of attention that night. Everybody comments on her body, which never fails to delight me.

Twenty paintings hang in the newly renovated gallery, an enormous space about the size of a football field. I have orchestrated the entire event, from invitations to cocktail napkins. I instruct the caterer to set up tables of live mermaids—scantily clad women decoratively surrounded by hors d'oeuvres. This makes a huge splash. Because Mark is opposed to alcohol (there is always a rumor circulating about an incident in high school where a bunch of drunk high school guys roughed him up), juice is served in champagne glasses. For dessert, chocolate chip cookies and milk (in champagne glasses, of course). Mark wears a bright red suit and really stands out among the crush of people. It's mostly a trendy downtown crowd, models and artists mixed in with "new" collectors—yuppies, stockbrokers, investment bankers, and lawyers—rushing to invest their recent bonus checks in the most talked-about art. This is art as commodity, and people are looking to make money quickly. But some serious collectors are lurking about, too, just in case they might miss out on an opportunity. The art scene had already gone through a wave of artists like Haring, Schnabel, Salle, Fischl, and Basquiat and everyone had seen their prices skyrocket, and none of these "new" collectors wanted to miss out on a golden opportunity. I'm busy squeezing through the crowd to find Mark so I can introduce him to editors and writers who want to meet him. For the first time there is a buzz about Kostabi and his work that puts him into the limelight of the art scene for a brief moment. At 2:00 A.M., when the last guest leaves, we have offers on four paintings, which we didn't even expect. Mark seems thrilled as we recap the night. "Did any celebrities come?" he asks me. "I don't think so, but I'll check," I tell him.

Kinderspritz

I'm bouncing back and forth from the art world to my other clients. The day after Thanksgiving—the biggest shopping day of the year—is my official William & Clarissa launch at F.A.O. Schwarz. For several weeks friends have been helping me assemble the product: folding boxes, inserting liners and the bottles, and sealing them. My entire apartment smells like citrus. There is no room at the store to do this, and the product can't be shipped fully packaged across the country without being damaged. I can't believe I am promoting a fragrance for children—what am I doing? Finally, we ship everything to the display booth at the store. I am supervising a manager and thirty employees part-time on-site, and am responsible for the entire production and success of the operation. The first day is a nightmare. Tens of thousands of people come through the store, thousands of units sell, and the display needs to be restocked constantly. I've unwittingly gotten myself into a full-time retail job. But it does pay well: $3,500 a month plus bonuses. What won't I do for money? I'm standing around crying children and spraying them with perfume. I can't decide which is more absurd, Kostabi paintings or children's fragrances.

A Nonalcoholic Toast

I leave the world of children's lotions, potions, and powders for a few days to chaperone Mark to an opening at the Hanson Gallery in Beverly Hills. I have never been so struck with how little real enthusiasm there is for Mark and his work among respected artists and art dealers. Scott Hanson is a slick dealer who makes "exclusive" deals with Kostabi World and sells Kostabi paintings in addition to limited-edition lithographs. These deals prevent other U.S. galleries from selling editions of Kostabi lithographs. Occasionally a couple of lesser-known stars from television will appear at an opening and be photographed with Mark, who has absolutely no idea at all who they are because he doesn't watch TV. People dress for these openings as if they're going to the Oscars. Some approach him and, almost as if they have a prepared speech, just deliver a curt compliment. Mark seems extremely uncomfortable tonight and walks around the gallery with his hands behind his back. At this show it's clear how much of a manufactured celebrity he is—he can dress for the part in an outlandish costume, he can be photographed in the role, but he doesn't know how to interact with clients. He's like an unsigned painting. These shows drag on for hours, until Scott takes a group of us for an uneventful celebration dinner at Spago, where he toasts to the success of Mark's newest show, even though there's really nothing that anyone hasn't seen before. Mark thanks him awkwardly, and there's very little dinner conversation. Soon Mark is yawning and has his elbows on the table, tired from jet lag, so the party breaks up unusually early. The next day I take the earliest flight to San Francisco, where I stop by the Wolf Schulz Gallery and buy a painting by Remi Blanchard.

Natural Blonds

After dinner at Stars, I come back to the Stanford Court Hotel feeling very drunk and horny. I take a cab to the Tenderloin, a seedy part of town, but I don't find much open except some bars. I love walking through this area because I have no idea what's going to happen to me. Small gangs of kids and drunks hang out on street corners. I can't find a cab (having forgotten that San Francisco doesn't really have cabs roaming the streets like in New York), and it seems to take forever to walk back to the hotel. I cruise the empty lobby waiting for some kind of action. Anything. It's unusually quiet except for two people behind the front desk whispering. They're working. They can't leave their post to come upstairs and fuck around with me. And I'm not going to ask them for suggestions for crazy things to do at 2:00 A.M. in San Francisco. I think about calling a cab and taking a ride across the Golden Gate Bridge, but I don't know what's to see on the other side. And anyhow, the point is, I'm horny. I want some kind of sex. Finally, I give up on the desk clerks, go upstairs to my room, and read an ad in a local newspaper for a Kurt and Karin. A couple into threeways. It appeals to me. Young, German, male and female. Attractive, twenty-three and twenty-five years old. I call and a guy with a slight accent answers. He describes himself—tall, muscular, good definition, six-feet-one, 180 pounds, smooth body, blond hair, blue eyes, well-hung—and his girlfriend—sexy, firm, five-feet-seven, 115 pounds, blond hair, blue eyes, 36D tits, 26-inch waist, great ass, tight pussy. I ask what they get into. He says just about anything except he doesn't get fucked and she doesn't get fucked in the ass. Straightforward. How much? $300 an hour, $150 for each additional hour. Cash. They can be over in about forty-five minutes. He has to call me back at the hotel to confirm. Here's the part where I have to give him my real name. No big deal. The phone rings and it's confirmed. Silly technicality. I start folding my clothes and putting them away and cleaning up the room a little bit. I drink an Amstel Light, put some coke out on a glass tabletop, and do a couple of lines with a crisp rolled-up bill. I bought this stuff from a friend in Los Angeles who promised it was pure. It's pretty good. I brush my teeth and rinse my mouth with the little mouthwash in the bathroom. I'm checking the clock and flipping through the channels in a trance. There's a loud knock at the door, and I panic for a second. It's the Germans. I run to the door, look through the peephole, and see the two blonds. I open the door and invite them in. I realize I don't remember her name. Kurt and something. Karin. They're very impressive—they look like they could both be on the German Olympic ski team. Kurt and I shake hands. I ask them if they'd like a drink or a line of coke, and they step right up to the table and do a line. Karin asks for a Diet Coke. The television is still on, some bad movie with Kurt Russell and Goldie Hawn. She's whining. We're all sitting on the couches feeling a little bit uncomfortable and talking about San Francisco; I make some stupid comment about earthquakes. They're just visiting the States for a year, living here for a few months and then going to L.A. I give Kurt three $100 bills, and he puts them into the pocket of his jeans and thanks me. I've been in this situation too many times before. Two months ago in Miami. Karin asks me if I'm here on business. I tell her I'm attending a medical conference; I'm a doctor tonight. My mother would be proud. Karin tells me it's a very nice room. So let's get started.

Kurt takes off his T-shirt and jeans, and Karin does the same. I pull off my T-shirt, and it gets stuck on my head for a few seconds, an odd moment. I step out of my jeans. We're all sitting in our underwear, just kind of looking at one another and snorting lines of coke. Kurt pours himself a vodka. Karin takes off her bra and out come these beautiful breasts. I think they're real. Kurt says something in German. It kind of sounds like va-va-va-voom. He scoops up a small amount of coke from the pile and puts it on her left nipple and licks it off and asks me if I want to do the same. I drop some on her other nipple and snort as much as I can, then lick off the rest. Finally he takes off his bikini briefs and she takes off her panties, the two of them get into the king-sized bed together, and they start kissing. I'm sitting on the edge of the bed. I guess I've paid for orchestra seats. I'm fascinated by how powerful Kurt's back and butt and legs look but also by how much control Karin has of him in bed. He starts fucking her. She's guiding him, taking his cock inch by inch and encouraging him the entire time. All in German, of course. Now I guess it's an opera. Her legs are wrapped around his waist and he is thrusting into her and talking to her in a sweet voice. He keeps asking me to come closer to watch his cock slide into her pussy. Finally, after about fifteen minutes, Kurt comes and fades into the pillow. By this time, my briefs are off, and I start playing with Karin, gently teasing her breasts and feeling like we've done this a hundred times before. She gets between my legs and starts sucking on my cock and I feel pretty high from the coke and I'm hoping that I can stay hard enough from the coke to fuck her. I'm fucking her and she feels so familiar to me that it's eerie. I'm thinking about fucking Allison and it feels good, but not as good as being with Allison. And her hair doesn't smell like Allison's hair, it smells like some kind of gel; Allison's smells like the most wonderful combination of oils and herbs. And Kurt's talking to us and coaching me to fuck her harder and his accent is getting stronger and he's sounding like an SS officer and then I think about Munich and having to ship paintings there and then I finally come. I have to go home to New York. Shit. $300 for a forty-five-minute fuck. Expense it.

The Short Gentile

Allison and I are being pushed further and further apart because of my intense involvement in my career. My mind is disjointed; my thoughts whirl; I have to be in three different places at once and feel like I can't turn down projects or invitations. When I'm in Los Angeles on business I can only stay a couple of days until I have to turn around and come back to New York to take care of a client or a press event because I'm only a one-man show. Things are moving unusually fast, even for me. Dr. Dworkin suggests that I make more time for Allison.

I become completely obsessed with improving our relationship because I am terrified of being abandoned. I do whatever I can to keep things going—taking her out to romantic dinners and buying little gifts, Limoges boxes and perfume—but these are gestures only. There are days when our staying together seems hopeless, when we are nothing more than roommates sharing an apartment and having casual sex. She does her nails and I watch TV.

But I just get more heavily involved in Kostabi World. As Mark gains more trust in me, he allows me more and more control. I start making new contacts with dealers and galleries around the world and begin negotiating for exhibitions and print deals, which seems to come naturally. The income for Kostabi World is phenomenal—we're making million-dollar deals—as is my commission, like nothing I've seen before. It all seems much too easy and I'm not complaining. Kostabi's motto, "A Kostabi in Every Home," looks hopeful. When he notices how big my commission checks are getting (10% on $250,000 deals), he starts feeling like maybe the arrangement isn't a fair one. He thinks he's losing money and I'm making too much. I constantly remind him that 90% is going to him and that he shouldn't complain.

That winter Allison spends weekends skiing in Upstate New York with some of her girlfriends from her job at a real estate company, where she's been since a brief break after leaving Dr. Giller's office. We're comfortable spending time away from each other, and she always recounts the fun she has on these trips over the few dinners we have together. I spend those weekends with Lauren and Jonathan, who have just gotten engaged, hanging out at their apartment or going to the movies or out to dinner. Jonathan is writing for *The New Yorker,* so he spends a lot of time with me listening to my unhinged pitches for possible "Talk of the Town" pieces about my clients, which actually end up appearing in this staid publication on a pretty regular basis. One is about a team of young brothers who are making a fortune putting on huge spectacles at weddings and bar mitzvahs with magic shows, singing and dancing. Jonathan puts his own brand of humor on the whole story, and it turns into more than just a profile.

One night I'm watching *Larry King Live* when Allison comes into the room and sits next to me on the bed. She seems upset and asks if we can talk—I have no idea what she is going to say, but it definitely doesn't seem like good news, and I'm frightened. She says what she has to tell me is difficult and that she hopes that I will forgive her. She looks petrified. It's simple: Allison's "girls only" ski weekends, in fact, are not girls only. She has met a guy, and they are meeting on weekends. I am furious—but even more, I am curious. I have a million questions. Who is this guy? Is she fucking him? What does he look like? Short? I bet. Jewish? No way! Who is taking my place after all of these years? Some short gentile? "I guess being tall and Jewish counts for nothing," I scream at her. I tell her to move out right away. She starts crying hysterically and packing, while I run to the bathroom and force myself to throw up because I feel like my insides need to be cleansed after hearing this awful news. I am still so curious who she has replaced me with, but she won't talk about it. Within a few hours, a friend comes to the apartment to pick her up. Her parents come the next day to collect her belongings and move her home.

I feel horribly rejected and deceived. I'm crushed. My friends rally around to support me, take me to dinner, and spend time with me at my apartment. Lauren, a big believer in self-help groups and talk therapy, immediately decides the best thing to do for me is go with her to a local Al-Anon meeting—it might be the right place for me to share my pain and find some support, but I'm not really comfortable addressing the issue in front of a large group of strangers. Over the next month my suffering eases, and eventually Allison and I arrange to meet for dinner. She leads me to believe that things are finished with the short gentile. I am relieved, able to forgive her. She decides to move back in with me. At the end of the month my sister gets married, and we're speaking again, and Allison and I attend the wedding together. Afterward, without giving it too much thought, I buy Allison a simple engagement ring in Soho. I hold on to it for a few weeks and give it to her on Passover. I don't know what I'm thinking, possibly that it will heal the tumult of the past two months and bring us back together, that all will be forgiven and we'll start from scratch. Two days later, after considerable thought, she agrees to get married and we go to visit her best girlfriend, who lives in Philadelphia, to celebrate our good news. About a week later Allison tells me that she can't go ahead with it. She returns the ring and moves out again. I am stunned but not sure that this is really her final decision.

Ménage à Trois

About a month later Allison and I, although we are not even together anymore, go to Lauren and Jonathan's wedding together on Long Island. We stay together at a hotel the night before and end up sleeping in the same bed and having the most awful sex in an attempt to patch things up. It's awkward, as if we've never been together before—we're a mess of twisted limbs, uncomfortable and unpleasant. I can't sleep the entire night. As for the wedding, it is an incredibly strange situation, too. Lauren has been putting quite a bit of pressure on Jonathan to marry her, but although they love each other very much, he still isn't ready for marriage. I think that there is no better couple—they are both attractive, smart, funny, and talented, and they complement each other perfectly.

I feel unanchored without Allison, and I don't want to let my two best friends out of my sight. Since this is the first time I've been single in years and I have no other plans, I decide to join the newlyweds in renting a simple guest house in Sag Harbor, kind of a posthoneymoon retreat for the three of us. Needless to say, spending a summer with a newly married couple is not the greatest idea, especially when there are no boundaries in the relationship. I am just the third wheel, calling out for attention. One day we all load into our shared Toyota and drive into East Hampton to do some shopping. We run into some acquaintances of mine from the art world, who are aware of my breakup with Allison. "These are my friends Lauren and Jonathan Graham," I explain. "They just got married, and I'm sharing a house with them in Sag Harbor this summer." It hits me. I'm feeling lost without Allison by my side. There's nobody propping me up. Could it be that I have no identity without her? To compensate for this lack of attention from Allison, I demand it from Lauren and Jonathan all summer long and create a ménage à trois. I become obsessed with my appearance again, working out four and five days a week and following a strict diet. Jonathan becomes an exercise fanatic with me, and we have fun suffering together.

After six months of tofu, tuna, and workouts, I lose more than thirty pounds and look like I'm in excellent condition, but I'm starving myself. I'm not building muscle, and I'm just getting weaker every day. I start bingeing again and gain all the weight back in a month.

I use the house that summer as a base for my PR, keeping track of my authors' book tours by phone and mapping out strategies for my other clients. Then I start traveling from city to city to meet new clients: author referrals from publishing houses, authors I've previously promoted, artists who have heard about my work for Kostabi, and mostly health and medical clients who've heard of me by word of mouth. They come crawling out of the woodwork. I take on an attractive and dynamic gynecologist who believes that hysterectomies are being performed unnecessarily in this country. She is a unique woman, and I want Jonathan to profile her for *The New Yorker,* so I arrange for them to meet when she comes to New York. The three of us have breakfast at the Plaza, and over poached eggs and hash browns, Dr. Schroeder starts discussing in detail the vagina, the labia, the clitoris, the ovaries. Vagina, vagina, vagina. I've never seen Jonathan with such a startled look on his face. That day I fly to Washington for a meeting that afternoon, then stop in Miami for two days to check in on William & Clarissa sales. I'm crisscrossing the country like a lunatic. I don't know if it's the tofu or the tuna fish, but I can't stop flying.

Berlin Holiday

February 1, 1990. 5:00 A.M.

I can't sleep. I'm lying in bed watching coverage of the Berlin Wall coming down on CNN and realizing that I absolutely must see this event in person even though I'm supposed to be in Los Angeles in three days. I don't care. I call TWA and book a flight for that evening. The only person I can think of who will possibly come with me to Berlin is Lucy, my friend from Wesleyan, who's moved to Paris. Of course she'll come with me. I call her right away and tell her I'm on my way to Paris and that I'd like to go to Berlin by train and check out what's going on there. "Are you sure you want to do this?" she asks me. "Yeah, I really need to," I tell her. "Great, I'm up for a little trip to Berlin," she says. I knew she'd be as excited as me! I take the last flight that night from JFK to Paris. I feel an intense urgency to complete this assignment; I can't sit still on the plane and keep going to the bathroom. Finally we land, arrive at the gate and I see a blond woman in a long black wool coat, holding a little sign with my name on it in bold letters. It's Lucy. I haven't seen her in months, and I've forgotten how pretty she is— she looks angelic. I feel like I've been sent on a mission and a beautiful secret agent has been sent to pick me up.

"*Bienvenue à Paris,*" she says in a Texan accent, which makes me laugh immediately. She's originally from Dallas, and throughout the trip she turns the accent on to get me to laugh hysterically; she's one of my funniest friends. She doesn't let me do any of the talking. "I have everything figured out," she says. "First, we're going to get you something to eat at Aux Deux Magots," she says. She grabs my suitcase, drags it across the street, and finds us a taxi. She directs the driver to the restaurant, impressing me with her French. "I'm practically a native now, as you can see," she says. At the café she orders us both a café au lait and a croissant. "It's actually just a crescent roll, if you weren't sure," she explains. Then she leans back in her chair. "I can't believe you got on a plane last night and flew all the way here to see the Berlin Wall," she says.

"Are you certifiably crazy?" "No, not yet," I say. "I just thought it might be incredible to see, you know, history."

Lucy tells me about her new life in Paris. She is living by herself and spends her days writing (she is currently working on a play that is later produced when she returns to Washington, D.C.) and reading. She has become part of a circle of Americans, with whom she socializes pretty regularly at dinner parties. She seems very at home. I'm starting to come back to life. After breakfast, we drop my luggage off at her studio apartment, a tiny space in an old apartment building in need of some repair. The room looks a lot like Lucy. Lots of lace, velvet throws, candles, and perfume bottles. But she has no time to waste in her apartment. "Let's go, let's go," she says. "There's nothing to see here."

Since I haven't been to Paris in years, Lucy takes me out on the street for her quick tour of the city: Pont des Arts, the Opéra, the Rue Faubourg St. Honoré, Shakespeare & Company, and Luxembourg Gardens. When we finally get tired of walking, we stop at a café and have another coffee. Lucy takes out a lipstick and mirror, purses her lips, and applies the lipstick with even strokes. "Pretty French, huh?" she asks. "Yeah, where'd you learn that trick?" I ask her. "Just been copying some of the French models I see at cafés," she answers. "You know, Lucy, I think you might be French," I tell her. This is the highest compliment I could pay her. "Why, thank you!" she says. We have a million things to talk about, everything from my breakup with Allison to Lauren and Jonathan's marriage to my work for Kostabi to old college friends to our sisters to our nieces and nephews to our parents. "I can't believe we're sitting here together in a café in Paris," I tell her. "Where's your favorite place to go for dinner?" I ask. "It'll be my treat." "Doudin Bouffant," she tells me. "You'll love it. We'll go tonight." We pay our check and take a walk to see the Nikki de St. Phalle sculpture fountains, which are playful and multicolored and make us both feel giddy. "We have to get to Berlin, if you still want to. The Wall is coming down," I say. "Sure I'll go anywhere," she says. We head to the station to pick up our train tickets.

The next morning, we take the train from the Gare du Nord

to Berlin and arrive at Alexanderplatz. We are immediately struck by how different the two sides of the Wall are. One side looks exactly like the West, colorful and modern; the other side is muted and gray. Hundreds of people are crowded around the Wall, many of them with axes and hammers, pulling off pieces of it as souvenirs. The area is infested with reporters. I'm unimpressed. But I have made it from my bedroom on the Upper West Side to the Wall in less than twenty-four hours. That is record time. Now all I can think of is my hunger. At an East Berlin restaurant, with hundreds of choices on the menu, we try to order several times, only to be met with shakes of the head from our waiter. There only seems to be one available item that day: rump steak. Lucy and I can barely contain our laughter.

Back in Paris, we visit the Musée D'Orsay and have a delicious dinner at Polidor. Although I'm having a fabulous time, I feel the pressure to move on to the next country—and to move faster. I make a list of things to send Lucy for her apartment: a fluffy bath mat, a big coffee cup, Advil, magazines, tabloids, peanut butter, and Samsara perfume. I also make a note that I need to spend time by a pool in a warm climate.

The day after I come back from Paris, I fly to Miami for three days.

Back in New York, I start going out every night—with friends to dinner, on blind dates arranged by my sister or friends, even on dates with Allison, who is still involved with the short gentile. I hang out in bars and clubs, snorting cocaine and drinking. My behavior is out of control, and I'm enjoying every minute of this craziness. I just don't feel responsible. I feel like there are no boundaries. One night I photograph Allison nude in Mark's studio. This is the last time we see each other, a rather strange and removed way of finally ending the relationship.

Chapter 4

A Proposition

Kostabi World has become my second home. I'm friendly with many of the employees, particularly Lis Fields, an attractive British woman in her midtwenties who is one of Mark's idea people and whose office is right next door to mine. Lis has a great sense of design and style, wearing fashions from London before they become popular here, like cinch-waist tailored black pants suits. She has short dark brown hair and ivory skin and wears bright red lipstick. She feels stifled by her job but sees it as a stepping-stone to her own career as a painter. And then there is Jessica Doyle, Mark's assistant, a WASPy, slender, blond woman in her early twenties, a tough girl from a good family with lots of street smarts who doesn't take crap from anybody, including the Kostabi brothers. Mark likes to bully her—he constantly accuses her of losing shipping invoices and faxes, and of not returning phone calls—but she doesn't let him get away with it; he's actually scared to death of her. Lis, Jessica, and I become an inseparable trio, finding humor in the goings-on of Kostabi World; we even laugh at the pretentious name. When Kostabi discusses his new proposal—for building the world's tallest building—and summons the think-tank artists to render sketches, we snicker behind his back. Still, we run the place like clockwork. Paintings get designed, painted, approved, signed, and shipped all over the world.

One of the painters at Kostabi World, Annike Brandt, has a particular interest in me. She is a petite German with frizzy red hair, ashen skin, an elfin grin, and an infectious laugh. She often hangs around my office talking about art and films. She is a conceptual and performance artist, who works under the pseudonym Lore Schopf. She seems interested in the sales aspect of my job— targeting a gallery, making a sale, and closing the deal. One day she casually and quietly asks me if I'd like to have a drink with her at the corner bar up the street, a place nobody from Kostabi World frequents. We make a plan to meet the next evening at 6:30, and for some reason I feel a nervous flutter in my stomach.

I arrive at the bar about fifteen minutes late because I'm closing a deal with a German dealer who is planning a big opening exhibition and party for Mark. Annike sits alone drinking a screwdriver. I see her reflection in the mirror behind the bar. There is a stool next to her and a screwdriver on the bar waiting for me. I thank her for the drink and apologize for being late. She asks me a little bit about my day while she puffs away on a cigarette. I notice how small her hands are, how covered with paint. As usual, she complains about the general working conditions at Kostabi World—the late paychecks, the long hours, the vile art, and Mark's childishness. I nod in agreement. She complains about the time clock that Mark makes the employees use when they come and go—but she's figured out a way to beat the system: employees just take turns punching in and out for one another. We have a few good laughs over the lousy art—she is just completing a painting of a faceless figure playing golf. The Japanese love this stuff. We do a lot of custom painting jobs for dealers and buyers: tell us what you want us to paint, we'll Kostabi-ize it! The bar is starting to fill up with people from the neighborhood, and Annike moves closer to me. Then the tone of the conversation takes a serious turn, and I become a little concerned. Annike looks down slightly and begins speaking softly. "I've been watching you for several months," she tells me. "And I feel comfortable that I can finally trust you." My hands shake with anxiety. I need another drink. I order another round of screwdrivers from the bartender. Annike tells me that she dislikes Kostabi very much for what he is doing in the art world and wants to play a small joke on him. "Are you interested?" she asks. "It depends. What kind of a joke is it?" She asks me first how I feel about him. I explain that he's my employer but I think that I had made it clear to her during our previous conversations that I think he's a fool. She looks around the bar for a few seconds and then explains to me a scheme she's been thinking about for months. "This is between the two of us," she warns me. "It goes no further." I accept her conditions. She explains that she will paint reproductions of Kostabi's work and sign them, and I will sell them to foreign dealers. "Are you talking about painting fakes?" I ask her. "You want me to sell fakes?" "Reproductions," she responds. "Reproductions, whatever," I say. She wants me to pay her a mutually agreed-upon fee for each painting. I will be free to charge my clients as much as I'd like for each painting. "Are you interested?" she asks. This exchange happens in what feels like a split second. I'm wondering if the screwdrivers have gone to my head or if I've just made up what I've heard. "Are you serious?" I ask her. She takes a puff of her cigarette and looks at me laughing. "Totally serious," she says. I'm at a loss for words. Without a bit of thought, I go ahead and tell her it sounds like an incredibly ingenious idea. I'm thinking it sounds like a lot of fun, too. All I can do is smile and giggle. It's a funny gimmick. And the next thing I think is that I no longer have to split 90/10 with Kostabi World. Now I'm the factory and can set my own prices, competing with Kostabi directly. I tell Annike I'll have to think about this and I'll get back to her over the weekend; can we meet Monday at the same time? She suggests a different location, the Film Center Café on Ninth Avenue. The whole concept seems entirely logical. This is the most exciting proposition I've heard in years, and I'm tingling. But why is she choosing me? She mentions something about my being an Aquarius. She gets up to leave and tells me to hang around at the bar for about five more minutes. She doesn't want anybody to see us leaving together. I feel very special for being chosen, like being singled out in elementary school by Mrs. de Lime. How could I turn it down? I wonder if this is a trick being played on me and she's wearing a wire and Mark is outside with the police waiting to arrest me, but I banish the image, just like I dismiss any thought of the consequences. I leave the bar in a frenzy of excitement and start doing some quick arithmetic as I'm walking up Ninth Avenue. It looks like it could be a pretty lucrative deal. I'm thinking we can produce fifty paintings that I can retail for $500,000. Maybe I can buy that apartment I looked at in the Century on Central Park West after all.

Around this same time Lauren has me interested in co-producing a documentary film about a group of homeless gospel singers and musicians that she had found singing in the subway, called Emmaus the Group. They actually live in a homeless shelter in Harlem called Emmaus House. She wants me to come hear them perform and convinces me that this is an important story to tell. I go uptown to meet the group and hear their music and am really moved; I know immediately I can't refuse. I agree to co-produce the project with her. We form a production company called No Roof Productions, and I put up the first $10,000 to produce *A Six Voice Home*.

The *Playboy* Survey

The breakup with Allison is still very much on my mind. My family and friends urge me to move on, to stay busy, and to start dating again, but I have been connected to this woman for more than twenty years, and I'm still living in the apartment we shared and among the things that we collected together. I cannot function without her. I feel sick. I took care of her for so many years, when she had the flu or when she was so badly sunburned on vacation. Where is she? I am losing control. I hear through a friend that she's found an apartment only ten blocks from mine. This is a difficult blow. She is surviving without me. Days later I learn through a mutual friend that she has become serious with the short gentile. I am enraged. Had it been a fling, I could have understood, but here she is seriously involved a year later with that same guy—the pain of the rejection is overwhelming. My behavior becomes tremendously obsessive in all directions. I begin dieting and exercising compulsively again and working twelve- to fourteen-hour days. And that day I become an official stalker. I am compelled to drive and walk by her apartment building, look up and

count to the tenth floor to see if her light is on. In an effort to respect her wishes that I not communicate with her, I never call to
chat, but I start sending gifts: expensive lingerie, a pair of earrings,
books—anything I see that I think she'll like. On one of my scout-
ing expeditions to her neighborhood, I see her getting out of a
Honda Accord with Connecticut license plates. The boyfriend's
car. Progress. I now know where he went to college and what fraternity he belonged to—he has stickers on his back window. I am
relieved that he has gone to a less-than-mediocre school in the
Midwest and isn't too bright. Now I have a marker—the navy blue
Accord. All traffic is rerouted by Allison's apartment for at least a
year. I know when the boyfriend is sleeping over, when they are
going away for a weekend, and if they are living together. I keep
notes. One day I'm sitting on a bench across the street, peering
over my copy of *The New York Times* like in some pulp detective
novel. I see them get out of his car and walk into the building. I
wait about three minutes, walk over to the car, and open the pas-
senger door. I check his registration: Kevin Parker. I have his address, too. Now I can contact him directly. I spend a few days
planning the call. One night I dial his number, identify myself as
a pollster from *Playboy* magazine, and tell him that we are doing a study about single men and their sexual relationships with
women. I ask him basic background information: address, age,
height, weight, college education, job, salary. He doesn't paint a
very impressive picture of himself. I'm wondering how Allison is
going to finance her lifestyle on his salary. I have a list of twenty
questions, ranging from the serious to the ridiculous. What part
of your girlfriend's body do you like the most? (Answer: Breasts.)
Like the least? (Answer: Feet.) I am certain now I have the right
guy. How many orgasms can you give her? (Answer: Fifteen.)
How many can you have? (Answer: Ten.) Now I'm certain that
he's playing with me; he knows what's going on here. Neverthe-
less, I'm surprised and aroused by his forthcoming responses and
start fantasizing about having sex with Allison, from his perspective. I tell him I'll call back if I need any more information and
about a week later I call back with follow-up questions. He's not

so dumb after all. He's trapped me. This time he is recording me.
Allison calls me the next day and threatens to call an attorney if I
don't stop the harassment. I'm frightened, yet somehow I feel like
I've won the battle.

Prozac: The Wonder Drug

I finally stop seeing Dr. Levitt because talking to him is like talking
to a piece of Danish modern furniture. All he wants to do is discuss my childhood, and my mother and father. But there's something wrong inside my head and I'm starting to think it's in my
system. I also give up seeing Dr. Dworkin because I don't feel like
I'm making great strides with him either. (Allison had stopped
coming with me months before our breakup, and I had continued
to cross the George Washington Bridge in the rain and snow to
trek from the highway to his house.) He's an incredibly nice guy,
but he's a problem solver and I think I'm in a crisis. When I arrive
at his office, I sit in a chair with a big cushion next to his. He proceeds to do what I call the intake—a process much like blood
work. Basic background questions to fill him in on the previous
week's activities. It just takes up time. "Andy," he says, "I think you
need to learn to listen more carefully to what people around you
are saying to you because you often make quick decisions that affect you and your relationship with them. The next time you find
yourself in an argument with somebody at work or even a friend,
just take a step back and listen to what he or she has to say. It'll
give you time to respond more accurately." I don't want this kind
of coaching. He's not giving me the slightest opening to talk
about how I'm feeling, about the crazies. I leave each session frustrated. At the recommendation of one of my general practition-
ers, I start seeing Dr. Howard Wexler, a middle-aged psychiatrist
who greets me at his office wearing a navy blue blazer, gray flannel pants, and a bright red tie, looking more like a maître d' at a
bistro than a psychiatrist. He's extremely stiff and smells like
cologne. His office is impeccably decorated in a contemporary
seventies style, glass and metal. Behind his desk is a realist oil

painting of a horse that looks like it should be hanging at a steak house. I take a seat on a black leather ottoman across from his glass desk and start right in with my psychiatric history. He scribbles on a pad as I speak and asks very few questions. He has an annoying tickle in his throat and keeps apologizing for it. I feel like he's just processing my story as opposed to probing it, and when I try to underscore my feelings of madness and depression, he just continues to scribble. At the end of our session, he comes to the quick conclusion that I have a narcissistic personality disorder and suggests that we see each other twice a week and that I join his once-a-week therapy group. I don't feel comfortable with group therapy, and more important, I don't like Dr. Wexler very much. I cancel our next appointment an hour before. Bills from him collect in my mailbox for years. I never pay them.

A few weeks after my twenty-eighth birthday I realize that something is not functioning properly, and I'm convinced I should go for a CAT scan. I feel like I have an abscess swelling deep inside my head—I imagine that there's pus within the depths of my brain—just waiting to explode. One day it's going to burst and some unfortunate cleaning lady is going to be called in to mop it up off the floors and scrape it off the walls. Or maybe I'll be on the crosstown bus and it'll splatter all over the other passengers and the windows. You see, it works like this. When I wake up in the morning, I receive a signal that tells me, for example, whether to pack up and head to Los Angeles or to catch the next flight to Morocco or to just lie immobile in my bed and watch CNN all day or scrub the bathroom floor and tub until my hands are blistered. The decision is already made for me. It's somehow predetermined. I don't have a say. I don't call my own shots. I'm not really in control anymore. I guess that's why I finally make the appointment to see Dr. Herbert Kleinman, a well-known psychiatrist on the Upper West Side. Because every other psychotherapist and psychiatrist has failed me in the past, I have no expectations of our first meeting. Actually I figure it will be another three-month relationship that will probably end in another unpaid bill, resulting in a collection agent coming after me.

May 15, 1990. Upper West Side.

My meeting with Dr. Kleinman is at 7:30 A.M. I've never heard of a doctor who starts seeing patients so early. I've had only three hours of sleep and barely pull myself together. I look like shit, unshaven and unshowered. I wet my hair down, throw on a pair of jeans and a T-shirt, and try to cover the dark circles under my eyes. Dr. Kleinman is an older man with a mysterious European accent, and I am struck by his kind manner. He makes me feel very welcome in his office, and he smokes a cigar, which relaxes me. He seems confident and ready to attack my problems. I tell him that I am quite disturbed over my recent breakup and that I'm trying to erase the thoughts through incessant activity—working, socializing, drinking, and doing drugs. I tell him that I'm hypersexual, and he tells me that he is not surprised, since I was used to having sex on a regular basis. I discuss the issue of not having control of my life. We talk for forty-five minutes, and he confidently tells me he thinks this is simply a case of depression. And he has the perfect solution. He prescribes a new drug on the market; it is called Prozac and has shown some very good results. He thinks it should clear things up right away. I leave his office with a prescription and an appointment to see him in two weeks, and a feeling of hope.

That night, I take my first 20-milligram yellow-and-green Prozac. I dream that Dr. Kleinman is driving an ice cream truck around the Upper West Side, passing out Popsicles in the shape of Prozac capsules, and people are lining up for miles. In the morning I check to see if I feel any different. The next morning I look into the mirror. No change. I take an extra 20-milligram capsule before I go to work, just to speed things up. About two weeks later I'm in the shower washing my hair and I realize that I'm in a really good mood for the first time in a long time. I feel like I could be doing a commercial for shampoo—lathering up my hair, singing and smiling in the shower. I go back to see Dr. Kleinman and he puts me on 40 milligrams a day. The Prozac seems to keep me on the high side, and I don't slip into any depressions. I also happen to be moving faster than the speed of sound. I call my parents and tell them about my success with my new psychiatrist and medication, and they are relieved.

The World's Tallest Building

June 27, 1990. New York.
I've got a million meetings today, and none of my list making is helping to keep things connected. A meeting with Ellen Salpeter, the young representative of Dyansen Gallery, a large chain of art galleries across the country, about an exclusive contract with Kostabi World to publish a limited-edition graphic series, which will mean huge revenue for Kostabi World and a sizable commission for me. A meeting with Lauren and the Du Art film-lab people—I don't know why I ever got involved in this project. It's costing me a fortune and taking up a huge chunk of my time, although Lauren is taking care of all the production details from hiring the cinematographer and crew to organizing the shooting schedule. But I love Lauren to death, and I promised to see the project through to the end—$75,000 at final count. But Lauren could convince me to jump out the window of a skyscraper without a net below me. And we're shooting footage in Pennsylvania over the weekend with Emmaus, and we'll all have fun driving in the van and shooting the lead singer performing at his childhood church. Then I've got an F.A.O. Schwarz presentation for revamping our William & Clarissa marketing plan. Dinner at Arqua with two Japanese dealers who are interested in a one-hundred-painting deal.

I've begun taking on tremendous responsibility for the direction of the studio's everyday operation. This includes production of paintings from the think-tank stage through painting, titling, invoicing, and shipping. I am also negotiating deals with the large galleries for orders of large numbers of canvases and limited editions of graphics. The goal is to raise enough money quickly— about $800,000—so that Mark can purchase an apartment at the CitySpire Building on West 56th Street. The Prozac is making me feel highly motivated and energized, and I'm more productive than ever. But while I'm traveling the globe trying to raise money for his apartment, Mark is completely focused on his project for the world's tallest building, where he plans to house the new Kostabi World as well as live. It will be a building for art, for artists, for galleries and museums. He spends his days drawing sketches of it and actually goes as far as hiring the architectural firm Kohn Pedersen Fox to draw the preliminaries. It's all he talks about. I'm pretty pissed off that he's wasting his time on this ridiculous project. When I press him about how serious he really is about it, he expresses surprise. This building has become his passion. His desk and floor are covered with blueprints, and the idea people are busy sketching the world's tallest building from every angle, around the clock. He is already starting to figure out how he'll divide the space in this multibillion-square-foot megastructure: between museums, artists, residences, commercial space, and public space. He is racing around Kostabi World in his suit and tie as if he were Donald Trump, not giving any consideration to how it's all going to be financed. I wonder what the architects are thinking about the whole thing. Mark points to the highest level of the building on a blueprint. "That will be my living space," he says— yet we still haven't figured out how to buy his apartment at CitySpire. Now I realize I'm dealing with a lunatic.

A Creamy Vanilla Dessert

After dinner at Arqua with clients from a new Japanese gallery, I take a cab back uptown to my apartment. It doesn't feel like I'm going to be staying here too long—I'm restless. No phone messages. There's nothing on television. The *T*-word is coming on— trouble. Drugs. Sex. I'm not going back downtown or out to a bar. I could order in sex. But I'm not paying for it tonight. I get on the phone and start talking to a few different guys on one of the phone-sex lines. Nobody too interesting. Finally I hear a guy who sounds good. Nice voice. Good laugh. His name is Jeffrey. "Bi-curious" with a girlfriend. Always the most fun and fucked-up kind. He's been partying for a few hours, smoking coke. We talk for ten minutes about lots of things. Work. (He's a television producer.) Sex. What else? What he likes to do. He's a top. He's a big voyeur. He gets off on beautiful bodies. He likes watching guys fuck girls. (We've got a few things in common.) Says he's in the mood to party and play. He's in the 60s between Park and Lexington. I figure I'll give it a shot. I take his number and call him back. He answers. Phone-line protocol. I take his address. Get dressed. Jeans. T-shirt. V-neck sweater. Take a few thousand dollars from the freezer. My frozen assets. Never know.

The concierge rings apartment 35B and announces my arrival. He's a bit curt. I get the sense that I'm not the first visitor of the evening. I nervously ride the elevator, slightly buzzed, wondering if I reek of the five or six vodka tonics I consumed earlier this evening. Fuck it. I've got nothing to lose. I ring the bell and the door opens. Standing in front of me is a good-looking guy, about thirty years old, six-feet-two, 190 pounds, messy brown hair, green eyes, a cleft chin, and a worked-out chest and arms. Real straight boy. Looks kind of like he could do a deodorant commercial. He's wearing a light blue UCLA T-shirt and a pair of jeans. He's barefoot. Next to him is Einstein, his golden retriever puppy. We shake hands and he invites me in. Big hands. Solid grip. Good eye contact. It's safe to go in, I tell myself.

Jeffrey's apartment is a bit of a mess. My first instinct is to offer to help him clean up a little. He invites me to sit down and relax and offers me a drink. Vodka and Scotch bottles and empty Diet Coke cans cover the glass coffee table in front of the matching white Palazetti couches. He brings me a glass with ice. I point to the vodka, and he pours me a generous drink. Einstein is under the table, which is littered with Marlboro Lights, full ashtrays, pipes, lighters, an old Blimpie sandwich, and back issues of *New York* magazine. He lifts his glass to mine. "Here's to good friends," I say. "Tonight is kind of special," he adds. We laugh. It's unusually quiet thirty-five stories high. The lights are dim. This guy is making me nervous, so I take a drink. He asks me if I'm in the mood to smoke some coke, and I tell him I'm *always* in the mood to smoke coke. I sound like an addict. He double-checks that all the shades are drawn. He puts on Blondie. "Heart of Glass." Much better. Time for drugs. He fills the pipe with some crack and takes a big hit. He's leaning back on the couch and lifting his hips off the launchpad, lips pursed, smiling. He refills the pipe and passes it to me. I take a deep breath of the white smoke, and it tastes like a creamy vanilla dessert—it's so rich and fluffy it goes straight to my cock and balls. They're tingling. I'm as high as I can go on my chart. Suddenly I care about Jeffrey and Einstein. They're mine. I put my arm around Jeffrey's shoulder and rub his neck. He puts his head between his knees and starts laughing. We laugh together. We just sit next to each other on the couch waiting out the high. I'm petting Einstein. I get up and go to the bathroom and spot a Cindy Sherman photograph on the wall that I really like. Shit. He's got a Cindy Sherman photograph. I don't say anything. Maybe I can get him so fucked-up that I can steal it. I piss in his sink and go back into the living room. We're both barefoot at this point, so now there are two sets of naked feet on the white carpet underneath the glass coffee table. We take another hit. He stands up, takes off his jeans, and throws them on the floor. He's getting serious. Of course this guy doesn't wear underwear. Faggot. I should have known. He walks around the room showing off his ass. Not bad. He sits on the couch and turns on the VCR and starts watching a video of a group of guys taking turns fucking a blond girl with big boobs. He lubes up his cock with some lotion on the coffee table and starts jerking off in front of me. He smiles. I guess this is what I came here for. I take a hit until I feel real turned-on and sit down next to Jeffrey. I pull off my jeans and briefs and start sliding my hand up and down my cock. Then I start stroking his. It's pretty massive when it gets totally hard. It looks like a missile or a rocket. I'd like to have one that big. I don't know what for. Just for show, I guess. Out of nowhere he asks me my last name. I stumble for a minute, then give in and tell him. He tells me he knows my sister. I guess my jaw drops. He starts laughing. Jeffrey has this incredibly deep laugh. Great. He knows my sister. Should we call her now or wait until we're done? I'm fucked now. Guess what? I just jerked off with your brother. I'm craving another hit of coke, so I smoke some more and get even more turned-on. On the coffee table is a framed picture of Jeffrey and another guy, who looks just like him. It's his brother. He probably has a big missile dick, too. They're with their mother and father skiing in Aspen. They've been watching this entire display of lewd behavior from the coffee table the whole time. I'm a little embarrassed for Jeffrey.

Jeffrey gets up and announces that he's going to take a shower and that I should make myself at home. I already feel at home. I'm in my briefs. Watching television. Eating popcorn. Einstein is snoring under the table. Once I hear the shower running, I start rifling through Jeffrey's desk. I feel like I'm on a game show desperately searching for clues to something. *Beat the Clock*. On his desk is a photo of Einstein with a ribbon on his head at Christmas. The frame is monogrammed with the initials PJB. Something's off. I find his wallet with his driver's license, an American Express card, a Citibank card, all bearing the name Patrick J. Bailey. I should have figured. The old use-your-middle-name-as-your-first-name trick. I'll deal with this. Then I find rubber-banded piles of pictures of him at black-tie events with lots of beautiful girls and boys getting drunk and celebrating with their arms around one another holding champagne bottles. There are even some of him with Calvin Klein standing near a pool—looks like Miami or Los Angeles. He's got about $1,000 in cash and a bunch of Chinese menus. And crack pipes. Lots of them. I go into the refrigerator, and it's empty except for some peanut butter and jelly and bread. I'm not in the mood for a peanut butter and jelly sandwich. I find his passport on top of the refrigerator. It's brand-new. He must be going somewhere soon. Bad picture. Looks like Marcus Schenkenberg on a bad day. Probably spent the night before partying. He comes out of the bedroom wearing just a robe and tells me he feels much better and that I should take a shower. He gives me a towel, a pair of sweats, and a T-shirt to change into. I jump into the shower and stand under the jet of some Sharper Image faucet gadgetry that pulses on my brains. I start coming back to life. I use his Kiehl's grapefruit liquid soap and feel like I'm sterilized and ready for surgery. I dry off and walk back into the living room, where *Patrick* is smoking more coke.

"What do most people call you?" I ask him.

"Just Jeffrey, I guess. Sometimes Jeff," he answers. "Does anybody ever call you Andrew?"

"No, just Patrick," I say. "My real close friends just call me Patrick."

He stares at me.

"You should let your friends call you Patrick, too. Then you wouldn't have to reprint your checkbook or passport, get new credit cards, monogram your picture frames or stationery or any of that kind of stuff," I add.

"Go fuck yourself," he yells.

I start laughing. Patrick turns on the television and starts flipping through the channels. He offers me a hit of coke, which I gladly accept, and it gets me going again. This time I feel refreshed. I'm wearing my new uniform—sweats and a T-shirt—and I feel clean and smell good. Smoking crack is like a sport. It should be an Olympic sport. I would be very good. But Patrick, I think, would be a gold medalist. He goes into the bedroom and changes into a pair of briefs and a T-shirt. He feeds Einstein and then gets on the phone with someone he calls Matt. Twenty minutes later Matt arrives at the apartment with more coke, and I insist on paying for it. He tells me to put away my money. I recognize Matt from some of the photographs. Patrick introduces me as a filmmaker friend from Paris. Matt is about thirty, a scaled-down version of Patrick, with short brown hair and sad-looking blue eyes. He's obviously a regular visitor, as Einstein makes a big fuss over him. Patrick asks Matt to take Einstein out for a walk, and the two go running for the door. On the way out, Matt and Patrick look at each other and smile. I quickly decide to put my regular clothes back on and leave, but Patrick insists that I stay. "Don't go—we'll have fun," he assures me. We're going to smoke more coke when Matt and Einstein come back. He convinces me. When Matt returns in about fifteen minutes, he puts on Blondie again. We're all getting high. "What do you do in Paris?" he asks me. Make films.

What kind of films? Mostly documentaries about fish. Flicks about fish? Yes, fish. *Poisson.* Matt laughs. Soon all three of us are sitting in our briefs. Tropical fish? Actually, all sorts of fish. Are there fish in the Seine? I laugh at the question. Matt seems puzzled and takes another hit of coke while Patrick and I laugh at him. Then Matt and Patrick start touching each other on the couch, and I go into the kitchen and start making myself a peanut butter and jelly sandwich on toast. By the time I'm done, the two of them are in the bedroom, naked, sucking each other's cocks. They're boyfriends, is my guess. Also that there is no girlfriend for Patrick. Or she's out of town with a touring company of *Cats* and she's not coming home for a few years. I come back into the room eating my sandwich. They stop midsuck. Matt sits up and asks me how I met Patrick. Same way you probably did. The Parisian fish-documentary story was just a little joke. Move over. Three naked guys in a bedroom totally coked-up playing with one another in the middle of the day. Or night. Einstein's confused. It's dark, but that's because the blinds are closed. It could be light. Patrick and Matt and I are smoking and the two of them are kissing and they look beautiful together and we all have four letters in our first names and we all have blue eyes but Patrick still has the biggest cock. I'm not sure if I should be watching or playing, but Patrick keeps pulling me closer to him and Matt and both of them start taking turns sucking my cock while I'm getting high. I wonder if anyone else is coming over to play.

Later Patrick decides to order in some Chinese food and asks what we want. I tell him anything he likes; I eat everything. I lie in bed with Matt and ask him if he's okay with all this. Sure. He inhales a huge hit of coke and blows it into my mouth; I get extremely high from it. Patrick watches the whole thing from the phone. The food comes, and we put on our briefs. Dumplings with hot sesame oil, moo shoo pork with pancakes, shrimp with walnuts, Szechuan chicken and eggplant with garlic sauce—and Diet Coke. We don't really eat much of it. But if I die in this apartment, I wouldn't want to be the one to have to do the autopsy on me.

David Letterman is talking to Chevy Chase, so I know it's after midnight, and still nobody has shot his load. Einstein's been out only once since I arrived; it's somebody's turn to walk him. Don't look at me. Ask the doorman or the concierge. All I know is that I need to be inside dimly lit enclosed spaces when I'm coked-up. Patrick throws on a pair of jeans and plays self-sacrificing dog walker. I end up with Matt in the bedroom—we're naked in a matter of minutes and together in the shower before Patrick is back. I met him on the phone. Me too. Matt's your real name? Yeah. Andy? Yeah; little boy's name, huh?

After Patrick returns, we start passing around the pipe again. I'm watching Patrick and Matt together and stroking my cock, and all of a sudden I can't hold back any longer and it starts building and building until finally I just let it all go and shoot all over the two of them and all I can see in front of my eyes is a big pinwheel going in circles. For about three seconds my brain freezes and everything shuts off—just the pinwheel, no sound. And I feel this tremendous guilt for having spent the last twenty-four hours in this apartment for these three seconds and six spurts of cum. So I clean up a little, put my clothes on, and say good-bye to Patrick and Matt, who are entangled on the bed. Einstein follows me to the door and looks up at me. I go into the kitchen and feed him and leave.

Another Round, Please

My friends decide that I need to start dating again. They figure I'm successful, good-looking, and funny and should be in a relationship and put Allison in my past. Lucy, who has returned from Paris, turns out to be a well-intentioned and dedicated matchmaker, but she doesn't understand that I'm incapable of connecting to anyone in a serious way. She tells me that she has the perfect woman for me and introduces me to a good friend of hers, an actress named Jane Fletcher, who works as a waitress at Elio's on the Upper East Side. The first time I meet her, for drinks, I'm immediately impressed—she's got a great smile, a wild laugh, and a quick wit. I think she's a bit nuts, too. We're well matched. We start dating, nothing very serious at first, but we end up spending most of the summer together, going out to dinner and the movies and having sex. Unfortunately, although I don't know it, I'm looking for a replacement for Allison and she seems like the right one. But the relationship runs into some trouble: first, she's not Allison, and second, we're both drinking too much. I'm also taking medication, and we're both flying high around Manhattan.

It's a Saturday, and I've spent a long day at Kostabi World getting a huge shipment of paintings out to a client in Japan in record time, and I'm not feeling too well. I've got a bad headache. When I get home, I take about five Advil with an Amstel Light and after about an hour I'm a little better. I'm looking forward to tonight because Jane has the night off from work and it's been a few days since I've seen her. I call her and tell her I'm going to be a little late and jump into the shower. The water turns cold. Shit. I dry off. I throw on a pair of jeans and a white linen shirt and head crosstown at about 8:30 P.M. Jane gives me a big hug and kiss when she sees me, and I wait in the living room while she's getting ready. A pop station is playing in her bedroom and I'm reading *People* magazine. She's putting on her makeup and offers me a drink; she's having one herself, so I take a beer from the refrigerator. When she comes out of her bedroom, she's still brushing her hair, wearing a pair of jeans and a tight black shirt and looking like she's ready for a night out on the town. "How do I look, seriously?" she asks. "You look great," I tell her. I'm attracted to her; she's a lot of fun and really amusing. She thinks I'm incredibly wild and likes playing on the edge with me. By now, we've had a few drinks and we're anxious to go out. We arrive at Punsch, the restaurant of the moment, on the Upper West Side. The owner, who knows me well, seats us and we order drinks. I start rambling about some of the difficulties I'm having with Lauren about keeping the film financed. "Honey, you're going to have to talk to her about it," she says. Jane has such glib solutions. I have never considered talking to Lauren about budget problems because she could outtalk me any day. Lauren would just persuade me that I have the money and should just keep paying; it's for a good cause, and anyhow, we're almost done. The waiter comes, and we both order gravlax and the duck. I don't know why we both have the same thing. He also brings us another round of drinks, and I order a bottle of wine. It's getting more and more crowded in the restaurant, and very warm. It's been pretty hot the entire week, and I'm thinking that maybe the air-conditioning isn't working very well. Jane looks pretty buzzed; she tells me I do, too. We're laughing at each other in our drunkenness. Alcohol is clearly fueling this relationship. Our dinner comes to the table and we eat ravenously and order another bottle of wine. I don't think I can walk out of the restaurant now. Somehow I manage to pay the bill with my credit card, and I'm trying to think of where we can go next. "What do you want to do?" I ask her. But my mania steers the course; we stumble into a cab and go downtown without a specific destination. "Keep heading downtown," I tell the driver. We pass by some bars that we nix and just open the window and breathe in the air and laugh at the last couple of hours. We're having a blast. "Take us to Gansevoort Street in the West Village," I tell the driver. He drops us off at Florent and it's pretty crowded, but we don't care. We're fearless; we order an after-dinner drink and share two desserts, and I'm already starting to think about our next stop.

Frequent Flyer

I'm obsessed with buying large quantities of cleaning products at the supermarket. Everything I can get my hands on: paper towels, sponges, bleach, laundry detergent, dishwashing liquid, scrubs, soaps, waxes, sprays, and oils. I hoard them in my kitchen cabinets in case I get snowed in for the next six months. Then I get to work. I put on my rubber gloves and scrub the entire bathroom until it sparkles—this can take an hour or longer. I move on to the next room, vacuuming dust from crevices, waxing floors, and polishing furniture. I set everything in its proper place. When it's all done, I'm exhausted. I'm obsessed with counting the number of words on a written page, usually after I've read it, but sometimes I have to count first. Sometimes this gets in the way of getting work done. When I leave my apartment, I check three or four times to be sure I've locked my door.

When I tell Dr. Kleinman about my obsessional cleaning and counting, he prescribes Anafranil, which puts a sudden end to most of the behavior within a matter of days. He still thinks Prozac is working well for me, although I tell him the combination of the two medications is making me feel like I'm moving faster and faster. I assume that means it's working, because I'm not depressed. I'm invited to an art opening that's happening in Los Angeles that very evening, and by 1:00 P.M. I'm at the airport. I'm selling art faster than I ever have before and feel like I have this magic power of attracting people to me.

I arrange for an installation of Mark's work at Charivari, the fashionable boutique on West 57th Street, which is great publicity for him. He paints the windows personally and exhibits some of his work in the store. I also make sure a $2,000 Dolce & Gabbana overcoat for me is worked into the deal. The next day Mark and I go to Cologne, where the Schulze Galerie is putting on a huge opening and exhibition for a few hundred people. It's a wild party. Everybody is having a good time, getting drunk and singing together, when a German artist named Charlie Banana approaches Mark, looking for a fight. "Your work is crap, *faelscher!*" he shouts—the German word for "forger." Although the next day Mark is telling people a humorous version of the story, the look of unease I read on his face tells me he's been unsettled. We fly together to Tokyo to attend an exhibit at Galerie Sho, one of Mark's biggest Japanese dealers. The Japanese are taken with Mark's work because it's so pop and so American. I've lined up a schedule of galleries to visit while in Tokyo. These are my first contacts in Tokyo, and my meetings with dealers are rather formal. My presentations are well prepared, and my pitch is the key to my sales success. When I promote Kostabi, I am confident when I tell them that he is the fastest-rising artist on the international scene. I call in at Art Collection House, a gallery I had contacted from New York, and sell them a huge program of Kostabi originals and lithographs and arrange for an exhibition that Mark will attend within the next two months. I also meet with two American dealers who run a gallery for a wealthy Japanese woman who owns Marrs Gallery and is extremely secretive about her business; she ends up buying paintings from me, including one from my personal collection. I leave Tokyo with a nice profit and fly back to New York for a two-day layover.

I've invited my family out to dinner at Erminia, a dark and cozy Italian restaurant on the Upper East Side, to celebrate my success in Tokyo. I arrive about ten minutes late and see my parents, Nancy, and her husband seated at a table in the corner, already having a drink. I have to catch up. I order a vodka tonic. They all stand up to hug and kiss me. Nancy is pregnant and really looks big now, and I've only been gone for ten days. I'm carrying four shopping bags of gifts from Tokyo, and I put them underneath my chair. Everybody seems excited to hear about my latest adventure. I tell them about my sale to one of the biggest galleries in the country and the individual sale of a painting from my collection for my price of $40,000. Called *Lovers,* it was originally owned by Sylvester Stallone but later returned to Mark during a feud with him. I knew to grab this painting, which I took in exchange for one month of PR work when I began at Kostabi World. After we order dinner, I give everyone their gifts: a beautiful white linen Yamamoto shirt for my father, a black quilted silk vest for my mother, a big blouse for my pregnant sister, and a sweater for my brother-in-law. I think my family leaves this pleasant evening believing my life is on track.

The urge to keep moving is insistent, so I make an unnecessary trip to visit Lucy and her boyfriend, Yves, who are temporarily, because of his visa status, living in Montreal. I tell them about the counterfeiting scheme over a long dinner, because I think it will amuse them and I want someone else to know. They warn me that it seems unwise, but I don't pay any attention to their advice. From Montreal, I fly to London on a ridiculous mission that Kostabi actually approves to recoup money from a dealer who owes him $80,000. There's not a chance that this dealer will pay, but I visit him at his gallery anyway. He refuses to see me or speak with me about the paintings he has on consignment. I'm not too concerned; it was just a good opportunity to visit London. I build in a few side trips—vacation days. I'm in the mood to see Paris, so I fly there the next morning and tell Mark I'm going to the FIAC art show. But I spend a few days shopping and hanging out in cafés. I get the urge to go to California, so I fly to Los Angeles and make a tour of the West Coast, visiting a few art galleries and some friends. It feels like I'm adding three cities to my campaign schedule and I just need to keep my body moving or I'm going to crash. I'm enjoying the manic pace. I come back to New York for a brief respite and then travel to the art fair in Cologne, using it as an excuse to go to Europe again. I spend about twenty minutes at the show and do no business at all. Whenever I travel, I pretend that I'm working like a dog. I want to go shopping again in Paris and visit Lucy, who's just returned from Montreal, but I somehow get on the wrong flight in Cologne and end up in Vienna on Thanksgiving Day. I'm a little confused. But I finally get to Paris and meet up with Lucy, who takes me to the apartment of her friends Deb Copaken and Paul Kogan, where a group of Americans has gathered for Thanksgiving dinner. My behavior is particularly wild this evening—I'm carrying a roll of canvases with me and unroll them for the group and pour a glass of red wine on one of the paintings, explaining that it will only increase its value. They're all amused.

Faking It

November 26, 1990. 5:30 P.M.
I arrive at the Film Center Café and there's a screwdriver waiting for me. It's a ritual. And for the first time I'm feeling scared shitless. Annike and I make some small talk, and then I just blurt it out: "I'm in." She stares at me blankly. I realize that I have to translate that bit of slang for her. "I'm interested in participating in your plan," I tell her. "I'm in." She smiles, as if she's expected that response. What would she have done if I'd said no? I tell her I'll ad-

vance her the initial $20,000 for the first twenty paintings—$1,000 per painting. She tells me that she'll start painting in her studio in Brooklyn. We will choose twenty images from the Kostabi "image bank," books and slides that depict the standard images that are repeated over and over, and I will start discreetly preselling to clients abroad. We decide to meet at my apartment in the next few days to choose the images, confident it's safe to go with the standard ones. There's so much repetition of these images that another five or six on the market won't make a difference.

Annike comes to my apartment on Saturday morning, and already we feel like coconspirators, a modern-day Bonnie and Clyde. It feels good. She asks me if I've mentioned our plan to anybody, and I tell her I haven't. She emphasizes that nobody should know about this. Now I'm wondering if I've told anybody yet. Just Lucy and Yves in Montreal. I had to tell somebody, and I'm dying to tell more people. Especially Jonathan—he'll love this story. I'm sure he'll think I'm as crazy as he is now. I'm excited to be involved in such a great scheme, and I crave the attention. I give Annike the first payment, $10,000 in $100 bills. We make a list of paintings that should be easy to sell, and on Monday I'll get on the phone and see what kind of interest I can drum up overseas.

Annike moves quickly. She starts sneaking supplies—canvas, paints, brushes, and slides of the paintings—out of Kostabi World late at night in small trips and brings them to her studio in Brooklyn. She shares a loft space with Tom Hogan, another Kostabi World employee, from whom she must hide her activities by only working in the early morning. She keeps me posted on her daily progress when I see her at Kostabi World, and in about a month she has finished the first series of paintings. They're all popular or classic Kostabis—faceless women carrying bowls of fruit on their heads, a seated faceless woman with her chin resting on her hand, faceless people playing golf, and a faceless man and woman embracing. I'm about ready to make my first trip to Europe to sell them and then on to Japan to negotiate deals for large gallery orders. Annike photographs each completed painting against the white brick background of her studio walls, and slides are created to show customers.

The night before I am to pick up the paintings in Brooklyn I rent a car, then I wake up at 4:00 A.M. to be at Annike's studio by 5:00 P.M. This will be my first time ever driving to Brooklyn, and I imagine myself being lost until sunup, but her directions are perfect. She is waiting for me outside in the cold and quietly guides me upstairs. We load two rolls of paintings into the car, constantly fearful of waking up Tom, and the first phase of the pickup is done. I drive as slowly and carefully back to my apartment as possible, all the while worried that I'll be stopped on the highway with the counterfeit paintings. Annike has already signed them— a task usually performed by Mark but sometimes handled by an assistant when he isn't available. That afternoon I title and date and sign the back of each painting and store them all in my downstairs bathroom, in plain view. My friends who come over or drop in are all aware of the paintings, but I don't make a fuss about them, just referring to them as my Kostabi reserve. About a week before Christmas I take the paintings to Munich, where I have several appointments to show them to dealers. I've invited my friend Pamela to come along; she thinks I'm out of my mind to be involved in this scheme, but she's never been to Munich and I want to make a vacation out of this adventure and have some fun. The paintings are rolled up tightly and taped, and I carry them onto the plane. Our Munich hotel room is the size of a cage—about twelve feet square, which doesn't offer much space to show paintings—so I realize I'll have to lay them out on the bed. Pamela leaves to go shopping while I prepare the paintings. When the first dealer arrives, I apologize for the viewing conditions. I am barely able to move around the bed. She isn't sure she likes all of them, but I give her a price she can't refuse and sell her three of them for about $15,000. (A real Kostabi, depending on size, would go for $5,000 to $10,000 retail.) I feel like I've just unloaded a couple of used cars. Later Pamela and I go out to celebrate and then meet Annike's sister, Heike, who lives in Munich, and to whom we are delivering an envelope containing a $5,000 cash gift from Annike. We have fun dipping into the profits that night, going out to a few bars and a great traditional German restaurant. The next day we take a train to Trento to visit Raffaelli, a Kostabi client, and take care of some legitimate Kostabi business. From there we are off to Milan for a brief stay, where I show the rest of the paintings without much luck and have my ear pierced on the spur of the moment on the street.

When I return to New York, Annike is just beginning to work on a new series of paintings and I am preparing to leave for Tokyo to work on a deal with Art Collection House, now one of our biggest clients. Annike is painting faster than I can sell, and I worry that I'll have a warehouse's worth of Kostabi paintings crammed into my bathroom. I'm too nervous to tell her to slow down. I have established a good working relationship with the staff at Art Collection House, sweetening deals by throwing in extra lithographs or paintings, or ordering custom-designed paintings—golf, urban landscapes, and futuristic designs—for the director. With a roll of canvases and sheets of slides—a combination of counterfeits and "real" Kostabis—I make my presentation to Art Collection House. I offer great deals on the paintings I've brought with me, and they pay for several on the spot. I also visit other galleries and make similar deals, selling paintings outright for cash. My knowledge of Japanese is useful, even though many of the dealers either speak English or use translators. They are still amused by my language skills, which I picked up as a high school exchange student and at Wesleyan.

After selling a significant number of counterfeits, I start confiding in several close friends about my activities because I feel a desperate need to share with them what I have been doing on these trips abroad. And I think it's an exciting and entertaining story and that some of them will benefit directly from the money. I was never concerned that anyone I told would report to Mark, and I was right. It wasn't the wisest thing to do, but I just couldn't contain the excitement of the secret and my success. But when I tell Lis Fields, she panics and says she doesn't want to hear any more because she doesn't want to get involved. Jessica Doyle hears us whispering and wants to know what we're keeping secret from her, and I tell her about the scheme. She is equally appalled yet somehow amused. I am surprised by how nervous they are about what I'm doing but also realize that it's too late to stop the game. Now I am confident that it's just a matter of time until I'll be caught. Something will show up somewhere because I've left such a paper trail. I feel as if telling the story before I am found out will protect me, will make me immune to later accusations. I tell Jeannette Walls, a columnist at *New York* magazine, the entire story, and she hints that I may have caused some trouble for myself. She suggests that I tell the story to John Taylor, another *New York* reporter, which I do, hoping that somehow he can salvage this mess in a nice, neat article that will portray me as the victim— or even as the hero. Although I certainly don't see myself in that role, I delude myself into thinking it's the spin the story needs. My medication has pushed me so far into a manic state that I believe that nothing or nobody can harm me. But Taylor is very candid with me. He tells me that his writing a piece about this affair will only serve to hurt me, and that I will probably get into legal trouble. However, this story is never written. I'm not the slightest bit concerned about being indicted because I don't feel like I've committed a crime. I feel as though I'm creating enough income for Kostabi, and in my mind I'm just playing out Annike's joke from the bar.

Uptown Boy

February 28, 1991. New York.
It's been a hectic week. I've only been back in town for two days, and I'm starting to get frantic about my situation. But I'm looking forward to Friday night's date. In fact, I've been looking forward to it the whole week. Sarah Jones is a well-known fashion designer whose clothes are sold in her boutiques all over the country and in department stores. I had met Sarah a few times at social functions, and finally walked up to her at a restaurant recently and suggested

I call her sometime for dinner or a drink. She seemed delighted. Things must be bad if she was so quick to say yes. I called her the following week from Tokyo and suggested Friday. Great. On Friday morning I call her at her office and tell her that I've made a reservation for 9:00 P.M. at Blue Ribbon, a popular restaurant and bar in Soho. She wears a black dress and bright red lipstick. I spend the latter part of my afternoon at agnès b. on Madison Avenue picking out a simple gray suit and a black shirt. I practically bribe them to alter the pants in an hour. Cuffs? No cuffs? I shave twice so that my skin is perfectly smooth and stay in the shower for half an hour. The entire cab ride downtown I'm extremely uptight. Is the suit too downtown? Do I look too uptown? Maybe I'm neither. Why am I going out with an older woman? Is seven years older too old? I spot her checking her coat and walk over and give her a kiss on the cheek. Totally uncomfortable for both of us. We try to laugh, relax. We both order vodka tonics. This is a good sign. Compatibility. But from the moment we sit down, we both just look at each other, expecting the other to lead the conversation. We have almost nothing to talk about. I notice that her red lipstick looks unnaturally bright with her dark black hair. Can I bring that up with her? Can I ask her if she's wearing something that she's designed herself? She waves to a friend across the room. Who's that? Another designer. A quick question, quick answer. Somehow we start talking about having children—a great subject for a first date—especially since she's seven years older than me. She makes it clear from the moment the appetizer is served that she wants children soon. Should I just relent and conceive a child with her tonight? After dessert. Luckily, people who recognize her stop by our table to chat and she introduces them to me. We both have the oysters. I have the tuna, and I think she orders just a salad. She tells me she doesn't want to talk about work—it's been a rough week. For a moment I'm stumped. I suggest we talk about the oysters. This is my best joke of the night. I'm lucky if any of my jokes get a slight smile tonight. Everybody in the restaurant sees me out on a date with her—even an old college friend who might not recognize me but who recognizes her—but it doesn't matter. I'm having the worst time of my life. There's a table of two couples laughing next to us. How can I find my way into their group and somehow push Sarah onto a group of people she knows? This date has already ended, but I don't know how to make it official. I tell Sarah I've got to get up pretty early the next morning, and she tells me she's going to go over and sit with some friends. She thanks me for dinner. I leave the restaurant and take a cab uptown alone, which is how I've been feeling for two years. I was just looking to have a good time over dinner and get to know somebody. Maybe I wasn't downtown enough. I shouldn't be so hard on myself. There was no chemistry between us, which I somehow failed to see from the beginning.

Quick Cash

One afternoon I'm approached by the brother of a friend of Nancy's. Nancy and I have been on very good terms for two years, speaking with each other very frequently, discussing business and our successes. Nancy is doing a favor for the salesman by sending him my way. I know my sister well and I assume she's also getting him off her back. The young salesman is a smooth-talking Texan who arrives at my office looking to sell me five thousand pair of recycled jeans with a patch of the Texas flag sewn on the knees. "Watch them fly out of here," he tells me. I imagine that I can resell them for $25 each and make $100,000 on the deal. So I quickly agree to buy the lot for $25,000 cash on the spot. A few weeks later, a truck pulls up to my apartment building and proceeds to unload sixteen huge boxes into my living room.

This isn't the only get-rich-quick scheme I undertake. I start sending my money to a broker who invests it in foreign currency. I'm losing a couple thousand dollars a month, though he tells me not to worry—it'll bounce back. I like the idea of sending him a monthly check because I can see how much I have invested with him written down on a statement and know how much I can hope to get back based on his calculations. It's a process that appeals to my highly neurotic sensibilities. I try not to pay attention to the statements and look forward to my weekly phone calls with him, when he pumps me up with his market forecast. I actually believe whatever he tells me and ignore the facts of the statements. He exudes confidence, and I have no reason to believe anybody would cheat me.

The Death of Gustav Faelscher

May 7, 1991. New York.

Annike and I decide we are finished with our counterfeiting scheme. At the moment we don't have any buyers—the market is flooded—and we are frightened about being found out by the authorities. So I put together a death notice and submit it to *The New York Times* for a fictional character named Gustav Faelscher that Annike and I create. I messenger it along with a check to *The New York Times* and am promised that it will appear in the next day's issue. I use the Kostabi World phone number as a contact. The death notice reads, "Gustav Faelscher. Art dealer, filmmaker. Passionately devoted his life to bringing the work of contemporary American art to the German and Japanese art worlds. Private burial in Stuttgart. In lieu of flowers, direct all contributions to Jedermann." "Jedermann" is a reference to Kostabi's *Everyman*. I am announcing the death of the forger, actually believing that this will put an end to this project and the possibility of any danger to me. When the death notice appears the following day, Annike and I are both amused and extremely relieved. I actually believe we are safe now because the forger is dead and cannot be prosecuted. But exactly one week later the real trouble starts.

Rikers Island

May 14, 1991. New York.

When my phone wakes me up at 5:20 A.M., I figure someone is in trouble. It's Mark, calling from Tokyo. I'm right. The someone in trouble is me. The game is up. "Don't go in to Kostabi World today," he tells me. "There's a problem with some paintings Heather and I have found at a small gallery in Tokyo." I know right away that I've been caught. My heart is racing. He vaguely explains that he and his "model" girlfriend, Heather, have found some unauthorized paintings, paintings that he didn't sign. He tells me that John Koegel, his attorney, will be calling me later this morning. I immediately call Annike to warn her, then I get dressed, take a cab to Kostabi World, and walk into the dark studio only to find that the lock on my office door has been changed. Shit. All of my files, my Rolodex, and my personal belongings are locked inside. I'm in deep trouble. I take a cab back uptown and wait until my attorney, Larry Fox, gets into his office. I call him in a panic and tell him about my emergency. I'm shaking. He tells me to come to his office and make sure to bring his $5,000 retainer. I take the full amount in $100 bills from the freezer, grab a cab to his midtown office, dressed in a pair of jeans with the flag of Texas on the knees and a T-shirt, plunk the cash down on his desk, and lay out the entire story for him. I'm trembling and pacing. He holds his head in his hands and smiles in disbelief but moves into action quickly. He calls John Koegel and begins the negotiation process in an attempt to keep Kostabi from pressing criminal charges. Koegel responds by telling Fox that Kostabi wants to see me "on Rikers Island." Not a good start. I wonder how I'm going to break this news to my parents and whether I'm going to go to jail that afternoon or if I will be arrested in a few days. I pace his office while I listen to one side of the conversation. Fox argues that Kostabi should seriously consider the offer of financial restitution because it's unlikely that a D.A. will want to spend time and resources on a case like this and because the legitimacy of Kostabi's art will become an issue. But Koegel doesn't think Kostabi will budge. After Fox hangs up, I ask him how much it will cost to make restitution, and I start thinking of how I can raise the money by the day's end. Who can I call? God, I hope I never have to tell this story to my parents. I beg him to do whatever he can to make a deal because I'm sure that I'm going to be arrested before the day is over. He tells me it doesn't seem hopeful.

Chapter 5

Spilling the Beans

May 14, 1991. 4:00 P.M. New York.

After going back and forth with Kostabi's attorney all day, we still haven't made any progress toward a resolution of the crisis. I'm starting to panic about where I'm going to be sleeping tonight. Koegel assures us that Mark isn't the slightest bit interested in a restitution deal; he has taken good care of me financially, he says, and I have been disloyal. And I was so positive that my attorney, with his superpowers fueled by my retainer, would have it settled by noon. Shit. This is a goddamn mess. I finally leave Fox's office and take a cab back to the Upper West Side. I ask the driver to let me off at Gray's Papaya on 72nd Street and Broadway, where I buy my last two hot dogs as a free man and walk home up Broadway enjoying the best hot dogs. Lots of ketchup and onions. At home I call Annike and my friends from Kostabi World, gathering as much information as possible about what's going on there, and they sneak out to call me during their breaks. All the locks have been changed, and Mark has hired a twenty-four-hour security guard. Jessica, Mark's assistant, has been fired. Mark and Heather are on their way back from Tokyo. The drama is getting more and more exciting every minute. Fox calls and tells me that there's no progress. I'm doomed. It's nearly 6:30 P.M. and I've almost forgotten that I've been invited to dinner at my sister's apartment tonight. My parents are going to be there. I get dressed quickly and grab a cab crosstown. I roll down the window to take in a few gulps of Central Park air. Gives me an energy boost.

The timing of this dinner couldn't be any worse, but for some strange reason I'm in an upbeat mood and I'm just going to break the news to my family as if I've just won a $25 million Lotto jackpot. I think that's the best way to handle it. When I get there, everybody is playing with my newborn niece, and I make small talk while we're having drinks. Finally, I call for everybody's attention. "You guys," I announce, "I was fired from my job today." They look at me blankly, stunned. I take a deep breath and continue. "And I may need a criminal defense attorney." My mother looks at my father, then they both turn and stare at me. Explanation. I quickly and excitedly tell them about producing fake paintings—I refer to them as "reproductions"—at a studio in Brooklyn and selling them abroad, leaving out as many specifics as possible. I'm enjoying the telling of the story and the attention that comes with it. I almost feel like it legitimizes my activities, and when I'm finished, I'm feeling good. They don't seem to fully grasp it—it sounds to them like I'm in hot water—but they quickly pledge their support. I can see in their eyes that they want to believe I've done nothing wrong; they want to believe that all of my recently acquired wealth has come from legitimate art sales. They ask me if I'll be needing to find the lawyer in the next few days. I tell them it's not urgent yet. Within a few minutes the tension seems to subside and the worst is over—I've admitted failure and confessed to my parents. It's like I've failed an important college exam. Study harder next time, son. But I can tell that I've really frightened them with this one. We sit through an uncomfortable dinner, and I tell them that I need to leave early. That evening when I return to my apartment, I look around to make sure nobody's been inside it. Hello, hello. No answer. I collect all of my Kostabi canvases—twenty or so—roll them up, get on the subway, and take the PATH train to Jersey City, where Annike has a new studio. When I show up at her door, she's surprised to see me standing there with my art collection slung over my shoulder. I tell her to put her paintings together quickly. She looks around her studio. Outside, except for some light coming from a nearby warehouse, it's completely dark as we walk down to a dock on the Hudson River, roll the canvases around some cement blocks, and hurl them into the river. Thousands of dollars of faceless images disappear from the surface of the water—it's going to take bringing in Coast Guard divers for the federal government to crack this case now. We're both laughing, and I feel relieved, actually believing I've remedied the situation for good. As I ride the train back into Manhattan, I start imagining the discovery of these paintings. The thought of their faceless images floating back up to the surface throws me into a panic. Maybe I should write my own obituary. When I get home, I go upstairs, grab a pad, and make a list of everybody I want to invite to my funeral. Eighty-two people. I want to keep it small. I figure some people might bring dates.

The Social Butterfly

The countdown to my arrest begins that night when I turn off the lights and go to bed. My brain becomes further unhinged by the stress of my legal circumstances, and the crisis makes me increasingly manic. I dart from one obsessive errand to another—I have all of my clothes dry-cleaned and shoes resoled and start compulsive shopping, buying all kinds of unnecessary kitchen utensils and household items. I involve myself in a busy social schedule— parties, dinners, and movies, a full lineup of events. Sarah Wells, a friend I know through dealing art, is in town and has invited a group of friends to Le Cirque for dinner. Most of the people at the table are dealers or artists, so we all have a lot in common. We talk about the art market. The price of Warhols. The auctions. No one brings up my legal situation. It's a perfectly fun night. I will schedule and multitask my life back into normalcy.

I write a fax to Annike, who has decided to take a three-week vacation in Germany:

Dear Annike,

Everything is still quiet on the Kostabi front. I think I told you that Heather left Mark. Maybe she found that he was a fake and not the real Kostabi. Carl [the receptionist] asks about you frequently. Jessica is on her way to Italy for a family vacation.

Nothing very exciting to report about that place. I wish I could tell you that a large bomb or fire had destroyed Kostabi World, but no! I am still waiting to hear about several of my deals. I feel very confident about the Rothko painting and Klimt painting. I have a buyer for the Monet painting. She is a client of Ellen's who lives in Chicago and I forwarded her the photographs of the piece that Ken overnighted to me today. It's a pretty close connection. All of the money I've made dealing art and counterfeiting art is just about spent—on sushi, massages, nights at the Mondrian Hotel, Armani and Yamamoto suits, French contemporary paintings, airline tickets to Europe and Japan, documentary films, and recycled jeans with the flag of Texas on the knees. I really need to figure out a way to earn some money soon. So the money issue for me is very scary, too, and we'll have to have a conference about it when you come back to New York. Annike, you say that there is almost no money at the sunny horizon, but of course there is. It just hasn't found its way into our hands yet.

Love,

Andy von Strudel

Late one night, I stand naked in the front of the bathroom mirror, holding a pair of scissors in my hand, and start cutting big pieces of hair from the bottom of both sides of my head, then just chop random pieces from all over. I just don't have the strength to overdose tonight or go out on an all-night drug binge. My hair is completely uneven and resembles a bad wig. I am perfectly content standing in piles of dark brown hair and am kind of pleased with the damage I've done.

I call an old friend from Wesleyan, Sabrina Padwa, because I know that she'll be up late, and tell her about what I've just done. I take a cab to her apartment on the Upper East Side, and when I arrive, she appears shocked at my appearance. We look at each other and both start laughing. One side of my hair is considerably shorter than the other and the whole thing is wildly uneven. She looks concerned and takes me into her bathroom. She sets up a chair in front of the mirror, covers the floor with newspapers, and puts a towel around my neck. She tries to even it out the best she can, but it still looks frightening, as if I've been put through some kind of fraternity hazing.

The next morning, I return to Sabrina's apartment, and we walk up Madison Avenue to Michael's, a barbershop that is famous for kids' haircuts. We're both amused by the horses and cars that the kids around us are sitting in. The barber takes one look at me, raises his eyebrows, and tells us that he is just going to have to cut off most of my hair. So he gives me a buzz cut—my first one ever. I thank him for a great job, refuse the lollipop, and we walk down the street; all the while Sabrina says encouraging things about my new haircut, and I play with my bristly hair. We convince each other that my trademark long hair is a thing of the past and that this is the most perfect look for summer.

Miss Veronica

Since I'm two months behind in my rent, my landlord is more than eager to let me out of my lease early. I move from my duplex apartment on West 89th Street to a cheaper sublet, a studio on West 81st Street. I sell all of my antique furniture back to the store on the Upper West Side where I bought it, aptly named Better Times, for about $6,000.

The new apartment is one empty room. Hardwood floors. It echoes. I bring just a floral Ralph Lauren couch that Allison loved, and I sleep in a Murphy bed. At night I sit and watch the traffic go by on Columbus Avenue. Every day I wait anxiously to be arrested. I've convinced myself that I'll be grabbed under the arms by two plainclothes cops in dark suits and thrown into the backseat of an unmarked car. Frightened about entering and exiting my building, I avoid coming and going as much as possible. When my intercom buzzes, I hide in the shower and wait five or ten minutes before I come out. I panic when I hear footsteps near my door and a Chinese menu comes sliding through. I wish they would just finally come and arrest me. I am frighteningly alone in this place, desperate for the waiting to be over.

One night I'm up late watching a documentary on early Hollywood film pioneers that's starting to bore me. I don't know what to do with myself. I'm a little stoned. Phone sex is not going to satisfy me tonight. I grab the Yellow Pages and look under "Escorts." "Manhattan Nights." Classy escort service. Upper East Side. Since 1985. I saw the ad a few weeks ago, and I remember I liked the graphics. It isn't a tacky limousine or a skyline of New York or a big apple. It's just the profile of a slender and bosomy woman. I call Miss Veronica. "Manhattan Nights," she says. "Hello, I'm calling about your ad," I say. She pauses and asks me to tell her something about myself, so I tell her that I'm a young professional in my early thirties, that I travel, and that I'm just looking for a massage. She tells me that it will cost me $200 for an hour-long session. "That's fine," I say. She explains that it's late but that she's still got a few girls available at her Upper East Side apartment. She describes a few of them for me: a former *Penthouse* model, a Brazilian beauty, and a statuesque Swede. "Tell me about the Swede," I say. "What does she look like?" "She's lovely. She's five feet nine, 125 pounds, 36 - 24 - 36, blond, and has beautiful, tan skin," she says. She gives me her address, and I tell her I'll be there by 1:00 A.M. I grab a couple of $100 bills, brush my teeth, and get into a cab. I feel a rush of anticipation and excitement because I've never been to a brothel. When I get to the building on East 79th Street, I ring her apartment and she buzzes me in. In the elevator I think about turning back. My heart is racing. The doorbell makes a weird sticking noise. I feel like running, but a flaming redhead in her midsixties, badly wrinkled from sun exposure, opens the door. She is wearing bright orange lipstick, green eye shadow, and orange nail polish and some type of housecoat that isn't particularly flattering. "You must be Miss Veronica," I say. "Yes, I am," she answers, shaking my hand and smiling. The living room is painted red, and there are three girls inside glued to the television. "You seem like an awfully nice young man," she says, with a slight Eastern European accent similar to Dr. Kleinman's. "I will introduce you to Monika now," she says. "Follow me. Oh, but first we must take care of business."

My hand is shaking; I take out the two bills and give them to her. She examines them as if they might be counterfeit. "Brand-new," I say. She laughs. She leads me to a dimly lit bedroom, where a blond woman with dramatic makeup—glossy red lipstick, green eye shadow, dark mascara, and rouge—and highlighted blond hair is sitting on the edge of a king-sized bed, wearing just a black bra and panties. "I hope you will enjoy," Miss Veronica says as she leaves the room and closes the door. Standing in this bedroom, sparsely furnished with a bed and night table, I feel pretty lonely. Monika helps me out of my clothes and instructs me to lie face-down on the bed. I look over my shoulder. She's taking off her bra and panties and standing above me. She begins working my neck and shoulders, taking warm oil from the night table and pouring it all over my back, massaging it in. She has long legs like a dancer, a flat stomach, and firm breasts that sway slightly as she bends over me. Her pubic hair is shaved, and she has a piercing. She's concentrating on my lower back and moving down my ass to my thighs, and I'm getting turned on wondering where this is leading. She's taking her time and starts teasing my balls from behind very gently. Then she motions for me to turn over and massages my thighs; my cock is totally stiff. She grabs it, pours some oil on it, and strokes it while I'm playing with her breasts. I guess it's okay for me to do that. After ten minutes of this, I come, and it's all over. We say nothing to each other. I get dressed, thank her, leave the apartment, and walk a few blocks to a diner that I know. I order a bagel and cream cheese and then have a banana split, which is what I probably needed in the first place.

Up All Night

Six months pass. Unemployment runs out. I've borrowed about $7,500, and now friends stop loaning me money. I am not getting any financial support from my family. So I pawn my watch, my camera, and my great-grandfather's silver flask at Century Pawnbrokers on Eighth Avenue. $500. It's not going to go too far. When Annike returns from Germany, we engage in a survival game together. She's nervous about the D.A.'s office, but we don't talk about it much. After months of subsisting on loans, pawned items, stealing from the deli, and the sale of my remaining Kostabi "products" (we still had some of my legitimate paintings and lithographs that we sell to some contacts in the art world), we realize we need to generate some income. One weekend my sister offers us the opportunity to paint an office space and earn some money. Nancy feels sorry for me and wants me to move on with my life, but in the meantime she tries to help out any way she can. Annike and I work well as a team: she is the leader, making the job estimates and dividing the work, as well as the real talent. I provide the energy, spirit, and enthusiasm. This leads to an abrupt decision to go into the contracting business together. We bill ourselves as Ivy League Painters. Our colorful flyers, which we post all over the Upper West Side, attract a tremendous amount of attention and get a good response. Soon we're doing a few jobs around town, including painting and plastering. If clients want wallpapering jobs done, we do that, too, although we have no experience. Electrical work? Not a problem. We're bringing in anywhere from $500 to $2,000 a job, so our financial problems are lessened. Finally we can pay some bills. But the work isn't steady and I'm not very dependable—I have a hard time focusing. I lose interest in a job quickly and slack off. We both want to be dealing art full-time and think this contracting work is beneath us.

I'm at the apartment of Sally Randall, one of Mark's favorite painters at Kostabi World and a well-known name in the downtown art scene, to celebrate her birthday. Sally is tall, with long black hair and pale skin, and is leaning up against the kitchen door. I can't quite get to her from where I am. The place is filled with familiar faces, and of course everyone there is aware that I am one of the alleged counterfeiters. They haven't seen me in months, and I feel a bit uncomfortable. I'm drinking a vodka tonic to control my agitation. I don't know why I decided to come to this party in the first place. But I make my way over to Sally to wish

her a happy birthday, and she seems thrilled to see me and lets out
a shriek: "Oh my God, you came! Thanks for coming, how are
you doing?" "Fine so far," I tell her. "We miss you," she says.
Doug, a painter who now has a crew cut, comes up to me and
shakes my hand. "Congratulations, you kicked that motherfucker
in the ass," he says. I laugh. "How much did you make?" he asks.
"Not enough to pay the legal bills if I end up in court," I tell him.
Another painter, Rick, who I don't know very well, asks me, "How
did you reproduce the paintings so exactly?" "In the same way
they're projected on canvas at Kostabi World," I say. I'm titillated
by the questions and want to talk about it, but at the same time
the apartment is crowded and I want to get out and into a cab. I
leave without saying good-bye to Sally. Tomorrow is Lauren's
birthday, but I already bought her a pair of diamond earrings and
I can't think of anything else to get her. She'd probably appreciate
a DustBuster as much as jewelry. I walk for a few blocks and get an
Amstel Light at a deli, then grab a cab and head to the Second Avenue Deli because I haven't eaten all day. I order a turkey and
chopped liver sandwich, which is enough for two people, so I take
half home and leave the other half in a bag on a newspaper box
hoping a hungry homeless person will find it. I'm thinking about
the possibility of being arrested: when it will happen, where it will
happen, what I'll be wearing, whether anyone will see me being
taken from my apartment, if I will be handcuffed. And I keep
hearing them read me my Miranda rights. Stop. I hail the next cab
and go to the Michelangelo Hotel off Times Square. There's a
Harry Cipriani restaurant and bar there, and I go in to see Franco,
my bartender friend, who is dressed in his usual black tuxedo. I
order a vodka tonic. "It's on the house," he says. "Thanks," I say. I
put down a $5 bill, which he immediately pushes back into my
hand. "Please, Franco," I beg him. The bar is full of theatergoers
and businessmen. "How come I don't see you around here too
much anymore?" he asks me. "I moved to the Upper West Side," I
tell him. "Very fancy," he replies. I finish my drink, leave the hotel,
and walk down the block toward Times Square. The same prostitutes are working the corner of 50th Street and Seventh Avenue

that were there a year ago. "Want a date?" a chubby blond girl asks me. "Not tonight," I tell her. I smile at her and look away. I'm walking at a frantic pace, and Times Square is crowded with pedestrians. I want to take a total tally of everyone within the periphery of Times Square and find out some statistics about each one of them and how they differ from one another. Do any of them speak Swedish? How many of them have O+ blood? How many are carrying guns? How many have sexually transmitted diseases? Are any of them twins? Then I give up trying to play this ridiculously obsessive game. All these people are the same. They all eat. They all sleep. They all fuck. They all masturbate. It's just a matter of how they do it and how often they do it. So I get into a cab and go back to my apartment and do chores. I pay bills (I owe Con Edison, New York Telephone, and Manhattan Cable for two months; it's going to be tough with only a little more than $500 in my checking account), make piles of clothing for the cleaners, write letters to friends about my legal troubles, and scrub the bathroom tub and floor. I'm hoping the crazies will go away and I'll be able to fall asleep. But I'm wide awake for about six more hours, lying in bed watching CNN until it's light outside. I'm dying for something to drink, but I don't have anything in the house. By now my body is aching, even though my head feels like I could start the day again without going to sleep. I'm agitated and decide to go out for a walk and find a diner to satisfy some craving. There are only about three or four people in the diner when I walk in, and I take a table by the window on Broadway. I order a Swiss-cheese omelette, home fries, and a bagel with cream cheese. The waiter brings me a glass of orange juice. Did I order that? The food resuscitates me, and I come home and try to fall asleep. But it doesn't work. After a couple of hours of watching porn videos and masturbating, I pass out from exhaustion and don't wake up until 4:00 P.M. the next day. My entire schedule is screwed-up.

The Anxiety Shuffle

February 27, 1992. New York.
Still no word about Kostabi—the quiet is getting a little bit scary. But as every day passes, I forget more and more what happened. It feels like a weird dream, like I was on cocaine the entire time and reality was distorted.

I hear through the grapevine, from Kostabi employees who bump into Annike downtown, that it looks like the Manhattan D.A.'s office is about to take some type of action against me. I panic. I need a criminal defense attorney right away. My parents find the name of one through a family connection. Stuart Abrams, a gentle but intense man in his early forties, was formerly an assistant U.S. attorney with the U.S. District Court in the Southern District of New York. He agrees to see me the next day.

February 28, 1992.
I shower and dress, take the subway to Grand Central, and meet with Stuart at his office in the Helmsley Building on Park Avenue. Legal books line his shelves, and files are piled high on his desk, next to photos of his children, who have red hair like he does. I stammer through the story, impressed with how calm and non-judgmental he seems. He doesn't even crack a smile. After about a half hour, he tells me he's relatively confident that my case isn't the type the D.A.'s office will take on because it's a ridiculous one with an unbelievable witness—Kostabi. He warns me not to speak to anyone who calls me about the case and to "sit tight and wait it out" and that "hopefully the case will be dropped." I leave his office feeling a confidence I haven't known in a while.

March 1, 1992.
Lauren and Jonathan are a great comic duo who play off each other quite well, and I'm always entertained by their humorous interaction. One night, when Lauren is nine months pregnant, she and Jonathan invite me over to dinner. When I arrive Lauren is in

the kitchen, frantically cooking her famous lemon chicken and rice. There always seem to be too many pots and pans covering the stove and countertops when she cooks. Everything is steaming and smoking and seems out of control. While she is slaving in the kitchen about to give birth, Jonathan is lying on the couch watching television and barely picks up his head to acknowledge me. "Hey, Jonathan, you could say hello to our friend," Lauren says. "Oh, yeah, hello, Drew, have a seat," he mumbles. I stay in the kitchen with Lauren. "What's wrong with him?" I ask her. "It's just him," she says. "But give him about ten minutes, he'll come back to life again." We both laugh. When we sit down at the table Jonathan suddenly perks up and tells us about his session with Dr. Kleinman today. He does a perfect imitation of Dr. Kleinman when he explains what happens when a patient starts a new medication: "He *vill* get high!" We all laugh. Lauren sees Dr. Kleinman, too. She's even sent a family member to him for crisis treatment. Lauren sees him for her anxiety and panic disorder, which have really come to a head during her pregnancy. She can imitate Dr. Kleinman well, too. "*Zis* anxiety, it *vill* go away," she says. But Lauren's anxiety is a real issue, and you never know when it's going to strike. We're about halfway through dinner and she gets up from the table with a look on her face as if she's seen an apparition. I'm not sure if she's joking or it's real. "Oh, no, here we go," says Jonathan. Lauren is starting to have a slight anxiety attack, and we walk her into the living room and sit her down on the edge of the couch. "There's no way I'm going to make it through this pregnancy. Oh, my God. I hope this baby will be normal," she says. She jumps up from the couch and starts yawning repeatedly, whistling, and sticking her fingers in her ears. Jonathan, in an effort to comfort her, mimics her motions. "Let's all do the anxiety shuffle," he sings. He starts laughing and dancing with her. He and Lauren are yawning, whistling, sticking their fingers in their ears, and dancing around the living room in circles. Their apartment has transformed into a mental ward. I finally convince Lauren to sit down on the floor in front of me, and I rub her shoulders until her anxiety starts to subside. We all end up laughing while Jonathan entertains us with his antics.

March 13, 1992.
In two weeks Stuart calls me with the good news. The Manhattan D.A.'s office has turned down the case. Tremendous relief. I can breathe. The assistant district attorney thinks the case isn't strong enough—there are obvious credibility problems and it will be difficult to prove that the paintings were unauthorized. But soon I'm contacted by a detective who wants to interview me, and we learn that the Eastern District (including Brooklyn and Queens) has taken on the case. The representative of the Japanese company involved is located in their jurisdiction, and this is where faxes were transmitted and monies were wired. I tell the detective I have been advised not to speak with him.

Offshore Accounts

In the meantime Annike and I have delusions of dealing art on an international level. Thoughts of vast sums of money being wired into my "special account" at Citibank and of transferring monies from my Swiss account to my offshore account fuel my fantasies. We actually set up shop in two different locations, my studio and her studio, with two phone lines, two faxes, and Rolodexes of dealers, galleries, and art journals, and we're ready to get to work. Annike is confident that we can combine my sales skills and her contacts in Europe to sell paintings. She knows many international art dealers and tells me stories about their incredible successes. These delusions of making hundreds of thousands of dollars are a part of my mania and serve to repress the nightmare of the whole Kostabi debacle. But we actually start to break into a network of dealers, agents, and gallery owners, meeting them mostly by phone, by referral from dealers we already know or just by cold calling, but also some in person. Since we have no direct clients who own actual works, we're fighting an uphill battle. For

instance, we might call a dealer in Dallas and ask him if he's looking for anything in particular, and he may tell us he's looking for a
specific Magritte. We'll call as many dealers as we know in search
of the painting. After a while, you get to know where to find
things. We're on the telephone and fax for most of the day and
night, trying to interest other dealers in works we "have access
to." But for the most part, everybody has access to the same product. We spend most of our time trying to make a deal happen—
FedExing slides and transparencies of artwork across the country
and around the world. We think we actually come close to making
deals, but the dealers are just playing the game and leading us on.
A dealer in Fond du Lac, Wisconsin, guarantees us that she has
gone to Western Union and wired us a deposit for an O'Keeffe
painting and that it will arrive the following day, but it never does.
She does this every day for a week. But there is really nothing
there. We sit and wait days for money to be wired into our accounts. But the only person who really has a client is the agent,
who'll keep the deal for himself. But we persist: van Gogh, Renoir,
Picasso—nothing is out of our league. My determination to make
a million-dollar deal is simply a way to induce a manic feeling. I
forget that it's impossible, playing along because it gives me a rush
to be working again and supposedly "getting close" to a deal.

   A friend who is a dealer in the Midwest hooks me up with
a young New York dealer whose family has a lot of money and
an impressive contemporary collection. He invites me to meet
him for lunch at La Goulue on Madison Avenue. I arrive ten minutes early and wait on the sidewalk. I spot him across the street
right away. He's wearing a navy blue double-breasted blazer, white
khakis, a white linen shirt, and dark sunglasses. His dark black hair
is slicked back, and he's sunburned. He looks like he's about
twenty-three. I walk over and introduce myself. "You must be
David. I'm Andy Behrman," I say. "Nice to meet you," he says.
The waiter seats us at a table on the sidewalk, and David lights up
a cigarette and blows the smoke straight above him. "Kate tells me
you're an incredibly brilliant guy," he says. "And you know how to

make money," he adds. "I know your whole story and I don't care. I thought it was absolutely genius." I smile. "I've got a number of clients always looking for good work at reasonable prices. Maybe we can do something together," he suggests. We order lunch, and I try to impress him with my knowledge of the contemporary French painting scene and tell him a little bit about my collection. "I'd love to see it," he says. "It sounds like something I'd like." He invites me to a party Friday night at his apartment, where he'll be showing the work of a new German artist. "Don't miss it. It'll be a good party, too," he says. In the meantime, he leaves me with some transparencies of works by some contemporary American artists, which I promise to show only to clients who have expressed a specific interest in them. He seems pleased by our meeting. I tell him I'll see him on Friday. The truth is, Annike and I don't have any clients interested in these paintings, and I return them to him at his party.

Annike and I have isolated ourselves from everybody, and now we enter the Tofu and Banana Period. It's all we have money for. That and the occasional stolen cheese and crackers from the corner deli. Annike has such an artful way of presenting tofu and bananas on a plate—she makes them look so beautiful, so delicious—that I look forward to each meal with tremendous delight. We are waiting to be indicted and still deluding ourselves that one of our million-dollar deals is going to come through at any minute. We're desperate. I even borrow $50 from the corner newsstand vendor I hang out with at 3:00 A.M. We're shuttling between my sublet and Annike's studio in Jersey City, paying rent on neither, and waiting to be evicted from both. One morning I do not receive my usual wake-up call from Annike. I can't find her all day. I leave message after message and fax but get no response. Later that evening my phone rings. Her voice is faint. She's admitted herself to Payne Whitney, a psychiatric hospital on the Upper East Side, and she assures me she's fine, but that they want to hold on to her for a few days for observation. The survival game has gotten to her.

When I go to visit her, she is wearing a white hospital gown with a light blue star print. Her skin is bright white, her lips dry and peeling. I ask her if she is hungry or thirsty. She tells me she's just eaten some eggs. I'm relieved. She tells me that they've put her in the same room Marilyn Monroe stayed in thirty years prior, a fact that appeals to her sense of history and drama. I pretend to be amused. But I feel isolated and alone. Annike has given up on herself and on me. She was the one who told me how important the survival game was, how we both needed each other. She didn't come to me when she needed me. I realize how selfish and sick I am. I need her, and I will be alone until they release her from this hospital. Now I have to eat tofu and bananas on my own.

Annike pushes to be released from the hospital and they let her go after five days. I'm even more protective of her now, like an older brother of his sister. I don't want her dealing with the same kind of stress she's had recently. I keep her with me at my studio for a while to keep an eye on her and stop her art-dealing activities for a few days. We're running low on money, and I start stealing more food from the deli by shoving it in my knapsack while no one is looking. It's pretty easy. When we realize we're still not making progress and the pressure is about to spill over, I finally borrow $2,000 from an old friend, telling him I need to get to Europe to close a business deal. Given the sums of money I used to deal with, it seems like such a small amount to ask for, but I feel like I've asked for the universe—and it'll certainly get us as far as we need to go. Annike and I decide to leave the country and go to the Basel Art Fair, then continue on to visit dealers in Germany. Our official intention is to meet some of the dealers we've been talking to, to solidify our relationships and to establish new ones, but we really have no specific business to address. The idea of leaving the country together is what's really driving us, and I fantasize that we will never return.

The Von Strudel Diaries

Annike's attorney warns her that her telephone line could be tapped, so we both become paranoid and stop communicating by phone, using only our fax machines to get in touch with each other. Our messages go back and forth day and night. Late at night, the sound of the phone ringing and the clicking noise of the fax machine wake us up.

> Will I come back to the United States if I go to Europe? Should I just flee the country now and avoid a trial? I was thinking of opening a laundromat in Istanbul or cohosting Jessica Hahn's fantasy show. Or maybe I'll just stay in bed all day and eat boxes and boxes of Mike and Ikes until I get sick.—Andy von Strudel

> I'm very scared about the buzzing and the knocking on my door this morning. I really have to relax. I have to pretend the D.A. and the I.R.S. are all on vacation.—Andy von Strudel

> I understand the fear—the confusion—the reaction to inner and outer pressure and that you don't sleep. You always sleep when I'm at your house at night. Maybe I should be considered as your sleeping pill.—Annike

> Why does it seem like when we're just about ready to starve—when we're right on the verge of collapse—money comes through from somewhere?—Andy von Strudel

> Before our flight—we have to take care of: the photos of the Hockney, the Picasso ceramics, close the O'Keeffe sale, make sure George's money is in the bank, buy airline tickets for Germany, pick up prescriptions from Dr.

Kleinman, pay the telephone bills, FedEx Rothko slides to Michelle and do everything else that is on our to-do lists.—Andy von Strudel

I got a prescription today for 100 Prozac—can we afford it somehow?—Andy von Strudel

I have a client who wants to put a 10% deposit down on the Atlantic Ocean. He needs to see a transparency first. I'll have David overnight one.—Andy von Strudel

I feel very lonely without you being here. The only communication I have is with Sylvia Plath and Gertrude Stein.—Annike

Do you think maybe it would be better if we separated and I went alone to Israel to live on a kibbutz to pick pears? I'm going to watch television all afternoon. I'm never going to eat food again. I think I want to die.—Andy von Strudel

My phone was just cut off today—but I can still dial out on my fax line.—Andy von Strudel

I have a 36 × 24 inch Warhol Soup Can (1964) from a very important collection. It's red and white tomato soup (most desirable). Our price is $320,000.—Andy von Strudel

I'm scared. My eggs are having two yellow egg yolks each. Is that a very American mutation?—Annike

Here's my advice. Take many deep breaths. Smell the fresh air. Drink chamomile tea. Life is very short. You spend more time in your lifetime dead than you do alive.—Andy von Strudel

I can pick up the money from Ted today—dance—sing—
celebrate. We can eat! Can we go to Bendix? No new
O'Keeffe developments. I am hungry and am saving my
$5 and four subway tokens until I see you.—Andy von
Strudel

Mr. Soap

(unsent)

June 17, 1992

Dear Mom and Dad:

I spoke to Nancy and she told me that you were a little bit concerned about me, since you hadn't heard from me since two
weekends ago when I saw you in East Hampton. I'm alive and
well—don't worry. I had to get away from my routine in New
York. I "fired" Dr. Kleinman because he medicated me like an
absolute lunatic, and after that I decided I wanted to take a
break from therapy. So here I am in Munich—I feel pretty
healthy and well balanced. I had a free frequent flyer ticket. I'm
staying with two German guys (Dietmar and Dieter) who I met
at a party of a mutual friend. I'm helping them organize tours
from Frankfurt to Majorca. It's not great money, but I will get
to travel and meet lots of people. They also own a chain of
laundromats in Munich called "Seifenmeister," which translates to Mr. Soap (I'm writing this letter from there now).
They're a bit eccentric and Dietmar has a wild collection of Indian headdresses on these weird non-Indian mannequins.
Dad—I took plenty of pictures. Dieter is Jewish. Dieter Metz-
ger—it means butcher in German. His parents met at a concentration camp and stayed in Berlin until the late '60s, when
they moved here. I met his mother for the first time and she reminds me a little bit of you, Mom. Please don't worry about
me—I'm fine. I'm sorry that it's taken me a month to write, but
I will write often. I put all of my things into storage and it'll be
fine for a year. I even took care of Dr. Ruben—the lump was

nothing—just overexposure to the sun. I'll be in touch. Here's my address: Hubert Alle 86, 8000 Muenchen

Auf wiedersehen

Dein sohn

Andy

Escape to Switzerland

June 18, 1992. New York.
It's finally the day to depart for the Basel Art Fair. I organize my suitcase carefully: my navy blue Yamamoto double-breasted suit, three dress shirts, and three ties. I pack my slides and transparencies, my last forty capsules of Prozac, and all of my canceled credit cards—I know I might be able to use them.

Annike meets me at my apartment, and we take a cab to Newark Airport, arriving early for our flight to Hamburg. We've spent most of the money we've borrowed on the tickets but still have about $600 left. She repeatedly tells me not to be concerned about money. I'm struggling to figure out how we're going to manage a weeklong stay on so little. Hotels. Car. Food. Gas. But I have faith in Annike, because she's never let me go hungry. As I notice people forming a line near the gate, I start to feel like I'm fleeing the country to avoid arrest. But this is just self-induced paranoia. I haven't been indicted yet, and I have a passport and am free to travel abroad. I'm just afraid that while I'm away something might come up and they won't be able to find me. I'm eager to board the flight and take our art-dealing show to another continent, confident that we're going to hit the jackpot this time with a million-dollar sale. I actually believe it will happen.

It's early morning when we arrive in Germany, and we rent a brand-new Volkswagen with my canceled American Express Gold Card. Nobody checks it through a computer. They just take an imprint. Not my problem. Stay calm. Hurry. Get in the car. Annike speeds out of the parking lot onto the Autobahn, and we're on our way to Basel. I'm having fun mispronouncing the names of the exits, and we're both laughing and giggling and I'm thinking at any minute we could be arrested or, worse, die, but it doesn't seem to matter anymore. It might relieve some of my pain.

We arrive in Basel and check in at the hotel, and I immediately become suspicious of any men with blond hair, which is kind of ridiculous, but I'm on the lookout for Kostabi, who never misses this show. I'm not quite sure what I'm going to say to him if I see him. Maybe I'll try to sell him a painting. Or maybe I'll sign his autograph for him. I take a quick shower and get dressed in my art-dealer suit—I'm an art dealer again. Annike puts on her female version—a taupe knee-length skirt, a beige silk blouse, and heels—which is very conservative for her. Briefcases in hand, we go to the exhibition hall, which consists of what seems like miles and miles of booths, in which exhibiting gallery owners and dealers are selling "our" wares—including our $25,000,000 van Gogh, the very same one we have received a slide of from a dealer in Chicago and passed on to another dealer who supposedly had a bank interested in acquiring it. There's not a chance that anybody will ever buy this painting through us; we just don't have those connections. After about two hours, I realize we're not making much progress. We have arranged some meetings with dealers and gallery owners in advance, but we haven't met anybody on our list yet and we're just looking at booths. I'm not finding this very helpful and I'm getting tired, so we decide to call it a day.

At 10:00 the next morning I meet with Stephen Curtis, a Los Angeles–based private dealer, to discuss the sale of a $3.2 million Renoir painting that his client is interested in purchasing. Annike is having coffee with a German dealer at a café, and I'm going to meet her for lunch at noon. We're sitting in the lobby lounge of his hotel having breakfast, and he assures me that his client is prepared to make a deposit on the painting and then view it. If he likes it, he'll wire the balance directly into Stephen's account and the deal will be done. I have access to the portrait of a mother with child through another dealer in Los Angeles, who tells me that she has direct access to its owner. There really is no reason for the meeting except it gives me a chance to meet him face-to-face. I really believe that Stephen has a client for the painting, and by the eager look on his face I can see he thinks I really do have access to it. So I give him another transparency and we agree to talk again when we get back to the States. In my mind I'm already calculating my commission; in reality I don't even know if my contact has access to the painting. I can only hope that she's not jerking me around. Basically, we're talking about something that might not even exist.

Things aren't exactly going as planned. I wake up the next morning and realize I don't know if Annike really has an itinerary for this trip to Europe. I tell her I'm a bit angry and am not sure it was worth borrowing the money to make it happen, and she calms me down, pushing me into the shower. When I come out I see that she has taken a thick black Magic Marker and drawn on the white wall a huge map of Germany complete with all of our stops and our route—literally our itinerary. I'm shocked and think she's getting a little crazy. But this is how she makes her point— she knows exactly where we're going. I'm impressed but at the same time somewhat nervous that the maid is going to walk into the room and see the wall before we leave. Now we just have to escape from this desecrated hotel room without paying.

We won't be deterred. We convince ourselves that the $20 left in my pocket is the mark of astounding success and it's time for us to leave Basel and head to Germany. Our first stop is Munich, to meet Annike's family. Her parents, a robust couple in their sixties, greet me warmly and offer us all kinds of food—meats, cheeses, breads, vegetables, salads, and drinks—in the middle of the afternoon. Annike's father is proud of his relatively good English, and her mother gestures very well. We accept their offer to stay overnight, and busy ourselves putting together slides and typing letters to dealers. I sense they actually believe we're dealing art successfully. After all, we have flown from New York to Hamburg, rented a car, stayed in luxury hotels, and brought them gifts.

Dachau is our next stop. I don't know exactly what to expect, but for some reason I imagine a huge sign with ten-foot-tall letters. Something like the HOLLYWOOD sign. I've been obsessed with Holocaust documentaries for as long as I can remember. It seems as though one day Jews are leading relatively normal lives, and the next they're being rounded up by the SS and shipped off to concentration camps by train. It all seems to happen so quickly. Now I'm standing outside one of those concentration camps. The trees are so unbelievably green, like the trees I grew up with in the suburbs. They're blowing in the wind and it's summer and it seems so peaceful. I'm confused by the beauty. I didn't imagine all of this color. We walk past the gates. MONTAGS GESCHLOSSEN. Mondays closed. That strikes me as very peculiar. Where do they all go on Mondays?

ARBEIT MACHT FREI, read the words over the gatehouse. "Work makes one free." I'm overwhelmed by the quiet. We walk over to the memorial to those who were murdered at the camp and tour the ovens and gas chambers. I feel like I've stepped onto the set of one of the documentaries and there's no one there to direct me. I feel like I'm on sacred ground. I'm looking for all of the extras in their striped prison garb, but there is nobody in sight. I guess they aren't needed anymore. This is a deserted prison camp, a graveyard that's filled in with green trees and grass. I look down at my feet. There is a dandelion growing between the cracks in the concrete.

Walking around the grounds, I feel numb, disconnected from what happened here almost fifty years ago. "I'm ready to leave," I tell Annike. I walk back through the gates and leave Dachau behind as an emerald-green memory. We drive on to Cologne and Düsseldorf, visiting private dealers and galleries, making more empty deals along the way, collecting more promises and adding more charges to my credit cards. When we finally return to the airport, we just leave the car in front of the terminal, so as not to cause any trouble at the car-rental return area. Someone will find it.

The Diagnosis

October 6, 1992. New York.

I'm not taking Prozac because I can't afford it—it's $3 a pill—and I'm not even sure it's doing anything for me. I don't have any way of paying for a psychiatrist, and I can't seem to articulate to my parents how urgently I need professional help again. My mother calls me and tells me that they're coming into the city for dinner and asks me to join them, so I meet them that night at Demarchelier on the Upper East Side. I'm not used to eating at restaurants like this anymore, so I feel a bit out of place. They ask about what's going on in my life, specifically the progress I'm making finding employment, and I tell them some concocted story about having looked for PR work with a couple of different agencies, with no luck. I tell them I'm looking into other things, and that I can't afford to see a therapist again right now and I desperately need to see one. But they've been through a rough time with me—my ongoing unemployment and my legal problems—and they're a bit confused about my mental state and where I'm headed and my future plans. I feel really uncomfortable about asking them to bail me out again like they have so many times in the past. They feel that I've seen more than my fair share of therapists and hope I'll find some type of job and make a living. They offer many suggestions. I should try something new. Something creative, perhaps. Or try to go to work for somebody in a stable environment. I could think about going back to school to get a business or law degree, or rebuild my PR company. They even talk about my going to work for my mother's recruiting business. They're extremely encouraging, but they want me to pull myself out of this ditch on my own. And I don't really expect them to rescue me this time either. That night I call my sister and I tell her about the severity of my situation. I try to explain my condition to her as best I understand it. She agrees without hesitation to pay for me to see a psychiatrist once a week. I'm shocked. This is an extremely kind offer on her part, since we really haven't had the closest relationship in years, but more important, it's a critical moment for me because I realize that my problem is very serious—serious enough that she will reach out this far for me. I set up an appointment with Dr. Golub, a psychiatrist on the Upper East Side. He's tall and lanky, in his early forties, and looks frighteningly like Abraham Lincoln, a physical resemblance I can't quite get out of my head. During our first session I start from scratch, again, repeating my psychiatric history, talking about my symptoms, and giving my background information. He asks if he can speak with any of my previous psychiatrists, and it just so happens that he knows two of them. In the meantime, without making a definitive diagnosis, he suspects that I might be manic depressive, and he puts me on lithium, Prozac, and Anafranil. It's the first time I remember hearing the term *manic depression,* and it sounds serious to me, conjuring up images of patients running around a mental ward half-naked in terrycloth slippers—it sounds like the word *maniac.* The first thing I ask is if my condition is going to degenerate. I just naturally assume his diagnosis is accurate and don't ask too many other questions. I'm more concerned with how he can treat me. He assures me that he can stabilize my condition with the right balance of medication. I leave his office feeling rather positive.

October 8, 1992. New York.
I call Sandy, an old friend and colleague from Nancy's PR agency, and ask her if she wants to get together to talk about starting our own agency. I know that she's relatively unhappy at her job, and after a few meetings we're confident that together we can find a few clients to promote and work out of my apartment. At this point my sister is doing well enough that my poaching an employee is not going to upset her, and we discuss it before the actual transition. Sandy and I give ourselves the name Agency 4, and soon we are promoting everything from authors and doctors to restaurants and gyms. After a few months we are doing well enough to move both our office and my apartment to executive office space on 51st Street and Seventh Avenue, next door to the

Michelangelo Hotel, a few blocks from Times Square. This isn't the safest location for me because I like to wander at night and because there is so much sex available. Soon I'm back to where I was years ago, but it only matters that I'm having a good time. I'm taking the Prozac, lithium, and Anafranil cocktail, speeding through my days and not feeling much of a change in my moods. In fact, I live life a little more dangerously again and my mania is back in full swing. I entertain friends—and strangers—at the bar and restaurant, where they extend me a tab, probably because I spend so much time in the hotel lobby and just become a regular. Big mistake. The hotel becomes my living room. I make drinks for customers, entertain and serve as the master of ceremonies at the hotel bar. After hours I wander aimlessly around Times Square, which at 2:00 A.M. looks oddly suspended between night and day because of all the neon lights. I stop in bars for drinks or porn stores looking at magazines and videos. I want to stay up all night and then have breakfast. This way I'll never die.

Going Cold Turkey

A bunch of Jonathan's actor friends tell him about an excellent therapist they all go to on the East Side. So after Jonathan has seen Dr. Solnick a few times and recommends him, I decide to give him a try. I cancel my appointments with Dr. Golub and tell him that I no longer can continue treatment with him for financial reasons. I'm also not feeling like I'm making much progress. Although I feel he has properly diagnosed me, I'm not responding well to the medication. Lithium is not effective for all manic-depressives, and Prozac is usually not used to treat manic-depressives; it can induce mania. I tell my sister that I have found a doctor I can afford on my own and make an appointment to see Dr. Solnick, who is opposed to treating his patients with medication. I am curious about this because I feel open to a new approach to my psychological problems. When I tell Dr. Solnick, a middle-aged psychiatrist with a hint of a British accent, about my pharmacological regimen, he immediately dismisses it as "overmedication" without really listening to my diagnosis of manic depression. He advises me to go off the lithium, Prozac, and Anafranil cold turkey.

Within a few days I notice that my thoughts are becoming increasingly unhinged. It's as if chunks of my brain have been scooped out, like the part that edits my thoughts before they become speech. I talk nonstop to friends and family about the case, babbling about anything that comes to mind. It's sort of like that nervous energy you feel right before you have to give a speech, or what actors must feel before they go on stage. Only I feel it all the time. "Andy, relax," my father says rather gruffly one morning when it's clear he's exasperated by my chatter.

I'm beginning to wonder if Dr. Solnick has done the right thing. But those times when I'm able to focus on winning my case, I feel a powerful euphoria wash over me, filling me with a sense of confidence that I hope will last through this trial.

Chapter 6

Easel Weasel

July 22, 1993. Brooklyn.

S tuart learns that the Federal Prosecutor's Office in Brooklyn is preparing to indict me, on one count of conspiracy to defraud and four counts of wire fraud. The day has come to surrender. I meet Stuart at his office and we take a cab to the courthouse in Brooklyn. It seems like such a formal event. I'm wearing my Yamamoto suit, but I wish I had been allowed to dress more casually. I have to appear before the judge to enter a plea. When we arrive I'm taken into custody and handcuffed by a police officer—a formality, I'm told—while I wait to be processed. I'm unusually calm. But this isn't good. I've lost control. It's getting hot in this room, and I'm sweating and I want to get this over with. After about half an hour they remove the handcuffs and fingerprint me, and I'm really feeling like I've committed the crime of the century. Guilty. Then on to be photographed. Head on. Sideways. Holding the ID board in front of the Yamamoto suit. Right from the movies. Then Stuart and I walk into the courtroom and go before a judge, a stern man who states the name and number of the case, *United States of America* v. *Andrew Behrman,* Case 93-0515—a whole fucking country against me—and asks how I plead. Per Stuart's advice I plead not guilty on all counts. The voice barely comes out of me. He sets the trial date. Throughout the arraignment my mood is one of high energy—though nervous, I actually enjoy the experience because after two years I'm finally dealing directly with the system and I think we're going to win this case. We head down the long courthouse steps into a group of local photographers and reporters who photograph me and ask Stuart lots of questions. Stuart comments to the press that "we all will be able to sleep easier now knowing that the government is going to defend Mr. Kostabi." The next day the *New York Post* captions a photo of me "Easel Weasel" and prints an article filled with errors about the story, such as "The forger is believed to be cooperating with authorities." The forger, Annike, is not cooperating with authorities and is not indicted by the government. Because I trust her, I am confident that Annike is not talking to the D.A. I feel relieved that the wait is over, and at the same time I'm on top of the world. I love the frenzy of the attention. My big secret is finally out—I've been indicted. It all appeals to my manic state of mind.

The newspaper and magazine articles generate a wave of interest from prospective clients—authors, doctors, musicians, even artists—who for some reason want to work with me now that I've been indicted. I'm flooded with requests from prospective clients and give Sandy notice that I want to go back to working on my own. I abruptly break the lease on the office/apartment. I also walk out on the $2,000 tab at Harry Cipriani (only to settle with them later when they track me down). I'm still off all the medications and am just self-medicating with alcohol. This causes me to make off-the-top-of-my-head business decisions without any real thought. I sign three new clients in a week, open a new bank account, and quickly become obsessed with building a brand-new business. I take an expensive office space on 57th Street and Fifth Avenue, which I can cover with the new retainers I am collecting. It costs about $3,000 a month for a space that is only about fourteen feet square, but it gives me a sense of security, and I turn it into my home and office, working and eating at my desk for marathon twenty-hour stretches, sleeping on the floor behind my desk on a roll of bubble wrap, and bathing and brushing my teeth in the men's room sink. There are other people working in offices on the same floor, but I'm sure I'm the only person in the entire building who sleeps over. Still, I'm tired of asking to sleep on friends' couches and imposing on them for their hospitality. One day I take my usual walk outside on Fifth Avenue to find some coffee, and the streets are virtually empty. I come back and start frantically typing a memo to Stuart.

TO: Stuart Abrams
FROM: Andy Behrman
RE: MY PREDICAMENT
DATE: November 1, 1993

I am obsessed with winning this case.

What can I do in the next five weeks to help you?—I'm feeling desperate!

If we need expert witnesses, let's get them. I'll find a way to finance this. If we need to bring up the original painting, *Give Leaves a Chance,* let's do it—it can be rolled and FedExed rather inexpensively.

If I need to testify—and you feel confident that I can pull it off—I'll do it!

If they convict me, and choose to indict Kostabi, what do I get for cooperating?

If I plead guilty to a lesser count today, and cooperate, what do I get?

Isn't our defense pretty solid so far?

Isn't his crime worse than the one I am accused of (worth more to the government)?

What's the jury going to think when I don't testify?

I spend the rest of the morning preparing press information for a client, an artist named Paul Rebhan, who paints small canvases and quietly hangs one in the Museum of Modern Art as a publicity stunt. Next to his 11-by-14-inch abstract black-and-white painting, he places a card that reads, "Gift of Mr. and Mrs. Donald Trump." The painting hangs for two days until it's discovered. I'm talking to a columnist at the *New York Post.* "Yeah, he actually put double-sided tape on his small canvas and stuck it on the wall without the guards seeing him, and it stayed up for two days," I tell her. The *Post* publishes the item the following day, as does *The*

New York Times. I get a call from an English rock band that is recording an album in New York and is interested in having me promote them. This is a new direction for me. I still have diet doctors calling me. I'm sitting back in my chair, drinking my coffee, wondering why anybody wants to work with an indicted art dealer. Annike calls to see how I'm doing. We haven't seen each other in a while. Nobody has called her from the D.A.'s office. She's teaching German to Americans now, and things are more stable for her financially. I tell her more about the upcoming trial. "I despise Kostabi," she says. She always says that. At about 1:45 P.M. I leave for a massage appointment that helps me keep my head together. I love being kneaded, twisted, and stretched. I've become one big ache. When I return to my office, I have quite a few messages to return, but first I call my friend Deb, who invites me over to dinner. Both my mother and father called to see how I'm doing. I look up at my door, and standing there is Jason, my escort/med-student friend, who is now a doctor. We haven't seen each other in a long time, and he's brought a bottle of Perrier-Jouët and two plastic glasses to celebrate my troubles and catch up. We get pretty drunk quickly. I put the answering machine on, and we reminisce about the eighties and our scandalous activities. "And look how far you've come," jokes Jason. "Shit, what the fuck did you get yourself into?" he asks me. We walk out together—I'm flying—and say good-bye. I head to Deb and Paul Kogan's apartment on the Upper West Side for dinner, a much needed injection of normalcy: a good meal, good wine, music, intelligent conversation, and friendship. I'm so tired, I sleep over on their couch.

Sleepless Nights

I'm thrilled with the media coverage and the rush it induces—it's as good as a manic high or a cocaine high. I enjoy seeing my name in print and being the topic of conversation around town. It's particularly exciting to me that the indictment has been given space in *The New York Times.* All of the New York newspapers have covered it, and the story has even appeared in *USA Today* and the *Los Angeles Times*. Some of the reports are ridiculously inaccurate: "A knowledgeable observer said the forgeries were of markedly lower quality than genuine Kostabis," reports the *New York Post*. Some are humorous: "The U.S. Attorney's office in Brooklyn, perhaps lacking an appreciation for dada, has shattered this house of mirrors by indicting Andrew Behrman, the salesman, on charges of fraud and criminal conspiracy. If convicted, he faces up to $250,000 in fines and 25 years in prison, where the Government may well envision him lovingly attending to license plates," writes the *New York Observer*. Everybody seems to know that I've been indicted. Stuart gets to work on the case immediately. He prepares our pretrial motion for dismissal. Stuart argues that the acts I'm charged with committing don't amount to a criminal offense under the wire-fraud statute. But the judge rejects this argument; we're going to trial. *United States of America* v. *Andrew Behrman*. We have five months to prepare our case, and there's a tremendous amount of material to review—government exhibits, documents, and grand-jury testimony (from more than a year ago)—in a short period. There's research and strategizing to do. The government has had a full year to prepare for this case and has a large staff and unlimited resources with which to prosecute me. Stuart and I meet regularly to discuss my defense. I continue to be in touch with Annike, who has not been indicted; because they don't see her as the mastermind of the scheme they'll have difficulty proving that she actually painted the paintings, and she can just flee the country. And I am the one who has carelessly left the massive paper trail—tons of invoices, receipts, checks, and wires that are all in the hands of the government. I'm feeling confident that we'll win the case and that no jury will find me guilty of producing or selling "counterfeit" Kostabis. There's just no such thing as a fake Kostabi, since he doesn't paint any of his own paintings. I don't believe a jury will buy the fact that these paintings are his creations just because they have his signature on them. So technically there can be no forgeries. The issue here is about "authorized" versus "unauthorized" paintings—what is a genuine

Kostabi? Is a Kostabi only genuine if it has the Kostabi signature, the Kostabi blessing? If we can prove not only that he doesn't paint his paintings but also that he sometimes doesn't even sign his own name on the paintings, I'm convinced the jury will have to find me innocent. Other times I fantasize that the jury will find me guilty, and I imagine myself eating bread and water for the next five years, banging my tin cup against the bars of my cell in some jail somewhere in the middle of the woods in North Carolina. And then I counter by asking myself, is a jury really going to side with a self-described "con artist" who makes millions of dollars paying people minimum wage to paint his ridiculous faceless paintings?

It all drives me crazy, and I fight hard to maintain some level of sanity. Because I really think I'm losing my mind. I spend hours at Stuart's office examining hundreds of pages of government exhibits, documents, and grand-jury minutes, filling him in whenever he needs a question answered or an issue clarified. I'm intrigued by the case and fascinated that these details that we are working with trace *my* moves over the last years, because oddly I feel as though I'm working on somebody else's defense. I agonize over facts, searching for loopholes that might help us win this case for "the defendant." Sometimes I'm stunned that someone has made such blatantly foolish mistakes committing a crime—having monies wired directly into his personal bank account, signing receipts for cash, and issuing invoices separate from those of Kostabi World. Clearly I wasn't thinking about the consequences of my actions. I set myself up for my fall. I stay up until four or five in the morning, looking for clues to help Stuart and this pathetic defendant. I seize every opportunity I can to make money. Obsessing about the case induces my mania, and I go for days without sleep, becoming less lucid and more incoherent. I start believing that this is the most important legal case of our time. Stuart realizes that I am a bit out of control and obsessed, but he never loses focus and lets me continue my own investigation.

When I can no longer handle my manic obsession about the case, I try to divert my attention to some other activity. I usually go on a strict 800-calorie-a-day diet of egg whites, tuna, and tofu and a vigorous exercise program, starving myself until I lose thirty or forty pounds in two or three months. Ultimately, I break down and gain the weight back within a month, but I get tremendous gratification from watching myself losing the weight. At my most manic period, I weighed about 175 pounds at six-feet-one, rather lanky. I returned to 195 pounds.

I go back to see Dr. Solnick. I tell him I'm feeling much worse since I last saw him, and he tells me not to worry, that this is a typical response to coming off the medication. Finally, after a month of talk therapy and downward spiraling, I leave his care. A year later I learn from a psychiatrist I meet that the infamous Dr. Solnick practiced without a medical license because of an incident in which he allegedly seduced a patient, and that he was not a proponent of medication because he was no longer able to write a prescription. I call to thank Jonathan for the recommendation, and he is rather amused by this story about his miracle shrink.

Stuart decides that I will take the Fifth Amendment because the prosecutor will have a field day cross-examining me. Certainly I will appear guilty. There's no reason for the jury to hear what they will hear from witnesses coming from my mouth as well. But the thought of sitting silently at my own trial drives me crazy. They might as well handcuff me, too. And I worry that the average juror will question why I choose not to testify. Stuart is a brilliant attorney and can handle the case without using me as a witness, but still I feel powerful enough to convince anyone of anything, including my innocence. My thinking is so delusional that I really believe I can bond with each juror one-on-one, explain exactly why I am innocent, and answer any of their questions face-to-face, without lawyers, in a friendly way.

December 5, 1993. New York.
The day before the trial I go to Carappan, a downtown spa, for a massage, to relax and psych myself up for the big battle. The masseur tells me that he can't work on me until I relax and take a few deep breaths. He asks me if I'm feeling *particularly* tense. I tell him I'm facing twenty-five years in jail so I am having a *particularly*

hard time relaxing. He doesn't seem to believe me and laughs. Honest, I tell him. Counterfeiting. There's an odd silence. I feel his hands working on my lower back squeezing the tension up through my shoulders and neck and pushing it out through my head. Breathe. I imagine I'm on the set of a game show where the judge is the host and Kostabi and I are the two contestants. The judge goes back and forth asking us trivia questions about the case. "Mr. Kostabi, how many of your paintings were sold at Christie's last year?" he asks. "Twelve?" Kostabi asks. "No, sorry," says the judge. "Mr. Behrman, how many lithographs did Kostabi World publish last year?" "Six," I answer. "That's right," he says. I'm ahead. The judge asks eight more questions, and I beat Kostabi 8–2. I'm surrounded by a border of flashing lights and I'm jumping up and down and the audience is cheering for me and it's obvious that I'm the champion. And the masseur's hands are working on my head, relieving all the pressure, and the lights are flashing and I wake up and I'm totally relaxed. Where'd I go? I won. I've been acquitted.

United States of America v. *Andrew Behrman*

December 5, 1993. Edgewater, New Jersey.

I'm sleeping at my parents' new house tonight. I feel revved up, like it's the night before a big field trip to the Museum of Natural History. Except this one's to the Federal Courthouse in Brooklyn to see a real trial with a judge in a black robe with a gavel. And I'm in this courtroom drama—I play the role of the defendant.

December 6, 1993. Brooklyn.

I decided yesterday that I will not wear a suit in court, just a navy blue blazer and a pair of gray flannel pants. I feel it makes me less slick, more innocent. The drive to the courthouse with my parents is somber. I feel like we're on our way to a funeral. It's a bleak day, and there don't seem to be many subjects that are safe to talk about. My father gives me a pep talk as we get closer to Brooklyn. "You've got the best lawyer. He's ready for them," he tells me. As we get out of the car and approach the Federal Courthouse, my mother's tiny hand squeezes my hand tightly and she tells me to be strong. Just be strong. We walk into the courthouse at ten minutes before nine and find the massive courtroom, where I can see through the windowpane of the door many of my friends, including Lauren, Jonathan, Lucy, Deb, Paul, Ken, and Pamela, and my parents' friends, already seated. My parents both hug me before we enter the courtroom. I sit to Stuart's right at the defense table, trying not to stare at the young prosecutor, and Mark and his brother sit across the aisle. Indrek is grinning at me, thrilled to see me in court. I'm most glad that Jonathan is here; he gives me a tremendous amount of strength, like an older brother. We wait for the judge to arrive. I try to avoid turning around and looking at my parents and friends, but knowing that they have come to support me gives me a sense of comfort. The door behind the judge's bench opens, and Judge Eugene Nickerson, a sprightly white-haired man in his seventies, walks in. Everyone in the courtroom stands, then sits down, and I feel my blood pumping. I'm ready to win. The judge greets everybody with a friendly "Good morning." So far so good. Maybe we should all just shake hands and go home. Jury selection begins. It's an agonizing process in which both sides interview more than thirty potential jurors for approximately ten minutes each. I take voracious notes and mark the jurors that I like and dislike for Stuart to see. I don't like the guy who works for the post office and owns the Picasso print. Scratch him. I like the guy who takes art classes. I like the Lithuanian woman who paints as a hobby. Suddenly I'm an expert in choosing a jury. After about five hours we finally narrow it down to twelve. We're ready to start the trial.

I sit in the courtroom waiting for the trial to begin, searching around the room, trying to avoid making eye contact with anyone, especially anyone from the prosecution team, being careful not to look at the jury too much. I realize for the first time that the government is extremely serious about prosecuting me. They've flown in witnesses from Los Angeles, Paris, and Tokyo to testify against me, including former friends from Kostabi World. They've turned what my attorney feels should be a civil case into a criminal one. And the only reason I can think of that they've made such a big deal about prosecuting me is that the climate in the art market is just peaking and they know this will get a lot of media attention. There are reporters from newspapers and magazines ready with their pads to take notes. I nervously doodle the words *federal case* on my legal pad. I realize that I am not on a field trip. But it all seems so unreal—this courtroom scene has the color and clarity of a made-for-TV movie.

The prosecutor, Jonathan Polkes, looks like he is in his late twenties. Probably a classmate of some of my Wesleyan friends. Short and squishy-looking, with glasses. His mother comes with a friend to watch her son at the trial. They sit up close. This makes me want to puke. The two attorneys are huddled in a conference with the judge when Stuart says he wants to introduce Kostabi's arrest record, for his fight with Morton Downey, Jr. "On what theory?" asks Judge Nickerson. "Mr. Kostabi, who admittedly is someone who believes that generating bad publicity is good for his business—I believe that is very relevant in his motive to what he has done in pursuing this case against Mr. Behrman, including giving testimony in this case," says Stuart. The judge does not allow this as evidence.

Polkes attempts to present a simple case of fraud, in which a defendant who has exploited his position at Kostabi World takes tremendous advantage of dealers and galleries to sell unauthorized paintings created by a Kostabi World employee. He details the counterfeiting process fairly well and explains the logistics of the deal making and negotiating: "You're going to learn that Andy Behrman didn't only confess to his friends Lis and Jessica what he was doing on one occasion, he had a big mouth and couldn't stop telling his friends Lis and Jessica what a great thing he stumbled onto. He told them, virtually every day for six months, every detail of the scheme as I have explained it to you, and that's how we know all about what happened. He's going to tell you how he thought it was such a brilliant idea that he and Brandt would create the fakes, which is his word for them, forging signatures on them to Kostabi customers, and how much money they were making. You're going to hear that from the mouths of his own two friends, Lis and Jessica, who will testify for you during the course of the trial." This doesn't feel like a good start for us. It's Stuart's turn to do some damage control. He stands up, walks around the defense table, and looks at the jury. "The evidence will show you that the engine that is driving this case is Mark Kostabi, vindictive allegations, and, I submit, the evidence will show to you, totally unjustified allegations of Mark Kostabi are what brought the case here. Mr. Polkes indicated that he [Kostabi] is going to be portrayed as some sort of victim. I submit, ladies and gentlemen, the evidence will show you he's no victim at all. One thing that I agree with the prosecutor about– there was fraud going on in this case. Yes, lots of fraud, and you'll see where the fraud was. The fraud was in the house of the man named Mark Kostabi, who I guess also has the name of Kalev Mark Kostabi, but he usually calls himself Mark Kostabi. That's the fraud. You will hear similar things about Mark Kostabi that the prosecutor didn't mention to you in his opening statement. That Mark Kostabi is a man who describes himself as a con artist. He is a person who says that only suckers buy his paintings and that you have to be a total fool to buy one of his paintings. That's the victim of this supposed fraud. In fact, ladies and gentlemen, the evidence will show you that Mark Kostabi is not an artist at all. Of all the frauds and cons going on here, the biggest one of all is this notion that the prosecutor made that there is such a thing as a fake Kostabi. To use a big word that I hate to use in courtrooms, that's an oxymoron. It's a contradiction in terms. It's silly. There is no such thing as a fake Kostabi. Why, ladies and gentlemen? The evidence will show you how Kostabi works. He doesn't paint anything. He doesn't think anything up. He hires people who think up ideas, make paintings, and he makes lots of money from them. There are no fakes, ladies and gentlemen. The evidence will show you that the paintings that are at issue in this case are no different from all the other Mark Kostabi paintings that Mark Kostabi sold and made lots and lots of money from. You heard that right, ladies and gentlemen. He didn't paint these. He didn't think them up. They weren't his ideas. He hired idea people who came up with ideas. He hired painters who painted them, and he made lots of money from that. In fact, ladies and gentlemen, the evidence will show you—the prosecutor didn't mention this—that Mr. Kostabi even acknowledged in writing that the paintings that are at issue in this case were Kostabi paintings. That's right, ladies and gentlemen. He acknowledged in writing, he wrote to people, that these were his paintings. The evidence is going to show you, ladies and gentlemen, that Andy Behrman is not guilty of any fraud. The only fraud that's going on here is Mr. Kostabi."

The first witness called by the government is Mitsuna Kawamura, whose testimony has been videotaped, since she could not attend the trial. She is the representative of Art Collection House in Tokyo, from which the government has recovered thirty-four unauthorized paintings, which have been entered as government evidence. She was my contact in Tokyo, and all of my dealing with Art Collection House went through her. She appears frightened to be testifying. The prosecutor quickly leads her through explaining that the gallery issued directly to me, for counterfeit work, two checks totaling $21,000, and an undisclosed amount of cash. Stuart, who is also present at the videotaping, makes a point that more than $200,000 was wired directly to Kostabi World, for legitimate work I sold to them.

Kostabi is the next witness. As he approaches the stand and sits in his seat, there is some whispering in the audience and I take a deep breath. I'm frightened to be in the same room as him and angry that he's taken the case this far. I keep my eyes focused on the prosecutor and just listen to Kostabi's voice. Polkes asks him about the counterfeit paintings in Tokyo and how he handled the situation with Art Collection House, which was afraid that clients would find out about forgeries in Japan and the reputation of the company would be destroyed. When discovering the "unauthorized" paintings, he jointly came up with the idea of sending handwritten letters with Art Collection House to buyers telling them that their painting was one of his favorite images and that he wanted to publish it in an upcoming book, but that he wanted to rework it to make it even better. "What did you do to them specifically?" asks Polkes. "I changed the signatures on the front. I changed the signatures on the back. In some cases I made drawings on the back. And I changed the title," answered Kostabi. There is some snickering in the courtroom. He is extremely agitated. I know he's going to have difficulty handling the cross-examination. Stuart starts by making reference to a *Village Voice* advertisement in which Mark refers to himself as the world's greatest con artist but also as somebody selling original forgeries. This puts Kostabi on edge. "Did you ever get someone to sign, a stand-in to sign?" asks Judge Nickerson. "No. I never hired anyone from this ad to fill this job description," says Kostabi. "Could you read the ad for the jury, Mr. Kostabi?" asks Stuart. "It says: 'Stand-in for Mark Kostabi, must sign paintings, autographs and sketches. Must give interviews and make public appearances. Must be willing to change hair color monthly. $3.75 an hour plus benefits. Hours vary, age range 18–21 preferred, M or F'—meaning male or female—'to Mark Kostabi, Inc., 361 West 36th Street, 3A, New York City 10018, attention personnel.' " Interestingly, on cross-examination Mark is not entirely certain of his signature on each painting. "If that's a Kostabi signature, it's a very poor one," he says. "It doesn't look like a good Kostabi." There is some laughter in the courtroom. Now Stuart questions Mark about my role at Kostabi World. "He was a very effective salesperson, was he not?" Kostabi answers, "That's a matter of opinion. I would have to say—he generated sales, but no, I wouldn't call him effective, no." "Isn't it a fact that he generated certainly hundreds of thousands of dollars in sales, if not millions of dollars in sales?" asks Stuart. "He's a criminal. I—" says Kostabi. Judge Nickerson gets angry and raises his voice: "No. Look, don't. Please." "Okay. I'm sorry," says Kostabi. "Listen to me," Judge Nickerson says. "Don't volunteer things like that. Did he, all you have been asked now is, did he generate hundreds of thousands of dollars, maybe millions of dollars' worth of business for you, for Kostabi World?" "Yes," answers Kostabi. Stuart grills Mark on cash payments that I picked up for him in Japan, but Mark denies that this ever occurred. In fact, he denies all cash payments from dealers. He seems confused. He doesn't see what Stuart is driving at. The point is clear. Any cash that I did pick up I often turned over to him. It's quite possible the cash payments from Art Collection House were also paid to him. "Now you stated that the—what you have described regarding these paintings had an effect on your reputation as an artist? I believe you said it had damaged your reputation?" asks Stuart. "Yes," responds Kostabi. "Isn't it a fact, sir, that your reputation is as a con artist, not as an artist?" he asks. "My reputation among my clients was damaged. I—I was—I wasn't referring to the general public who watches shows like *Lifestyles of the Rich and Famous*," says Kostabi.

December 7, 1993. Brooklyn.

Jessica Doyle, Mark's former assistant, and now a costume designer living in Paris, is flown to New York by the government to testify. She testifies very reluctantly. Her demeanor toward the prosecutor is bordering on rude—she gives him one-word answers and barely acknowledges him. She does tell him that I told her that Annike and I were producing unauthorized paintings and that I was selling them in Japan and also in Germany. "What did he say to you about his state of mind about this, about how he felt about what he was doing?" asks Polkes. "He told me he was nervous. He told me that he knew that it was a crazy and silly thing," she tells him. She describes my personality as very highly strung. "Did you ever personally witness Andy Behrman sign any of the fakes in your presence?" asks Polkes. "No," she responds. But she also supplies important information about people who signed Kostabi's name on canvases. She goes on to testify that I had Mark sign blank certificates of authenticity, which I supplied customers with for my unauthorized paintings. She also admits lying to the police about knowing anything about the case when first questioned, " 'cause I was being loyal to my friend Andy." Then Stuart asks her if she was ever at Kostabi World with me and Hiromi

Nakano, the photographer, when I was writing the name Kostabi on a painting. "Not to my recollection," she answers.

Lis Fields, a former idea person in the "think tank" and now an assistant to a film director, comes from Los Angeles to testify. She has the most difficult time on the stand—she's unable to fight back tears while being grilled by the prosecution and explains that I had confided in her about my counterfeiting activities with Annike, after she begged me not to tell her anything about what I was doing. She has received an immunity deal to testify, having lied to the government previously about knowing anything about the case. She tells the prosecutor that I had "a mixture of fear and excitement" about the scheme. Curiously, she has kept two different sets of notes of her version of the story—one a cover story that includes some untruths and omissions that would make it look as though she didn't know anything about the case, the other an entirely truthful rendering of what happened and what she knew. In the first set of notes she actually wrote, "I had no idea he was doing anything wrong." She testifies that my behavior was manic and that I was taking medication. For some reason, maybe because I hate to see her go through such a stressful situation, I thank her when she passes by the defense table.

December 8, 1993. Brooklyn.
Today is a half day in court because of Hanukkah. Hiromi Nakano, the Kostabi World photographer, testifies that the slides of the counterfeit paintings were not taken by her, because she doesn't use a white brick wall as a background. Annike overlooked this detail. She goes on to tell the jury that she saw me late one evening, in a panic with Jessica, signing Kostabi's name to the front of a canvas. "What did you see Andy Behrman doing?" asks Polkes. "He was signing paintings," she answers. "Signing names on paintings?" he repeats. "Kostabi names on paintings," she says. This seems like the most devastating evidence to be introduced by the prosecution. Fortunately, the prosecution's own witness, Jessica, has no memory of the incident.

The prosecution calls Mark Zimmerman to the witness stand. Formerly a Kostabi groupie, "Maz" is now the operations manager of Kostabi World and says he does "basically everything." He describes the studio's perfectly organized system of record keeping. But Stuart questions him about signing Mark's name on a check, and he admits to having done it before. This is the first bit of hard evidence introduced that points to Kostabi allowing an employee to sign his name.

Hiroshi Yokohama, the owner of Hama Gallery in Tokyo, testifies about our meeting at which I sold him four paintings, which I shipped to him when I returned to New York. He also testifies that I gave him instructions to wire the money into an account at Marine Midland Bank, which happens to be my personal account. The prosecutor asks him if he ever meets Kostabi. Yokohama says yes, but that he left and came back again and asked him to take the frames off the paintings. "They said that something is strange," he said. "So Mr. Kostabi said he wanted to take these back to the United States, and he rolled them up." In an effort to suggest to the court that it would be okay for me to accept cash for the sale of paintings from my own collection, Stuart asks Yokohama if he is aware that I have my own personal collection of Kostabis. Unfortunately, Yokohama has no knowledge.

December 9, 1993. Brooklyn.
Stuart calls Kostabi's accountant, Mel Kaplan, and questions him about the purchase of Kostabi's $1 million apartment at the CitySpire Building. Kostabi has bartered artwork to satisfy part of the mortgage, and it has not been recorded. Stuart also finds out from Kaplan that Kostabi drew no salary in 1991, which implies that the proceeds of unreported cash sales went to him.

Outside the courtroom, during the lunch break, I see my mother talking with a woman in her midsixties. The woman inquires if this is my first trial. Yes. She assures my mother that I'll do just fine. My mother responds by telling her that I am the defendant and not the attorney. They both start laughing.

Ron English, a former Kostabi painter, testifies that Kostabi offered him a couple of certificates of authenticity so he could make his own Kostabis. English testifies that he never took him up on his offer.

It's time for the prosecutor's summation. He shuffles up to the jury box. "Now, let's say I find a basketball in a closet. If I went to sell that basketball, I could probably get five bucks for it. Let's say I take the same basketball and sign Jonathan Polkes on it. Probably then I'd get a dollar, but, of course if I put Michael Jordan's name, then it's magic. Now let's suppose I take the basketball and I take a Magic Marker and I sign Michael Jordan's name and I try to sell it to you for a couple of thousand bucks, I'd be cheating you. That's exactly what this case is about. Mark Kostabi has the same ability; sign something which is a piece of canvas and turn it into something worth a lot of money. The defendant gets nervous again when Kostabi goes to Japan," Polkes says. "And what's Behrman's reaction? After all I did for him, I can't believe he fired me," he says. "That's the twisted mind. This guy has been cheating Kostabi, and his only reaction, all I did for him."

A woman in dark Muslim garb appears in the back of the courtroom while the prosecutor is making his closing arguments. She sits right behind Lauren and Lucy, who are both frightened by her. At first I'm curious what her connection to the case might be until I realize that it's Annike, who has disguised herself to come see the last day of the trial. She has borrowed the outfit from a mosque in Jersey City. At first I'm shocked, imagining the worst— that she will be discovered as the co-conspirator and arrested on the spot. But then I realize the ridiculousness of this entire scenario. I chuckle and smile at her.

Stuart starts his summation with a simple question: "Did Andy intend to defraud anybody?" He questions the money I received from Art Collection House. Miss Kawamura's testimony supported, he argues, the fact that I had my own extensive collection of Kostabis and was entitled to any monies that I received. He accuses Kostabi of lying to Art Collection House customers by writing letters requesting to correct their paintings. "The government is accusing Andy Behrman of engaging in criminal fraud, and what does Kostabi do? He writes letters to people saying these are real paintings. These are really my paintings. I want to, quote, change them, and he doesn't tell them that he's claiming now that they are fakes. What is his explanation, basically? I lied in the letter," says Stuart. "Judge Nickerson will explain to you what an attempt to defraud means, and the government has to prove that beyond a reasonable doubt. So he can get up here and say, see, all this evidence, eyewitnesses, people saw him signing, you got all these ten different ways that we showed people signed and it wasn't Kostabi. Big deal. Where is the proof that Andy Behrman believed that what he was doing was not in accord with—and I hesitate to use this word but I will say it—normal, within the realm of what was normal at Kostabi World? It's so appropriate that they call it Kostabi World because that's what it is, it's like some other world where concepts that apply in this courtroom about truth and honesty have no meaning; where a man says he's the world's greatest con artist and makes a lot of money by saying it." Then Stuart brings up the issue of how the two Kostabi brothers treated me at Kostabi World. "Before any of this ever happened, they used to go around accusing him of being a thief. There was pressure on Andy to get more sales. Not only that, ladies and gentlemen, they owed Andy a lot of money."

After lunch in the cafeteria, I'm in the elevator with my father and some friends when my knees buckle and I nearly collapse, but my father grabs me before I fall. I'm a lot more anxious than I've realized. I'm huddling with my parents, holding their hands, wishing the trial could go on for a few more days and that I could have a chance to say a few words to the jury.

All the jury knows is that somebody has painted Kostabis and forged a signature. They are never introduced to any co-conspirators. They aren't even sure which paintings are fake. Kostabi isn't even sure. But I can tell them apart. Judge Nickerson instructs the jury on how to determine the guilt or innocence of a defendant and sends them to the jury room. They deliberate for only an hour before he dismisses them until the following Monday to start deliberations again.

December 11, 1993. New York.

My friend Paul takes me to see *Wayne's World* to get my mind off the trial and the deliberations, and for two hours Garth and Wayne manage to keep me focused—it is a good diversion. I go to a party at Larissa's, a friend of Deb and Paul, on the Upper East Side, and the intensity of my week disappears in the crowd of partygoers. Everyone is curious about how the trial is going, but I don't have the best perspective. "We're doing great," I say, just glad to be out of the courtroom and in a room full of people smoking and drinking.

December 13, 1993. Brooklyn.

I pace the area in front of the courtroom waiting for the jury to return with the verdict. I am surrounded by my family and friends and make calls to other friends on the pay phone to keep them posted. At 4:30 P.M. Judge Nickerson enters the courtroom and everybody quickly assembles inside. He asks for the verdict from the foreperson. I am frozen. "How do you find the defendant, Andrew Behrman, as to count one, guilty or not guilty?" asks the clerk. "Guilty," says the foreperson. Ouch! The clerk runs through counts two through five quickly, and I am found not guilty on each count. The clerk polls the jury. Judge Nickerson releases me on a personal-recognizance bond and sets a sentencing date for May 20, 1994. The prosecution team has mixed reactions, Stuart seems let down, and I'm just glad that the jury has come to a verdict I had predicted an hour earlier. I was pretty confident they wouldn't convict me of these other counts because none of them involved unauthorized paintings.

I am now officially labeled a felon. There doesn't seem as much of a stigma associated with being a felon as I thought there would be. So I won't be able to buy a handgun. A few days after the verdict I'm contacted by *New York* magazine writer James Kaplan, who is working on his story of the "Kostabi affair." He has attended the trial and wants to interview me, but Stuart asks me to decline being interviewed by him or any other member of the press because I haven't been sentenced yet. Nonetheless, I agree to meet with Kaplan because I feel like I can trust him and desperately want not only to be a part of the story but to exert some control over it. He agrees not to quote me. I meet Kaplan one afternoon for lunch on the Upper West Side at Lenge, a Japanese restaurant, and give him my version of the story. The article, complete with a bizarre nude photo of Kostabi, is published. It's a cover story. My reaction to the story and the response I get is extremely positive—calls from friends, family friends, and clients are all very supportive. The article portrays me quite fairly and does not paint the most flattering picture of Kostabi. " 'With Mark, Andy got a tabula rasa,' says a friend of both men. 'When Andy wasn't there to make him do tricks, he was boring. Where with Andy, everything was a joke, Mark had absolutely no sense of humor. He was almost like a trained dog—he'd always talk about how Donald Trump was his big hero.' " Kaplan asks Kostabi, "Would you ever forgive Andy Behrman?" "If he served a sufficient number of years in jail, and made financial restitution, and offered a sincere apology—under those circumstances, and those only, I would forgive him." Kaplan writes, "For one who has often portrayed *himself* as a con artist, for one who claimed that people who bought his paintings were fools, Kostabi pursued Behrman with remarkable single-mindedness. His determination seems all the more striking when you realize that until May 1991, Kostabi had considered Behrman one of his closest friends. Oddly, Behrman seems to have felt the same. After he was indicted, Behrman told a friend, 'I'm scared this is going to be a movie of the week, and I'll be played by Andrew McCarthy.' "

The media's attention to the trial only fuels my mania more, instilling me with an extra shot of confidence. I'm tremendously relieved that the jury has issued its verdict and that I can finally put an end to this chapter of my life. Concealed in this defeat, I think, is a small victory. I have been convicted on only the first count— conspiracy to defraud. Since I'm clear on the other four, that means I'll spend less time locked up. So I tell myself not to worry and I go about making the best of my time before my sentencing, allowing the wounds of the past few months' time to heal.

Chapter 7

Jack Daniel's in a Paper Coffee Cup

February 24, 1994.

U.S. Probation is going to visit my parents at their house in order to prepare a profile of the family for the judge, for the purpose of sentencing. It's about 9:30 A.M. on the appointed day, and my parents and I have just finished breakfast and are nervously awaiting our visitor. My father is straightening up newspapers, and my mother is cleaning up the kitchen while I watch television. My father and I both wear khakis and a sweater; my mother is dressed in a skirt and jacket. A guy who looks no older than nineteen arrives to interview us, and we greet him as if he's a salesman. My father invites him in, and he sits on a chair next to the couch and begins to ask us questions about our educational backgrounds, employment and financial histories, and our living situation in general. We must appear to this interviewer like a relatively stable family. I don't think he's going to leave with the impression that I come from a family of crime, and he ends up putting together a picture-perfect report of the family for Judge Nickerson. But I'm actually not living at this quiet, safe, and cozy home—I don't want to stay in New Jersey. I'm just bumming around at night or sleeping in my office or on friends' couches in Manhattan. And I'm running around drinking excessively, talking to complete strangers that I meet in bars and on buses about my recently acquired felony conviction. I'm not lucid. In fact I'm losing it quickly.

At night I roam the streets, spending my time in bars and clubs, ending up in diners at 5:00 A.M., begging one waiter to serve me Jack Daniel's in a paper coffee cup because it's after hours. I find myself talking incessantly and feeling agitated, constantly needing to be on the move and involved in several activities at once. My friends are becoming more and more concerned about my mental health, and one of them insists that I see her therapist for a consultation. At this point I can't even keep track of how many doctors I've seen, but I figure I'll give another one a shot. Dr. Rector is a young therapist who after about a half hour of talking to me gently tells me that there's nothing that he's going to be able to do to help me with my problem. He feels strongly that I need to see a psychiatrist and arranges for me to meet with a colleague on the Upper East Side, Dr. Caroline Fried. I feel like I'm being bounced back and forth from East Side to West Side. How many times will I have to cross Central Park before someone will be able to help me? But this is the first time I've been referred to a female psychiatrist or psychotherapist since my days at Wesleyan, and I feel oddly hopeful about seeing a woman.

When I arrive at Dr. Fried's office, I decide not to judge her on her bad magazines: *Redbook. Parenting. Colonial Home.* She shares the office with another psychiatrist, and I'm hoping that they're his. She opens the door to her office and smiles. She looks like she is in her late thirties. I sit down on a small leather couch and spend the first few minutes of our session trying to figure out who she reminds me of. I decide it's Sally Field, with her short, dark, straight brown hair and her friendly but serious nature. She's petite. She has a contagious laugh. Glasses. I take an instant liking to her. I'm in the right place. She seems to approach the session like a science project. She's methodical in her questioning and collecting background information. She asks me about my spending habits (which surprises me), my drug and drinking habits, my sleeping schedule, and my sexual promiscuity. I even offer to talk to her about my suicidal thoughts and my impulsive behavior in general. I tell her that there are some days that I feel like jumping in front of a bus and back away at the last second. Nothing I say frightens her. I feel her taking an imaginary giant breath to figure out how she is going to attack my problem. She doesn't panic, but

I can tell she's not exactly sure how bad my situation is yet. At the end of the session she prescribes Klonopin, an antianxiety medication, for the time being, to try to stabilize things. I make an appointment for another session and leave her office feeling that I have found the doctor who's going to rescue me from hell. No other doctor that I have ever met is ever going to help me. Not even Dr. Golub. He was going to treat me like another one of his twitching psychiatric patients in his waiting room. Over the next sessions, Dr. Fried and I talk about everything from my recent conviction to my manic trips around the world to my obsessions with food, spending, exercise, and sex. She asks lots of questions. During the third session she starts talking to me about moods. Mood swings. Highs. Lows. Cycles. What is this mood thing she's talking about? The more I talk about my activities—sleepless nights, drug and alcohol abuse, sexual promiscuity, overspending, and breaking the law—the more convinced she is that I have manic depression, or bipolar disorder. Her diagnosis sounds so definitive that it feels like a life sentence. Hearing it from her, I'm frightened that this "energy" floating around *my* brain and attacking *my* neurons, this force that has already wrecked my life, is going to continue to destroy me and that she won't be able to help. There's got to be some combination of medication to quickly put an end to this hopelessness. Her goal now is to stabilize me on medication before I am sent away to prison. We've got some time to work things out before I'm sentenced. But the Klonopin doesn't seem to do anything for me, and I start to abuse it, randomly popping a handful every so often. One night at dinner with Pamela at E.J.'s Luncheonette I order an ice cream sundae and just for fun sprinkle ten or twelve of the little blue pills on top and eat them off the top with the whipped cream. I don't really seem to care what happens or if I have to be taken out by an ambulance. It's just an urge I need to satisfy, a chance I take. I joke to myself that I shouldn't be too anxious after I'm done with this sundae.

A week later, my mind racing as if I'm on speed, I tell Dr. Fried that I'm fighting off sleep and feeling manic and suicidal again. She prescribes Depakote, a mood stabilizer and alternative to lithium. My problem with Depakote, the peach pills, is that I take too many at once, too, sometimes up to ten or twelve at a time—not because they're addictive, just because I can't resist the urge. I like experimenting with the medication to see what kind of reaction I have, and my mania seems to shield me from fear. I'm aware that I'm sabotaging my own treatment. I report back to Dr. Fried that I obviously can't be trusted with either Klonopin or Depakote, and that anyhow they both make me dull. Usually it's the doctor who makes the decision that the patient isn't trustworthy, but in this case I do. So we switch to lithium, which I haven't been on since Dr. Golub prescribed it for me, and after a while my racing thoughts slow down. I see Dr. Fried twice a week but give her daily updates on how I'm feeling so that she can adjust my medication. Soon I feel stabilized, more centered and without any dramatic highs or lows.

Dr. Fried insists that I see a psychotherapist as well, since my stabilized mental state allows me to think more coherently about my situation. She refers me to Dr. Arlene Marks, whom I start seeing once a week for therapy. We have so much to talk about: impending incarceration, IRS problems, manic depression, medication, suicide, sexuality, family, career. My level of anxiety has registered an all-time high. I'm still dealing with the aftershock and fallout from the trial, sorting through the hype from the *New York* magazine article and a television segment that has just aired on *Eye to Eye with Connie Chung,* am juggling five clients at work, and am extremely frightened about the sentencing. I'm also in the process of giving up the office space on Fifth Avenue after three months because it's not practical and I need a real apartment to live in. I move to a one-bedroom apartment in a new luxury building on 86th Street and Broadway, which I also plan to use as an office. I actually draw a flow chart for Dr. Marks and include "dry hair" as one of the issues I feel we need to address in our therapy. I'm under attack from all sides—there's almost too much for this woman to sort out and deal with once a week. I feel like I'm overburdening her.

In a letter to Dr. Marks, I write, "My seams are coming apart and my insides are on the outside. I can't feel my being, I can only think of freebasing or masturbating—of getting high. Nobody loves me. I can't perform. I'm waiting for the drugs to take effect and to send shocks into my brain. I am suffering."

March 11, 1994. New York.
I am becoming paranoid and having psychotic thoughts. I won't answer the telephone and think that the words on the pages of books and newspapers can hurt me like sharp objects. I'm walking down Broadway to the cash machine when all of a sudden I start feeling a razor blade slicing my tongue from all different angles. I twist my face in agony and hope that nobody notices. The psychotic episode only lasts for about thirty seconds, but I can't get the image of razor blades out of my head, or the belief that my tongue is a bloody mess. It creeps into my mind every so often and frightens me when I least expect it. After I call Dr. Fried in a panic, she puts me on the antipsychotic Risperdal, which relieves me of these visions but has several bizarre side effects. For instance, I become very stiff and walk with a shuffle, I lose facial expression and don't blink, and I can't urinate in a straight line any longer (I spray all over the toilet). I have a noticeable tremor in my hand and find it difficult to hold utensils or write. I'm put on Propranolol to counterbalance the tremor, which seems to help a bit, and Symmetrel for the stiffness. I am taken off the lithium and put on a different mood stabilizer, Tegretol, but it makes the backs of my hands itch and gets me revved up, so I have to stop using it. I'm talking very fast and under more pressure since I'm about to be sentenced.

11:30 P.M. Rihga hotel bar, New York.
I'm sitting drinking a Pilsener Urquell, just for a change, when I hear a couple speaking German, sitting on a couch nearby. They're in their midthirties and dressed in jeans, black turtlenecks, and boots. They have blond hair and tans. They're splitting a bottle of champagne and smoking, so I walk over to them. "Can

I borrow a cigarette?" I ask, even though I don't really smoke.
"Sure, do you need a light?" the man asks. "Thanks," I answer.
"Are you from New York?" he asks me. "Yes, just waiting for a
friend," I tell him. "We're here from Germany for a week," he
says. I've now gotten myself into a conversation. "What do you do
in New York?" he asks me. "I do public relations. I used to be in
the art business," I say. "Oh, what kind of art?" she asks. "I work
for a gallery in Düsseldorf," she says. Small world. "I used to work
for an American artist named Mark Kostabi," I tell them. They
look at each other and start laughing. "Kostabi? Kostabi?" he asks.
"Such crap. You're not the guy who reproduced his paintings, are
you?" he asks. I nod. "We hate that stuff, but we would love to
own a fake one," he says. I'm not sure if he's joking. "Here, have
some of our champagne," he says as he asks the waiter for another
glass. We spend the next two hours talking about the entire saga.

Sentencing: The Electric Chair

May 20, 1994. Brooklyn.
Five months after the trial, after a sleepless night at my parents'
house, I return to court with Stuart, my sister, my parents, and the
same loyal group of friends who had attended the trial. I have no
idea what kind of sentence Judge Nickerson will give me, but I've
been considering all the possibilities for the last five months, and
I'm hoping for less than a year in prison, although there is the possibility of as much as five years. Stuart goes before the judge and
speaks for quite a while about the case and about my character.
"Andy, in his own mind and heart, has difficult feelings about what
happened here but, in any event, honestly didn't believe that he
committed a crime, and I realize that that issue has been resolved.
But that is the feeling of the person, and I've come to have some
exposure to that," he says. "I think that under any view, Kostabi
World was an ethical swamp that Andy Behrman had the misfor-
tune to be working at."

Judge Nickerson has been provided with letters from my

friends and family asking for his leniency in sentencing. I read a prepared statement, which I have written out on note cards. "Your Honor, I'd like to start by saying that I do respect the decision of the jury, and I do take full responsibility for this incident. I'm sorry I have to rely on these note cards. My nerves. It's been more than three years since my involvement with this case began. From that time on, the normal routine of my life came to an abrupt end. My conviction in December and the anxiety of waiting for this day has devastated myself, my family, and my friends. Not only am I sorry for what has happened, but I take full responsibility for it. In 1990, while I was working eighteen-hour days and closing $2 million deals for my employer, on the outside my life seemed perfectly in control. Inside, however, I was falling apart. By early October of 1990, my mental health reached an all-time low. I was bouncing between manic episodes and, at the same time, working in a world in which it was not uncommon to attend an opening in Munich one night and one in Tokyo the next. I was drawn to a world whose rules were different from any I had known before. Because at the time my manic depression was not being properly treated, I was wide open for trouble. I clearly remember the day that I was invited to a neighborhood bar near the art studio. There, I was presented with a plan that ultimately led to this case. I constantly remind myself that I had the choice to say no that day. For reasons I still don't entirely understand, I didn't. This was the greatest mistake I ever made. Because of this mistake, I am the convicted defendant in *United States* v. *Andrew Behrman*. I have humiliated myself, but even worse, I have shamed my family. I will never be able to forgive myself for this. I hope that I will be given the opportunity to prove to the court that I have something of value to offer the community, and that this mistake in judgment does not define my character. I am deeply sorry for what I have done. I take full responsibility. I am sorry for the pain I have caused others. Regardless of what happens here today, I will carry the burden of this mistake for the rest of my life."

Then I wait for him to speak. "I've thought a lot about this case. And I must say, I am very impressed with the letters that were sent to me. Extraordinary, they were, on the whole, and I believe them—most of them. I get a lot of letters for people up for sentencing, and mostly they are concocted. They don't have a ring of sincerity about them. These did—a lot of these did. You've obviously done good things in your life, and I've thought a lot about that," says Judge Nickerson. Among the letters included in the submission to Judge Nickerson is one particularly moving one from my friend Suzanne Yalof:

> Andy is the most giving and selfless person that I know. I think the best example of this is his devotion to my friend Ken Johnson, who has been diagnosed with AIDS. Andy has not only spent every day with Ken in the hospital since his admission but has created a support group for Ken which has kept him comfortable and financially independent. I truly do not believe that Ken would be alive today were it not for Andy's support, caring and strength. I was surprised to hear of Andy's involvement in this case. I cannot emphasize enough how terrible it would be for so many people not to have Andy around, particularly Ken Johnson, whose life depends on him.

Jonathan wrote:

> Andy is the best friend one could possibly have. There he is, at my daughter's birthday party, wearing an alligator costume, passing out Barney-inspired party favors for the two-year-old boys and girls. Oh, and here he is, helping my wife and I when we recently moved from Manhattan to Brooklyn Heights. At the hospital, he holds your hand and gets the coffee when your wife is in difficult and protracted labor. He calls your mother in Washington, D.C., on her birthday; he helps your twenty-three-year-old brother get a job after a year of fruitless searching.

One of the letters comes from Robert DePasquale, who was featured in the documentary Lauren and I made, *A Six Voice Home*. Robert writes:

> I've never told this to him but Andy Behrman is a fine individual whom I will never forget. The year of 1988 and our encounter was a blessing. I am in an unusual position. Twenty years ago I needed friends to attest to my character. Conversely, I am now pleading that a friend be given every possible consideration. An individual, frankly, who does not fit the accusations made about him. Your Honor, Mr. Behrman quite possibly gave me back my life.

Judge Nickerson straightens out some papers on his desk and leans back in his chair. There's a painfully long pause. "I'm going to impose a sentence of five months' imprisonment, two years' supervised release, a special condition of home detention, another condition of two hundred fifty hours of community service, as directed by the probation department, to commence only following the period of home detention. And I'll impose the minimum fine of $7,500." I'm relieved that he has not sentenced me to the maximum five years. In fact, I'm thrilled. I think he's been extremely fair. In the next few weeks my parents line up a "sentencing advocate," who for a fee of $7,500 will negotiate that my sentence be served in a CCC—a community corrections center—with work-release restrictions. Without the recommendation of the sentencing advocate and the approval of the judge, I would be sent to a minimum-security prison somewhere in the Northeast. This particular CCC, Esmor, provides residential care for individuals who have been referred by the U.S. Department of Justice, Federal Bureau of Prisons, U.S. Probation and Parole Service, U.S. courts, and other legal jurisdictions. It's something like a halfway house for assistance in the transition from institutional to community life. It's supposed to be a step up from a minimum-security prison, and it's closer to home. The judge approves the advocate's recommendation. I leave for Esmor at the end of August.

The Calvin Klein Prison Collection

August 16, 1994. New York.
In preparation for serving my sentence, I put all of my possessions in storage and move back to New Jersey with my parents. I enjoy the comforts of home—good food, a comfortable bed, and a clean bathroom, luxuries I doubt I'll see again for the next five months. My parents, concerned for my safety at Esmor, make me feel as though I am going off to battle. Luckily the facility is in midtown Manhattan and not someplace in Bumfuck, Pennsylvania, making it easy for friends and family to visit. Everyone is sad here. Scared for me.

A few days before we leave for Esmor, my mother suggests we take a short drive over to Riverside Square, an upscale shopping mall in Hackensack, to pick up a few things. Like what? I wonder. She keeps her eyes focused on the highway as she drives us to the mall, looking like she's about to break into tears at any moment. We park the car, and I can smell the heat rise from the asphalt as I follow her inside. It's a hot day in August, a year after my indictment, and the mall welcomes us with a blast of cold air. Our first stop is the men's department at Bloomingdale's. My mother immediately reaches for a black cotton DKNY sweater, which she waves at me from behind a mannequin. She looks at me for approval. We'll take it. She strides around the store at a rapid pace, a woman with a mission. She holds up a pair of Ralph Lauren khakis. Try these on. I grab them and try them on in the dressing room, and when I come outside I see that she's made a pile of button-down and polo shirts. Is there anything else I need for the next five months? For God's sake, Mom, I want to say. I'm not a freshman going to college—I'm a convicted felon going to prison to serve his sentence. But I'm not sure if reminding her of this would make her laugh or cry, so I just keep trying on the clothes. It makes my mother happy to see me try on everything and put together a few good outfits. She starts grabbing packages of Calvin Klein briefs. I don't need that many. She doesn't pay attention, talking and reaching for white sweat socks. You were "best-dressed" senior in high school, and you'll be the best-dressed prisoner at Esmor, damn it, I think to myself. She pays for the clothes, and we stop in a restaurant at the mall. We both order Caesar salads with grilled chicken and Diet Cokes. And we're both happy.

Jonathan calls me from Washington and tells me that he's leaving the East Coast. Somehow I find humor in the fact that he'll be in treatment in the Midwest and I'll be in a prison at the same time; in our own ways, we'll each be on sabbatical from the New York scene. I didn't think it would end up like this. He was going to be the famous novelist, and I was going to make a small fortune and retire by forty. Lauren and their daughter, Nicole, who is now two years old, are living far away in Denver. She is encouraging about my situation.

I don't want my friends to forget about me over the next five months. Two nights before I have to surrender at Esmor, I throw a party for myself at the Merc Bar in Soho. I design invitations using the famous Lichtenstein image of the crying woman, which I caption, "Come Shed a Tear for Andy Behrman," and enclose free-drink cards based on Monopoly "Get Out of Jail Free" cards. I invite all the friends, acquaintances, contacts, and media people I know in New York. I'm having fun organizing the party and making sure everyone is going to have a good, memorable time. I arrive in an upbeat mood and am energized by the crowd and their support, but I immediately realize that I've forgotten what I've done to be in this room—I've been handed a five-month sentence in a minimum-security facility and five months under house arrest. The evening is a celebration of a huge loss for me as well as a good-bye party, and there is an undertone of sadness beneath the good mood. "I've got to leave early—early morning flight to Miami—be good," says one friend as he shakes my hand. Nobody knows what to say to me, and nobody talks about where I'm going. We just talk about the phenomenon of having a going-away-to-prison party. I hug and kiss friends and make the rounds to everybody who has come to send me off and toast to the next five months. "Here's to prison," I say. Everybody laughs. I'm walking around, a little spaced-out, when I see Katie, a "friend" of mine. I met Katie on the bus a month earlier and in the first five minutes of our conversation invited her to my going-away-to-prison party. She has come with a guy she met in front of Grace's Market, on the way to the party. I realize there are lots of people here I don't know, and they all seem to be having fun at my prison send-off bash. The bar is crowded and friends are handing me drinks and I'm getting pretty drunk for the last time and this party isn't making much sense to me. Somehow I feel like I've won a prize I don't really want.

The night before I go to Esmor, I dream that I am sent away for five years of hard labor and that I find myself working at Kostabi World as a painter. I am standing in the studio, wearing a pair of paint-splattered overalls and a cap. I work around the clock, churning out painting after painting of faceless images; Kostabi signs his name to them as fast as I can produce them.

Chapter 8

Doing Time

August 31, 1994. New York.

E arly on this sweltering afternoon, my parents drop me off at Esmor, on 31st Street between Fifth and Madison. It used to be a single-room-occupancy hotel, and by the look of the façade it was probably a magnificent place in the early twenties. It's as if my parents are dropping me off at a hotel for the weekend—except for some reason we're all crying. I walk up the steps to the building and into the lobby, a dingy area with walls that are painted two shades of gray and speckled brown carpeting. There's been a little mistake. My travel agent has obviously booked me into the wrong hotel. I identify myself to a security guard at the front desk, a young Latin man in his early twenties wearing black pants and a wrinkled white short-sleeve dress shirt. He has me fill out registration papers—I guess they're expecting me. I'm dripping with sweat, and my hands are shaking from fear and all of the medication I am taking. Everybody around me is speaking Spanish. Latin music blares from a radio behind the desk. When I'm finished filling out the papers, I give my suitcases to one of the resident supervisors to put into storage. I am pushed into a small room and asked for a urine sample. It takes me a few minutes to pee because I'm so scared, and when I do it spills over the tube onto my hands. Too much. Then I pick up my suitcases from storage and am guided to my room on the fourth floor by a resident supervisor. It's a small room with a TV, two single beds, two dressers, a closet, a locker, and a bathroom. One side of the room is occupied. I follow the resident supervisor back downstairs for

sheets, blankets, a pillow, a towel, and a handbook. I go back upstairs and make my bed the best I can—it's a three-inch-thick
green plastic-covered mattress, and the sheets keep slipping off. I
unpack my clothes and put them away. I organize my books and
magazines on top of the dresser. I glance at the handbook and
read the list of prohibited acts; the first three are killing, assault-
ing, and setting a fire. I put all of my pills in the top drawer of the
dresser and take a Klonopin to calm myself down and stop shaking. I hide my medication in my socks, as a precaution against
theft. I walk outside my room and laugh when I hear Tony Or-
lando and Dawn on the radio singing "Tie a Yellow Ribbon Round
the Ole Oak Tree." Nobody else is laughing.

I walk through the hallways and pass by small groups of men
just hanging out in shorts and tank tops, sweat dripping from their
faces, trying to cool off in front of their fans. A large group has
congregated in the first-floor smoking lounge. The room is filled
with smoke, and *Cristina* is blaring on a television in the background that's competing with the heated tones of two residents
arguing in Spanish. Three pregnant women in shorts and slippers
stand near the vending machine in the corner; one is kicking it—
she's just lost two quarters and is intent on getting them back. The
women live on different floors from the men. I can't stay in this
room much longer without being noticed—I'm the only white
person in here—unless I can find a big-enough cloud of smoke to
hide behind.

I take the elevator upstairs, but there's someone blocking the
doorway to my room. He's drinking a Pepsi, a pack of Marlboros
sticking out of the waistband of his shiny green sweatpants. It's
my new roommate for the next five months. He's muscular and
tattooed with multicolored serpents and hearts; SONYA is written
in script on his right shoulder, and dark green-and-red swirls are
emblazoned on his torso from his pectorals down to his navel.
He's wearing two thick gold chains with medallions. Didn't I see
him on *Geraldo*? He reminds me of some kind of Latin superhero
action figure. He introduces himself as Pippo and extends his
hand, glittering with gold rings and bracelets. He offers me a ciga-

rette. No, thank you, I don't smoke. Pippo finishes his Pepsi, opens the screen, and throws the can out the window. He throws all his garbage out the window. He takes a picture out of his wallet of his girlfriend and their kid, a seven-year-old girl. He smiles. Two more months in this place, he tells me. He walks into the bathroom to smoke a cigarette, since we're not allowed to smoke in our rooms.

It's nearly 95 degrees. He nods at me to follow. He offers me a cigarette again and lights it. I'm wearing a pair of khakis, a white Ralph Lauren Polo shirt, and a pair of loafers. My pants are sticking to my legs, and my shirt is clinging to my back. The shower curtain is clear vinyl with a seashell print. The floor tiles are loose and some are missing. The sink is cracked. I'm trying to explain my crime to Pippo. Looking for key words. Art. Fraud. Counterfeiting. Japan. Inhale deep. I'm choking on smoke. He starts laughing, so I start laughing. Soon we're both laughing. I'm still choking on smoke. I don't know if he's laughing at my crime or because I'm choking, but I keep laughing with him and then he starts mumbling in Spanish and laughing even harder.

Esmor is run by Mr. Hughes, a cruel black man in his midforties who manages a staff of resident supervisors—a group of young social workers who are poorly trained and command little respect from the residents—and a pathetic and nasty employment counselor, Mr. Gordon, who picks his nose and advises me to apply for a job at a nearby toy factory. He is the target of hatred and the butt of residents' jokes since he treats us like animals. He is known for meting out harsh punishments for ridiculous infractions, like weekend lockup for five-minute lateness. The second Sunday I'm there, all of us residents assemble in the cafeteria for an hourlong meeting with Mr. Hughes, in which he begins by discussing policy and the past week's violations. He talks about the importance of curfew, keeping a neat and orderly room, and respecting the staff. "Respect. Respect is key," he says. He paces in front of us, telling us we're lucky to be in a place like this and that we all belong in the "big house" and he has the power to send us back there. Then he starts screaming insults and demeaning random residents in the group. "If you hadn't had such blatant disrespect for the law, you wouldn't find yourself here, so I have no pity for you," he says to a dark-skinned young Muslim wearing a skullcap. The man stands up and lunges for Hughes, starts choking him, pulls him to the floor, and sits on his chest. The resident supervisors finally pull him off, and the police arrive in about ten minutes to take him away. The meeting is quickly disbanded.

There are about one hundred men and women confined to this facility. A majority of the residents are transitioning—they've spent time in "real" prison serving longer sentences, mostly for drug-related crimes. The majority are Hispanic or African-American, although there is one Orthodox Jew in for diamond fraud. I definitely stick out in the crowd; residents are constantly stopping to ask me questions as if I work here or asking me to sign passes for them. I feel like a fool.

I am prepared for my stay at Esmor with a month's supply of medication, which I am able to administer myself. I am taking lithium, Depakote, Risperdal, and Ambien to sleep at night. I've been committed to keeping a consistent regimen, taking my medications at the right dosages and the right times. In my dresser drawer they're easily accessible to anyone, but I'm never concerned that any of the residents are going to steal my medication, although sometimes I do double-check to see if any are missing. On my first day—I introduce myself to as many of the residents as I can—it feels like freshman orientation again. I feel a huge surge of energy as I sit drinking a Diet Pepsi (unfortunately they don't have Diet Coke here) in the smoking lounge after dinner with a few new friends. It's almost 10:00 P.M., time for lights out, and everybody starts returning to their rooms. It's ridiculously hot and I get into bed in my underwear and lie flat on the three-inch mattress. Pippo opens his top drawer and pulls out a flag, the flag of Puerto Rico. He gets into his bed and covers himself with the flag. The resident supervisor comes into our room for the head count and calls out my name. I answer "here" and thank him, and he slams the door shut. For the next twenty minutes I hear doors slamming. I can't stand the noise. I feel like I'm being locked in my cage. And I'm petrified of falling asleep next to this scary guy underneath his flag of Puerto Rico—I feel like he's lying in his coffin.

Each day, when you are outside Esmor, you are required to make two "contact calls," one between 10:00 A.M. and 2:00 P.M. and the second between 4:00 P.M. and 8:00 P.M. They're fifteen-second calls—all you are required to do is to state your name and your location. A silly technicality, but sometimes it slips your mind. When you leave in the morning and when you return in the evening you have to sign in and out in three different places. My signature becomes abbreviated, and I even drop the loop in the *D* in my middle name because I have to sign it so many times.

The first night I come to Esmor I call my friend Lucy and tell her that I'm on work release; can she help me find a job? She calls her friend Susan, who has just opened a new, upscale café in the Village. This phone call establishes a pattern between Lucy and me—we speak every night I am at Esmor, sometimes a couple of times a night, and she visits me several times a week, constantly reassuring me that there will be an end to this five-month sentence. I make an appointment with Susan at the Cake Bar and Cafe and have my meeting approved by the staff. I've never worked as a busboy before, and I guess thirty-two isn't too late to start. I fill Susan in on my status and she seems somewhat amused; I promise that I will be an incredible worker and a tremendous asset. Susan is a lawyer by training, and it was her dream to open this café. She's very understanding and certain things will work out just fine. From my first day, I become obsessed with clearing dirty plates and lipstick-smudged cups and glasses off tables and wiping them down like an automaton. I am proud when I'm promoted to the position of waiter, and I excel at serving my customers. It's a pretty simple job, but I manage to turn it into a rather complicated one in my mind and make it a challenge—I give myself ridiculous goals related to clearing plates and glasses: I estimate that it will take three trips to the kitchen to clear off six tables, or I can carry everything in one hand from three tables. It keeps me occupied. My attitude is always friendly, probably because it feels like a volunteer job, but I'm efficient and move quickly. A young couple comes in and orders carrot cake and cappuccino, and I can tell that they're in a rush. I hold my other orders and get to theirs right away. The first day, I wait on chef David Bouley. This makes me slightly nervous. No problems. Good tipper. $5 on $20. During the day, in this world of chocolate-mousse pies, banana rhum tarts, cappuccino and espresso, I'm a totally free man—except from my obsessions—but when the kitchen closes, I'm forced to return to the world of urine tests, shakedowns, and confinement. Since I have to give 25% of my earnings to Esmor and I have taxes to pay, I'm not earning too much—about $150 per week—so I decide that I'm going to have to come up with some freelance public relations work to do so I can put aside some money for my release. Since most of my PR work is done on the telephone anyway, I figure it shouldn't be a problem for me to handle two or three clients from prison.

The smell of disinfectant in the cafeteria is so strong that it's almost impossible for me to eat without getting nauseated. Beef stew and rice that smell like ammonia are hard to stomach. It doesn't seem to bother anybody else, so I don't say anything, I just don't eat. I buy most of my meals at places like Burger King and Wendy's in transit from my job, or I settle for Oreos or Lay's potato chips from the vending machines in the lounge. Today in the cafeteria I push the food away, go upstairs, and take a cool shower—it's like an oven in this building—then sit in front of the television and ask Pippo if he minds if I watch *Melrose Place*. He looks confused. He's obviously never seen it or heard of it, but he's hooked after the first show. He thinks Amanda's a big bitch. We watch *Party of Five* next. I don't bother trying to explain this to Pippo. I don't think he gets it. Sometimes when there's nothing on television, Pippo puts a tape in his boom box and dances around the room while I'm reading a magazine or writing in my journal. He pretends to be dancing with a partner and makes snapping and hissing noises with his tongue. I can't imagine this happy dancing man transporting kilos of cocaine across the border, and I stay away from the exact reason that he is here.

One evening Pippo isn't feeling well and can hardly move in bed. He is sweating and cursing in English and Spanish, and finally I go downstairs to get help. He is taken away in an ambulance, and I never see him again. The rumor is that Pippo has spinal meningitis, so for weeks I'm obsessed that I, too, have contracted this fatal disease and am going to die in this shithole. Mr. Hughes replaces Pippo immediately with a new resident, Tony, who has served a long sentence for some type of business fraud that we never actually discuss. Tony comes from a tough Italian family. He finds a job at Williams-Sonoma, doing cooking demonstrations. They make him wear an apron on the sales floor, which really humiliates him. I wish I could see him wearing it just once. He is lonely and desperate to go home, and all he wants to do is talk about the injustice of his trial and how his co-conspirator walked away without having to serve any time. We hang around in the lounge together playing "What's His Crime?," a game in which you pick out a resident and guess his crime and then find out why he's really here. The closest guess wins a Pepsi.

In the months preceding my admission to Esmor, I was still actively pursuing new PR clients. I'm not quite sure what I was thinking I was going to do when the time came for me to turn myself in and be cut off from the rest of the world. But I do have the telephone. The telephone has always been my most important tool. I prefer it to the press release, the press kit, the memo, and the letter. It is quick and efficient. There is one pay phone per floor, calls are limited to ten minutes per call, and the lines for the phone usually have ten people waiting. So I get on line one night to use the pay phone, and there are about four or five guys ahead of me, each speaking loudly in Spanish and for much longer than the allotted ten minutes. I just need to make a quick call to an artist to confirm an appointment to meet at the café tomorrow. He knows about my situation and is actually quite comfortable with it. I get him on the phone, and he tells me that he's decided to go ahead and use me. He asks where he can drop off a check quietly, and I tell him to do it at the café, because I can't receive money while at Esmor. I make a call to a couples therapist who has been referred to me by another client; she is interested in doing national television appearances. We talk briefly, and the whole time I'm frightened there's going to be a fire drill or someone is going to scream something out in Spanish.

September 18, 1994.
It's Sunday morning. Sundays we're allowed out for two hours for religious worship. I decide to go to St. Patrick's Cathedral on Fifth Avenue, since it's only twenty blocks from Esmor and I can easily take a bus there. Since I'm Jewish, I have really only been to church for weddings and funerals, so I'm not really sure what to expect. When I go in the Fifth Avenue entrance along with a large group of tourists, I'm overwhelmed by the size of the cathedral. I follow a young tourist in shorts and dip my fingers into the holy water and pretend to cross myself, then take a seat in the back. I'm engulfed with loneliness, but at the same time I feel surrounded and supported by so many people in the church. I feel like I've found refuge and there is no reason to return to Esmor. I pray that my incarceration will be over soon. An elderly woman attached to an oxygen tank is sitting a few rows in front of me. This makes me feel fortunate. But praying at St. Patrick's doesn't make the sentence go any quicker. Soon I realize that the Tivoli Diner on Third Avenue is closer to Esmor and I can pray there just as easily and have a toasted corn muffin and read the Sunday *Times* all in the same two hours.

September 30, 1994.
I scrub the shower so that we'll pass inspection today. Yesterday Rodriguez, one of the resident supervisors, wrote us up for "too many hairs." I figure I'll scrub the toilet and sink again. It's almost impossible to make this bathroom look decent—it's such a vile pit. I'm a pro when it comes to disinfecting. Tony is still asleep, and I don't want to disturb him. He'll be relieved not to have to do any of the cleaning when he wakes up. I think he expects me to do it. He's served four years already, so I think he has seniority.

The room is like an oven—well, at least a toaster oven. It's dark and dingy and it smells like the Chinese restaurant behind the building. I go into my dresser to pull out some clothes. I'm shocked. Everything is missing. Jeans, khakis, polo shirts, button-downs—gone. I look all over the room, which takes all of five seconds. I start looking in Tony's dresser, and he sits up quickly. Like he has some type of automatic alarm system connected to his property. I tell him all my clothes are missing. He laughs and tells me we're living among criminals. What do you expect? At dinner I see Alvarez, a big guy with a Latin Kings tattoo on his knuckles, dressed in my Ralph Lauren striped button-down shirt. Tony tells me to keep my mouth shut.

October 21, 1994.
We got an incident report for "too many hairs" again this morning. Getting an incident report here feels like being convicted of another felony because you're the defendant again. It's like going to court. I'm fighting this one with Ms. Black. I tell her that this is a ridiculous charge and that Rodriguez is obviously doing this to fill his quota and that I'm not going to accept the punishment for it this time—scraping the wax off the cafeteria floors. She tells me that she'll look into it. I come face-to-face with Rodriguez, who tells me in front of Black about the big clump of hair he found in the drain. She sends me and Tony to the cafeteria for the punishment, where we get down on our hands and knees in front of a crowd of residents and start scraping off the wax.

November 7, 1994.
In my journal I keep track of the days as they pass. I break my sentence down into all different types of units—weeks, months, percent of sentence served, blocks of ten-day units, anything to make things seem to move faster. I track the change in seasons by the holiday displays at the Duane Reade drugstore on the corner. These are motivational because they run so far in advance of the actual celebration: pumpkins, witches, and goblins start appear-

ing the first week in September; snowmen, reindeer, and Santa Claus the first week in November. The street vendors are hawking their wares on the street—"Nintendo games for Christmas" in November. I'm thrilled that December is right around the corner. I'll be out of here in January!

November 10, 1994.
I am approaching the halfway mark of my time at Esmor—two and a half months—and I write to Judge Nickerson asking him to consider releasing me early so that I can begin my community service and put the remaining two and a half months on the house-arrest side of my sentence. In my letter I tell him that "I feel as though I have been adequately punished." I mail it off and patiently wait for a response.

November 15, 1994.
The crazies are coming back. I tell Dr. Fried during our weekly appointment today about my fantasies of committing a mass murder or shooting at Esmor. The target of the murders is usually the staff, but most of the time it doesn't matter and I think of killing anyone in the building. These feel a lot more like well-thought-out plans than fantasies. Dr. Fried increases my Risperdal, which seems to alleviate some of the problem. I've also been walking on the curb to avoid the sidewalk as much as possible because I'm scared of wearing out my heels on the sidewalk and I'm frightened of looking into the eyes of strangers.

November 18, 1994.
Judge Nickerson rejects my request for a reduction of my sentence. It was a long shot.

November 22, 1994.
Several months before I am to leave, I start looking for a full-time job that pays a real salary that I can begin immediately and continue post release. I interview for a job with a nonprofit organization called the Center for Alternatives to Sentencing and

Employment Services (CASES), in a public relations and fund-raising capacity. The organization provides educational and employment opportunities to young people in lieu of serving time. I get the job and work with a dynamic group of dedicated people, including many young lawyers, who feel strongly about the mission. I am forced to leave my waitering position at the Cake Bar.

November 24, 1994.
It's Thanksgiving Day, and I travel with my family to my aunt and uncle's in Connecticut. The day confuses me, as I'm not confined to either Esmor or the café. It's entirely strange to be eating a civilized Thanksgiving dinner with linen, silverware, china, and crystal with my family after three months of Salisbury steak and peas on Styrofoam plates. Of course, everybody is curious about this "prison" to which I am confined, and I choose to tell them lighter and funnier anecdotes about residents like Hank, who braids his long silver hair like an Indian chief and walks around with a sullen face, or Georgie, the black transvestite who is obsessed with Diana Ross and has posters of her plastered all over his room and a library of books about her on his dresser.

November 28, 1994.
I'm watching CNN and see that Jeffrey Dahmer has been killed in jail today. For some reason I start fantasizing that I'm going to be killed, too.

December 8, 1994.
I wait in line for an hour to call home to tell my parents that my sentence is officially two-thirds complete. They're thrilled.

December 15, 1994.
I've become popular as the community advocate and letter writer. I help other residents write to their attorneys and judges and do my best to help explain the system. Residents line up outside my room after dinner. I'm paid with cigarettes and Diet Pepsis.

December 20, 1994.
I walk up Fifth Avenue to see the big Christmas tree at Rockefeller Center. I only have about an hour to get back, but I stand there and watch all of the tourists and the skaters circling the rink, listen to the music, and realize how pathetic my situation is. In the cab ride back, I pass store windows magnificently decorated with gold and silver trimmings, toy soldiers, and Disney characters. I know that I'm not going to be buying any gifts this year or going to any parties this season. When I turn onto Esmor's block, I think about telling the driver to keep going downtown, but I know that I have to sign in by 7:00 P.M. I walk through the dimly lit lobby with the shabby, musty carpeting and into the smoking lounge. It's loud and smoky and smells like sweat. They've Scotch-taped a torn reindeer to the vending machine.

The Taste of Freedom

January 27, 1995.
I hear on television that it's the fiftieth anniversary of the liberation of Auschwitz. It's also my release date from Esmor and my thirty-third birthday—such a special one for me. I have packed up my suitcases the night before and stay up all night waiting to go through the release procedures at 6:00 A.M.—signing my name in a hundred different places. When I'm finished, I thank the administrator and walk out the door and down the stairs, feeling perplexed about being officially released. I'm relieved to see my father waiting in his car. That night there's a very small celebration with just my parents and Lucy, who has been a constant voice of reassurance and support during my confinement at Esmor. I didn't want a welcome-home party the way I wanted a going-away party. The dinner is at Patria on Park Avenue South, and it's a peculiar feeling knowing that I'm celebrating blocks away from Esmor. Part of me feels that I need to make some sort of transition—first be fumigated and detoxified and then given two weeks' rest. Knowing that I'll be spending the night at the apartment I've recently found for myself on the Upper West Side and

never having to sleep on that awful mattress again is strange. I haven't been out to a real restaurant in five months, and it feels odd to be having choices and ordering dinner that doesn't come with a gift or prize. I'm a bit paranoid, wondering if anyone can tell where I've just come from, and the conversation is a little difficult at first for me because I really just want to cry. The theme for the night seems to be liberation. My father makes a toast: "To health, happiness, and the future." I can't believe it's over. I'm looking around the restaurant at all of the smiling patrons eating and drinking, contrasting this scene with what's going on blocks away. That night, when I return to my new home, I double-lock the door. I'm immediately struck by the quiet. I can only hear the humming of the refrigerator, which I have filled with Diet Coke, orange juice, cream cheese, milk, butter, and eggs, and the freezer with two pints of Häagen-Dazs ice cream. It's a start. I line up my pills and take them one by one. I wait for someone to shout out my name. I get into the shower and stand under the hot water for a half hour. My phone starts ringing, and I am talking to Lauren in Denver. I'm thrilled that people can reach me at home now. It seems miraculous. I'm naked on my bed, eating Häagen-Dazs rum raisin ice cream from a pint container and watching television. I am a free man with HBO and Showtime.

Chapter 9

My Adult Spaceship

February 1995. Upper West Side.

Worn out and tired from my experience at Esmor, I'm pained to think that my sentence is not yet over. I still have to serve a five-month term of house arrest. The feds call it home detention, a name that seems much too kind and gentle. It isn't quite incarceration, but it isn't freedom either.

I'm restricted to my one-bedroom apartment on the Upper West Side for twenty hours each day, with a beeper-sized electronic monitor continuously strapped to my left ankle, for 152 days. On the first day of my house arrest, Mr. Henry, my probation officer (P.O. in prisoner jargon), arrives exactly at 9:00 A.M. He's a strong black man in his midthirties, perfectly dressed in a jacket and tie. He shakes my hand with a powerful grip. He's carrying a canvas bag with the equipment—the ankle bracelet and a stationary monitor called a Home Escort, which looks like a simple cable television box. In fact, Mr. Henry's not too much different from the average cable guy. In a matter of minutes he installs the Home Escort near my front door. It's connected to a central station in Boulder, Colorado, operated, I like to imagine, by a bunch of middle-aged, female crossing-guard types. The Home Escort tracks my movement and lets "Boulder" know when I've gone out of my apartment. I'm asked if I want the bracelet on the right or left ankle. It's an easy decision. I choose the left, because I want it on the same side as my heart—I think they will work well in unison. Mr. Henry adjusts the bracelet on my left ankle so that it's comfortable but secure. I feel like he's a tailor hemming my pants as I stand looking down at him fidgeting with my ankle. It's a simple procedure, and when he's finished he takes out a booklet and reads to me. The rules are straightforward and few. I am allowed outside to see my doctors, and, in addition, for four consecutive preestablished hours each day. I can have visitors, as long as they are law-abiding citizens, and I will be allowed time during the day to complete my court-ordered community service. I have chosen to work with dying AIDS patients at St. Clare's Hospital because it has a well-structured volunteer program, and it turns out to be a welcome relief from being trapped inside, as well as providing me with some real perspective on suffering. Mr. Henry smiles, wishes me good luck, and squeezes my hand again. I'm all wired up and ready to go. I feel like a contestant on some silly British game show that I think I've seen before on cable.

At first the ankle bracelet is a novelty with which I entertain my friends. Soon, though, it makes me feel kind of strange, like a life-sized action figure with a battery pack. Then it feels like a growth. I am forever fiddling with it. Wanting it off. When I'm inside, it reminds me of my confinement and I just want to take it off for a few seconds to hold my naked ankle, and when I'm outside, it reminds me of my curfew.

The device goes everywhere I do, like a sinus condition. I sleep in it, eat with it, have sex in it. But it is showering that underscores the humiliation of house arrest: even after the last article of clothing is off and I am standing under hot water, there is still a black metal contraption soldered to my body. Even naked I can't feel completely undressed. My clothes don't hide the thing. When I go out, people stare, point, and whisper. Some approach me and ask point-blank if I am under house arrest; others ask me if it's an odometer. It becomes a great conversation piece for my strolls down Broadway and Riverside Drive, almost like a rare breed of dog or a baby carriage with triplets. Strangers ask me out for drinks, coffee, and even dinner. I never thought the ankle bracelet would become a topic of conversation, much less a dating service. A pretty young lawyer from Miami drinking a cup of coffee next to me at Zabar's is fascinated by it. "Do you mind if I ask you how you earned that piece of equipment?" she says. "Conspiracy to defraud—counterfeiting art," I say. "Do you want me to get you another cup of coffee?" she asks. "Sure," I tell her, and we chat for forty minutes.

Because I am confined to my apartment, my manic world comes inside. I am like a butterfly trapped beneath a glass dome. I devour information, reading newspapers and magazines and watching the news on television for most of the day, keeping myself current in my isolated world, the grown-up version of my childhood spaceship.

I'm obsessed with masturbating; I spend hours watching videos, looking at pornographic magazines, and talking on phone-sex lines. Sometimes I can actually miss a whole night's sleep—inducing a tremendous high from the adrenaline rush—only to experience sleeplessness and tremendous depression the following day. The mania is fueling this intense sex drive that I cannot control. Dr. Fried increases my dosage of Risperdal, which seems to help, but, as before, the side effects are unbearable. I start getting day and night confused; they seem to run into each other. I'm a prisoner trapped and paralyzed with a supply of porn and fantasies big enough for an entire fraternity house. Masturbating with the ankle bracelet feels like an invasion of my privacy, as if the ladies in Boulder are watching on a remote camera.

I compulsively vacuum every square inch of my apartment to see what collects in the vacuum bag. I fantasize about big globs of hair, paper, pins, pills, rubber bands, toenails, paper clips, eyelashes, and dead skin. I start my mission in the bedroom and use the hose to suck up the dust in the corners and edges of the room first, then under the bed, where I find the largest dustballs. I move on to the kitchen where I come across onion skins, crumbs, rice, and wilted lettuce. When I get to the living room, I sweep the floors with a broom first, suck up the neat pile of dirt in the center of the room, and then work the corners and edges. The entire process feels sexually gratifying; it's an act with a purpose and an end result. Once my apartment is officially dust-free, I'm ready to take on the apartment next door. Would it be inappropriate to ask neighbors or friends if I could do some vacuuming for them? I have to think about the ethical issues here. It wouldn't be a sexual thing or anything. Purely a friendly gesture, of course. I open the vacuum bag over the garbage. Out comes a big wad of junk, mostly gray matter, with some colorful speckles, and my pulse races with glee. I can't wait to do it again tomorrow.

I'm having difficulty even going to my job at CASES because I don't seem to understand my job responsibilities and can't focus on what it is they want me to do there. So, I pass as much time as possible pretending that I am working, reading lists of potential contributors, and the rest of the time talking on the phone to friends, reading the newspaper, and going out with my office mates for lunch.

February 6, 1995.
I visit Dr. Fried because of my depression and suicidal thinking. She starts treating me with Effexor. I'll give it a chance.

March 6, 1995.
Effexor is helpful in terms of my suicidal thinking but destructive in terms of the total loss of my libido, so I drop the Effexor and the lithium after a month. I start taking Luvox for depression and obsessional thinking.

March 13, 1995.
Luvox causes me to have retrograde orgasms (an orgasm in which the semen moves backward and is not released), which scare me to death, and I stop taking it.

March 20, 1995.
I mix alcohol and about ten Ambien and Klonopin to relax, not the safest combination, fill the bathtub with hot water, and fantasize about killing myself by floating beneath the surface—hoping that I'll be too drowsy to resist drowning. I spend hours in the tub. I can't give up this pleasure because it relieves so much of my pain.

I tell Dr. Fried about these fantasies, and she prescribes Paxil for depression, but I become anorgasmic and refuse to continue taking it.

April 3, 1995.
I start getting confused, and my thinking becomes psychotic. When I speak to Dr. Fried, I use numbers for words—*five* translates to "happy"; *seven* translates to "tired." I start threatening both of my doctors that I'm going to commit suicide and begin to curse uncontrollably to myself—*shit, fuck, cock, pussy.* I urinate on the kitchen floor because "it's the thing to do," I tell Dr. Fried. I ask her about trying some more medications. "We've been through all of it," she says. She is clearly becoming frustrated about not being able to find the right combination of medications for me. The last few weeks have been particularly difficult, because I'm experiencing mixed moods, extreme highs and lows that literally change from hour to hour. She has experimented with more than twenty-five medications—mood stabilizers, antidepressants, antipsychotics, sedatives, and sleeping pills—but no combinations seem to work. Because she is growing more and more concerned about my condition, she sees me twice a week and speaks with me sometimes two or three times a day by telephone. At this point I'm embarrassed that nothing is working, feeling like the bad patient, paranoid that I am somehow sabotaging my recovery. During one office visit I discuss suicide as a serious option with her. I talk to her about my feelings of despair. I believe that I will never improve and that I will live like this forever. I leave feeling dejected. She tells me to call her that night. I walk through the park toward the Dublin House on 79th Street and Broadway. I get an Amstel Light from the bartender and some quarters for the jukebox and play some Billy Joel songs that put me in the suicide frame of mind. The bar is empty. It's about 4:30 P.M., and the more I drink the easier I feel like it's going to be to die. I just don't have any hope that anyone can help me straighten out my brain. I thought it would be Dr. Fried. And how many more doctors can I see? I can't keep going like this. It hurts too bad. I'm not going to

slit my wrists. I think I'm just going to swallow an entire bottle of Ambien and Klonopin and mix them with alcohol. I'm thinking about my parents and Nancy and her family and my friends, but in the end I'm the one suffering, and I can't go on. I walk out of the bar with a beer in my hand and stumble home two blocks. The police are at my apartment looking for me. They've gotten in through the fire escape via my neighbor's apartment. Of course, I'm frightened to find them there. Dr. Fried tried to call me at home but became worried when she couldn't reach me, so she sent the police to look for me. She is relieved that I'm alive, and I feel very special that she cared so much. I talk to her at home after the police leave, and later we spend a lot of time during my sessions talking about my suicidal thinking.

Madison Avenue Meltdown

April 9, 1995.

It's the middle of the day. Perfect weather. I'm taking a walk up Madison Avenue. I'm in front of Barneys. My skin starts tingling, and I feel as if my insides are spilling onto the sidewalk. Everything moves in slow motion. I can't hear. The taxis driving by are a blur of yellow. I rush home and curl up in my empty bathtub in my jeans and black turtleneck. I lie still for hours. I'm cold. Barefoot. Nothing seems to be working for me. Not the lithium, not the Depakote, not the Wellbutrin. I'm ashamed and frightened that the manic depression is growing wildly out of control. It feels like someone is pouring cement into my skull. Nobody can help me. The next episode is going to kill me. I can't make it go away. I'm trying to ease the pain from the most recent plunge. The bathtub is too small and hard for me, but I feel safe here. I call Dr. Fried and explain that I'm in serious trouble and need help. I need relief from the pain. She tells me to be at her office at 5:00 P.M. and to ask my parents to come with me. I call my parents and wait for them to pick me up.

We arrive at Dr. Fried's office early and sit in the waiting room until she finishes with her last patient. We're all scared to death. Dr. Fried brings us into her office and begins by telling us that we have tried every possible combination of medication available and my condition has still not been stabilized; I have reached a critical stage. So I ask the question about the last resort—electroconvulsive therapy, or electroshock therapy, as it is more commonly called. Dr. Fried has mentioned ECT before, but she has always been very much against treating me with it because of the side effects, particularly memory loss. There is an odd silence, and Dr. Fried looks at my parents. It's as if I've asked the wrong thing. But we've all known all along that it could come to this, and we all know that that's why we're here. Dr. Fried explains that ECT is used to treat depression, manic depression, mania, and schizophrenia and that it causes a seizure in the brain by passing a mild electric current through the head. She tells us one of the main criticisms is that there is no convincing scientific explanation of how it works, only a number of unsubstantiated theories. I'm not too worried about the memory loss, I tell her, and I'm not that interested in hearing these theories, but she explains them to us anyway. According to the *neurotransmitter theory*, ECT has effects similar to those of antidepressant medications, altering levels of important mood-related chemicals in the brain, such as serotonin, dopamine, and norepinephrine. Proponents of the *anticonvulsant theory* contend that the seizures induced by ECT actually condition the brain to become seizure-resistant. The *neuroendocrine theory* holds that ECT-induced seizures affect the hypothalamus, the part of the brain that regulates important functions such as sleep and body temperature, prompting it to release a chemical that stabilizes mood. Finally, there's the controversial *brain-damage theory*, which postulates that the shock from ECT literally causes brain damage, creating for the patient the illusion of mental stability. Brain damage scares the shit out of me. Am I going to become a permanent zombie, forced to return to the suburbs to live with my parents? After listening to Dr. Fried talk, I wonder if I shouldn't just try to administer the shock myself at home, possibly using my hair dryer in the bathtub. I don't like the sound of the brain-damage theory, but what other choice do I have? My situation has become so critical that I have nothing left to consider. ECT is really my only possibility. I say I'm so desperate that I'll do it because I have nothing to lose at this point.

Dr. Fried refers us to a well-respected specialist, Dr. Charles Wallenstein. I feel if I make the decision to go ahead and have the ECT, I will no longer be responsible for having the manic depression—that I will have chosen the most barbaric treatment and in return will be relieved of the burden of responsibility for having this illness. Hopefully, all of the guilt and shame I have about bringing this illness on myself from all my neuroses, compulsions, and obsessions will fade away.

The next afternoon we meet Dr. Wallenstein in his Park Avenue office. He's a tall, lanky man in his sixties with a soothing voice. He reminds me of my childhood pediatrician, and I feel at ease with him right away. He tells us he has reviewed my case with Dr. Fried and he feels strongly that I am a good candidate for electroshock therapy and that it will improve my condition. He tells me that my manic depression would be difficult to control with medication alone. These strike me as being stock lines, but I'll try anything. There's almost no discussion about the actual process, but Dr. Fried has filled us in enough. He just tells us where to show up and that I'll be in the hospital for seven to ten days (I'll have to have this approved by probation). There is something about ECT that sounds adventurous, like a scary ride at an amusement park, and even glamorous—I am reminded of celebrities like Vivien Leigh, Gene Tierney, Frances Farmer, and Ernest Hemingway, who were locked up in insane asylums and jolted. My parents seem calm and allow me to do the talking, but I can see that they realize the severity of the situation. We're about to make a decision together about my having electroshock therapy the next day at Gracie Square Hospital, and we know very little about it. It's as if I'm being asked something as simple as how much milk I want in my coffee. Just a drop, please. I'm so dulled that I can't even feel how frightened I really am.

Electroboy

April 11, 1995. 8:00 A.M.

The light is streaming in through the dirty windows on the terrace floor of Gracie Square Hospital on the Upper East Side. I'm waiting in a hallway outside of the operating room wearing just a light blue hospital gown with a group of about ten or so other depressed souls, schizophrenic crackups, manic-depressive freaks, and confused Alzheimer's patients who come in an assortment of colors, shapes, and sizes. Some of them are talking to themselves, some are talking to each other, some are busy reading old magazines without covers, and some are just sitting nervously staring. The hallway is shabby—the paint is peeling, the early-sixties furniture is dingy, and there are long black scuff marks on the floor. I'm trying to assign a person and date to each scuff mark. A woman in her late sixties sitting next to me tells me that this is her fifteenth electroshock treatment in four months. It's an impressive number. For some reason I'm staring at the two gold chains around her neck while I'm talking to her. One has a tiny heart hanging from it; the other has a cross. Her name is Lena, and she tells me that she was diagnosed with depression more than ten years ago. She has dark circles under her eyes. She claims that ECT has saved her life. This is one of her worst bouts in the last few years, but I don't really care too much about her psychiatric history; I only want to know if I'm going to feel any pain. "You have no reason to worry," she assures me. "You won't feel a thing." "Easier than root canal?" I ask. "No comparison." She smiles. I look down at the palms of my hands. My skin looks gray and pale, and I can only focus on the blue and green veins crisscrossing the inside of my forearms and wrists. My mouth is dry and I ask one of the nurses for something to drink, but she tells me that I can't drink until after the treatment. The doctors and nurses keep using the term "treatment" as if we're at Georgette Klinger. It sounds so pleasant—could it be? That would be nice. Could it be as relaxing as a massage? As refreshing as a facial? What am I getting so

worked-up about? I'm not usually this scared going to the dentist.
But I'm not getting my teeth cleaned. I'm in a hospital about to
get electroshock. I never imagined this illness would land me in a
mental hospital. I hope they call me toward the end of this morning's group. This way I'll be able to see if the first few survive the
treatment. It looks like they've already processed another group
before us because I see a man in his forties stumbling out of the recovery room, clinging to two nurses for support. He doesn't seem
like he's in such good shape—he looks like a lifeless rag doll, utterly confused and lost. Oh, my God. Am I going to be permanently damaged by ECT? Am I sure this was a wise choice?
Dr. Wallenstein told me there was really no other alternative. ECT
is a last resort in my case. There is no more medication to try—
we have been through the endless combinations—Depakote,
Neurontin, Wellbutrin, Risperdal, Zyprexa, Trazodone, Effexor,
Klonopin, Zoloft, Paxil, Serzone, Tegretol, Artane, Ativan. The
heaviest of the many Jamaican nurses comes around and takes my
blood pressure and then puts a sticky round "tag" on my chest to
monitor my heartbeat. It gets connected to some wires in the
operating room later. Amanda, who is no older than twenty-two
and is bandaged from wrist to elbow because she has sliced up
her arms with a knife, is the first one called. She whistles "Heigh-
Ho, Heigh-Ho" as she lies down on the gurney closest to the
operating room and is wheeled away by two male attendants,
through the swinging doors and into the operating room. She
waves good-bye to the group. As the doors open, I can see down
the hall into the O.R. and recognize Dr. Wallenstein, and feel reassured that he showed up for work today. Everything is okay for a
moment. Dr. Wallenstein is here. He must be treating all of us. I
ask Lena. She tells me Dr. Wallenstein is her doctor, too. He is
wonderful and I should calm down. I am in good hands. He has
been doing this for twenty-five years. Pressing a button for twenty-
five years. Michael, a guy roughly my age, leans toward us and
tells me that this is his fifth treatment and that "Dr. Wallenstein is
a pro. Trust me, you won't feel a thing. It's actually kind of cool,"
he says. I thank him and try to imagine how fucking cool it's going

to be. He looks down at my leg. "What's that thing around your ankle?" he asks me. I tell him that it's a monitoring device and that I'm under house arrest. "Cool," he responds. "Mr. Behrman," calls one of the nurses. I'm saved from telling the saga of the art fraud. I stand up and hop onto the next gurney in line, lying down on my back and resting on my elbows. I ask the nurse how long I'll be in the operating room. About ten minutes. In recovery? About an hour. She asks me if this is my first time. Yes. You'll be just fine. Now I realize I can't stop talking. I have a million questions about what's going to happen. She holds my hand with her chubby hand. I signal back to Lena, giving her the okay sign, and she whispers something to me that I can't quite make out. I shrug. She crosses herself. Exactly what I need to see before I'm wheeled into an operating room. I wait to be rolled past the swinging doors. I feel as if I'm waiting for either the scariest roller-coaster ride of my life or my own execution. I'm convinced that if I live, my brain will be reduced to a blank Rolodex. I look down at my bare feet. A flawless loafer tan line.

Inside the O.R. I notice Dr. Wallenstein standing to my left. He's wearing a jacket and tie and those black sneaker-like shoes, and he's next to what looks like an old stereo component system. He shakes my hand and introduces me to the anesthesiologist, the nurse, an assistant, and a group of residents. He seems too slick and charming to be doing what he does. He should be working at Goldman Sachs. He's humming, like he's out for a walk on the beach or working in his garden. I guess he feels at home here. It's making me feel very uncomfortable, but I put my head back anyway. Everyone is hovering over me. Standing room only. I'm making small talk to keep my mind off the fact that I'm about to have my brains jolted with 200 volts of electricity while ten note-taking residents gawk. I'm thinking about the electric chair and being struck by lightning, and joking incessantly to fight off the terror. Is it too late for the call from the governor? No call. The show must go on. "Got an Amstel Light?" I ask. No response. I give the thumbs-up. An I.V. of Brevital, an anesthetic, is stuck into my arm, silencing me. The room has a peculiarly sterile smell. I feel like I've just smoked cocaine and drifted high into the clouds and am struggling to stay awake. It's a losing battle; I eventually lose consciousness. But I've been told what will happen: an I.V. of succinylcholine chloride goes in next, relaxing my muscles to prevent broken bones and cracked vertebrae from the seizure that will occur. The nurse sticks a rubber block in my mouth so I don't bite off my tongue, a mask over my nose and mouth so my brain is not deprived of oxygen, and electrodes on my temples. All clear. Dr. Wallenstein presses the button. Electric current shoots through my brain for an instant, causing a grand-mal seizure for twenty seconds. My toes curl. It's over. My brain has been reset like a windup toy.

I wake up thirty minutes later and think I'm in a hotel room in Acapulco. My head feels as if I've just downed a frozen margarita too quickly. My jaw and limbs ache. But I am elated. "Come, Electroboy," says the nurse with a thick Jamaican accent. I take a sip of juice as she grabs my arm and escorts me downstairs in the elevator to my room, where my parents and sister are waiting for me. They stare at me like I've just returned from Jupiter. I start doing jumping jacks. They look surprised. "I feel great," I announce with delight. My mother's eyes well up with tears. I take a break from my jumping jacks and give her a hug. It's one of those moments when I realize that I'm oddly larger than my mother. I put my head on her shoulder. She smells like Fendi. My father gives me a gentle kiss on the forehead and holds back his tears. Nancy kisses me and starts to cry. Expected. All I can do is smile and laugh. I feel so fucking good. It's over. Someone finally repaired my brain this morning.

I'm glad that my whole family is here with me in my hospital room. I feel like a hostage who's just been released after six months of captivity. But it doesn't seem right for me to cry at this moment because I've never felt like this. I've never felt this happy—or is it this *healthy*? I feel incredibly different than I did pre-ECT, which was just an hour ago. Like the hard concrete that filled my brain has been liquefied and drained from my skull. I'm curious as to whether I look as good as I feel. You look fine, my parents and sister assure me. But the looks in their eyes betray them. I go into the bathroom to check things out in the mirror. I look awful. More specifically, crazy. Absolutely nuts. Like a lunatic. My eyes are glassy, and my pupils are all dilated. I hope that goes away. I go back to the room and start asking lots of questions. Do I have a job? Yes. An apartment? Yes. A dog? No. The questions sound insane to me, but I really don't know the answers. I feel like my memory's been erased. I'm a little unsteady on my feet, so I grab onto the bed and I climb in and prop my head up on the pillows. The sheets are unusually stiff—they remind me of the sheets at Esmor. My sister looks more frightened than my parents, like her little brother has become Randle P. McMurphy from *One Flew Over the Cuckoo's Nest*. She looks beautiful but very pale. She pulls her hair back behind her ears nervously and hands me a box from an oversized glossy navy blue Ralph Lauren shopping bag. I feel like it's my birthday and the family has come to visit their crazed son in the mental hospital, and now I'm a little embarrassed. I open it up—it's a pair of navy blue Polo sweatpants. I am now officially designated the most fashionable mental patient at Gracie Square Hospital. I wonder if the nurses will let me wear these during my next ECT treatment. I'm not sure that these are intended to be worn by a patient undergoing a course of electroshock treatment in a mental hospital; sweats are more of an outdoor thing. They seem too athletic—too healthy—too sane—too American for the mental ward. They've got a neat little American flag on them. You can't shock someone with a neat little American flag on his sweatpants. It would be like burning the flag. Entirely un-American. I thank my sister for them and go into the bathroom to try them on. They will serve as a symbol of sanity to guard me in the hospital through this nightmare. Or I'll just pretend this hospital stay is a Ralph Lauren commercial for the insane.

Later I'm stretched out in bed and my parents and sister pull their chairs up alongside me. For a brief moment I'm confused as to where I am. I think I'm in Connecticut, and I forget what I'm doing in the hospital. My father reminds me that I've had ECT and that I'm "at Gracie Square Hospital on East 76th Street in New York City." I laugh. My brains have really been scrambled. I'm very confused. I feel like these well-dressed people have walked into the middle of my dream. I hold my mother's hand. If I could just snap out of this fog I'm in, I'll be okay. I'm happy to be with my family. It's nice that they're all here. But most important, I'm glad that the pressure in my head has been relieved. It feels like one big pipe in my head has been cleaned out with a plunger and everything is finally circulating. I hope that I can hold on to this sensation for a little while longer. I wonder how long this ECT treatment will last. I tell my parents and sister as much as I remember about the operating room, about seeing Dr. Wallenstein beforehand, and about waking up in the recovery room. But I can't tell them anything about the actual ECT—it's almost as if I missed the second act. But watching them shift in the fiberglass hospital chairs, I can tell how frightened they are. My sister walks out of the room for a soda, and I'm alone with my parents. My mother is drinking a Diet Coke and holding my father's hand. I'm focusing on her wedding band and her engagement ring. I feel like I've done something horribly wrong to my parents. I've dragged them across the George Washington Bridge into this mental hospital. I feel tremendously guilty about having this invisible illness. I should just be able to shake it. Sweat it out. Make it go away. I wish I were here for something concrete, like an inoperable tumor in my brain that the doctor could show my parents on a CAT scan. Do they even buy this whole manic depression story? I'm not even so sure I believe it yet. I just don't want them to be angry with me. I must be putting them through hell. I think back to them watching my trial and visiting me at Esmor. Technically, being hospitalized is the third strike. They should just give up on me now and walk right out of this hospital. But they're hanging in there again. How much more shit can they take? I'll do whatever I can to get better and get out of this place quickly and get home and get back to normal for them. I'll try to fix whatever I've done wrong that's landed me here and make this whole situa-

tion better. I feel like I'm ten years old again and I've done something terrible like taken their car for a drive around the block and
smashed it up. But for now all I can really focus on is the pain in
my aching arms and legs, and I ask my father to rub them. He
kneads my calves, and the pain from the voltage that I've been
zapped with slowly dissipates. When I was thirteen and going
through a painful growth spurt, he sat with me every night until I
fell asleep. This is the same ache. And he's relieving my pain.
We're talking to each other, and I realize that I'm not hearing anything except their telling me "we really think you have a chance to
get better here." Well, of course, isn't that why I'm here? My sister
comes back into the room with a Diet Coke. Now we're all drinking Diet Cokes except for my father. The three of them get up and
huddle outside my room in the hallway and leave me alone to rest.

After my parents leave the room, I notice that the manic depression that was cycloning in my head hours before is now sleeping like a baby. I'm frightened of waking it, so I lie totally still,
flipping the TV channels with the remote.

That evening Dr. Gelman, the ward psychiatrist, knocks on
the door. He's a soft-spoken man in his early forties. My stories of
my ankle bracelet and house arrest make him laugh. But he's
more curious about the success of my first treatment. I tell him
that I think it went extremely well and that I feel great, with the
exception of the aches and pains and the memory loss. The pressure in my head is gone and I'm relaxed. I admit that I enjoyed the
premedication quite a bit—the Brevital's real good stuff. Can I get
a private session with the anesthesiologist? He chuckles. He tells
me he'll speak with Dr. Wallenstein but that we'll probably wait
another day until I have a second treatment. How many treatments will I need? He tells me he's not sure yet and that it'll de-
pend on how I respond to each subsequent treatment. Like Dr.
Wallenstein, he's a believer in voodoo ECT. So am I.

The next day my parents escort me into the dining room,
where they watch as I inhale some turkey and mashed potatoes
for dinner—I haven't eaten since last night, and I'm starving. They
pass on regards from family and friends. It feels like another visit-

ing day at Esmor and I'm locked up again, just counting the days this time instead of the months. I always seem to be eating or drinking something in these visiting situations, and we always end up talking about such normal things—movies, restaurants, trips, and the grandchildren. And they are always so well dressed in these institutional settings. Visiting hours are about to end, and my parents tell me that they're going to meet friends for dinner. Their imminent departure throws my situation into stark relief, and I feel cheated that I'm eating dry turkey and gluey mashed potatoes while I know they'll be eating at a restaurant that's just been written up in *The New York Times* this week. I'm the one doing the time again. I'm just not the lucky one in the family. (I'm also the one in the family who had the allergies, too.) I wish I could get a pass to go out to dinner with my parents. I slowly start convincing myself that I'm really okay and that further treatments are no more necessary than a salt rub.

Once my parents are gone, I walk the long hallway back to the patients' lounge. The television is blaring, and all the nuts are sitting around it in a semicircle. I focus on their faces instead of the television. Lena is staring out the window watching the traffic go by. Michael is peeking through his hands at the television. Amanda is fidgeting with her bandages. Bob, my roommate, a schizophrenic in his fifties, is sitting off to the side mumbling something about the CIA. By degrees I realize the extent of my illness. I'm not sure what I was thinking before, but this place isn't Canyon Ranch. I'm not here for herbal wraps, mud baths, facials, or five-mile hikes. After thirty-three years it hits me that there's something really wrong with me. I have a mental illness.

When we get back to the room, Bob starts speaking rapidly and incessantly. I try to avoid contact with him as much as possible, mainly because I'm so tired but also because he frightens me. He talks nonstop about the government plotting his death, and I don't even have the energy to respond, so I just ignore him. "Do me a favor, go downtown and check and see if the Statue of Liberty is still there," he barks at me. "If it's not there, we'll overthrow the damn government," he screams. "Bill and Hillary

Clinton are trying to kill me—slowly," he says. *Quickly,* I hope. If I were manic, I might play along with this game. For the first time I'm comforted by my condition. He's in much worse shape than me.

10:00 P.M.
Bedtime at Gracie Square. Lights out. Doors shut and locked. I have trouble falling asleep because I've slept all day, so I ring for the nurse and ask for a sleeping pill. She brings me an Ambien. I go over to the window and watch the cars driving by and the rhythm of the traffic lights changing. I'm controlling it with the blink of my eyes. I try to time it perfectly and keep my eyes shut in time with the red. Green means "go downtown." I dream that I put on my jeans and a T-shirt and jump into a cab and go downtown and meet some friends for a drink even though it's 2:30 A.M. Shit, I'm wide awake. Does this mean I'm still manic? Maybe this ECT isn't working. Bob is talking in his sleep. I can barely understand what he's saying, but he sounds more relaxed. Nobody's chasing him. There's no CIA, FBI, IRS, NRA, or KGB. Maybe ECT is working for him.

It takes about twenty minutes before I fall asleep. I dream I'm lying naked on a stainless steel gurney. Two guards wheel me into a room where a team of doctors start working on me while I'm conscious. I'm in a car wash. I'm hosed down first, shampooed, soaped up, hosed down again, dried off. My hands and feet are manicured, my teeth scrubbed. When I'm done, I'm wheeled into recovery. I come out wearing a tuxedo.

The next day I'm even more scared waiting in the hallway before my treatment. Although I'm looking forward to the anesthesia, I still fear what they're going to do to me while I'm unconscious, although most of the thoughts are ridiculously crazy. Maybe they'll electrocute me by accident. Maybe they'll cut into me and remove a kidney or liver. Maybe I'll never wake up. But what frightens me most is the control the doctor and his team have in the operating room—they rule the anesthesia, the oxygen, and the electricity. They can kill me.

I've become addicted to the premedication—the high is as good as freebasing. It brings you up to a certain height and suspends you there for a few brief seconds. It re-creates the euphoria of mania. It's a substitute for everything I ever liked to abuse—alcohol, cocaine, marijuana, sex. When I'm wheeled into the operating room, the first person I greet is the anesthesiologist. He's my favorite guy in there. We're in this together. He's the only one on my side. He's not only keeping me from feeling any pain, he's making me feel real good.

When I wake up after my next round of ECT, there are about ten people lying on gurneys in the recovery room, all in different states of alertness, all fighting for the attention of the nurses. I just want to know where I am. It sounds like an army hospital—patients are moaning, whining, and babbling. We're all lost and confused. It feels like a battlefield. I should have bullet holes in my stomach and shoulders. I should be bleeding through my gown.

My brains feel scrambled. I can't imagine what a straight line looks like or the shape of a circle. I don't think I can write without trembling or walk without shuffling. I'm out of order. My memory is totally fucked, too—I have difficulty making any connections and associations to stored information. The wires aren't hooking up with one another. I struggle to remember even the most simple details like my middle name and address. But oddly, I feel fine-tuned and tremendously relieved. The tension and clogged feeling in my brain has now completely disappeared. I imagine the neurons that were so jammed up in my head now floating free like tiny islands in my brain matter.

Dr. Gelman asks me about my mood change after the second treatment. I can't really tell the difference between the first ECT and the second. Maybe I feel slightly better. It's kind of like the fine line of distinction between your first beer and your second. After each treatment, my brain tension is almost gone and the pressure inside is reduced. It's as if a masseuse has worked the knots and kinks out of my brain. I'm focused on the dramatic relief of being able to breathe.

Even though physically my sense of balance is quite off, emotionally I've never felt more stable. It feels like there's an equal amount of cells on the left side of my body and the right. An unusual calm and quiet reverberates throughout my body. I can hear my voice and other people's voices more clearly. The ECT dulls my ability to feel depression or mania. I feel somewhere in the middle, functioning at a normal pace, a pace that seems unusually slow to me. Everyone seems to talk and move slowly. I also feel like my speech has been slowed down considerably, and sometimes I catch myself doing things in slow motion—I'm a calmer version of myself.

But this process is demeaning. I have no real curiosity about my treatment because I'm too confused to ask the doctors questions and don't know what I would ask them anyhow. I have no idea what's really going on once they inject me with Brevital. All I know is that I keep having these shock treatments every other day. I no longer have the capacity to be anxious. I hear everybody around me saying that they hope I won't have to have more than five treatments (five is somehow the magic number) and that I'll be pronounced well enough to leave the hospital and get into a cab and go home. My condition is supposed to be stabilizing more and more after each treatment, but it's difficult for me to assess because of the confusion. My memory worsens with each treatment. I often wonder where I am, what I'm doing here, why people are coming to visit me, and where I live. I'm afraid they're going to keep doing this to me endlessly. Maybe it was a big mistake to sign myself in.

After my third treatment I walk into my bathroom and stare at myself in the mirror. I wonder what the inside of my head looks like by now, if the ECT has actually changed the shape of my brain—really shaken up neurons like the doctors told me it does. I imagine the neurons bouncing around like in one of those big bingo tumblers.

My brain feels like a piece of Silly Putty. I feel tempted to take it out and play with it and think it'll come out my left ear or out one of my nostrils and I'll roll it around in my hands and make some adjustments to it and then reinsert it and correct the manic depression permanently. I believe that this is called do-it-yourself brain surgery. Maybe this is something I should suggest to one of the doctors the next time I go for a treatment. A treatment, singular, sounds like a massage or facial; treatment, by itself, sounds like chemotherapy.

———————

Many of my friends visit me at Gracie Square, including Annike. One afternoon she arrives wearing a brown skirt and blouse, bringing a small gift for me, a drawing of hers, and a candy bar from Germany. She is glad to see that I am feeling better but doesn't like the course of treatment or the hospital environment for me. "You've got to get out of here," she says. "I'll be out soon," I tell her. "You don't need to be in here," she says. I ask her about the D.A.'s office. She tells me that she seems free from any prosecution, and I'm relieved that they're not pursuing an indictment. I didn't think they would. Our meeting is very brief, but it is good to see her. I don't think she realizes how sick I am.

There's not much to do in the hospital. I talk a lot on the phone to friends and otherwise lie in bed and think of stupid things like how many chickens were used to make all the chicken salad sandwiches I've ever eaten in my life and how many eggs were used to make all the egg salad sandwiches I've ever eaten and how many tea bags were used to make all the iced teas I've ever drunk. I write the numbers down on a pad. Very important. And maybe someone will give me a dollar for each one of those chickens, eggs, and tea bags. Or maybe someone will send me to a mental hospital just like this one.

Sometimes I lie in bed wondering if putting my head in the microwave for thirty or forty-five seconds wouldn't do the same thing as the ECT. I guess it's my fault for not asking enough questions about exactly what's going on in the operating room with those electrodes and that voltage. But no, I'm hopeful that I'm making progress, that the depression is leveling off and I'm on the road to recovery.

Michael and Amanda, my friends from the ward, come to my room to visit me. They look like a happy couple on vacation in hospital gowns. But just this morning they were hooked up and jolted with 200 volts. It's amazing. They ask me if I want to play backgammon. I tell them I hate backgammon. I hate the name. I hate the triangles. So we don't play. They pull up some chairs. "Cool sweats," Michael says. "My sister gave them to me," I tell them. Michael's a lawyer. Amanda's a senior at college. There's a long silence. We all just stare at one another and start laughing because we're sitting around in our robes with nothing to do. "Let's play backgammon," I say.

My parents have brought me a huge stack of books and magazines, but I have difficulty reading and can only look at the pictures. I read a paragraph and then forget what I've read, reread it, and then forget it again. The fashion layouts and the advertisements are easy for me to digest. My poor memory frustrates me, and I don't know when and if it's going to come back. I only remember who has visited or called or who has sent flowers because I keep a journal I've brought with me because I've been warned that I will probably forget everything.

One afternoon, about a week into my stay and a few hours after I have rested following a treatment, my father takes me for a walk outside the hospital. I'm wearing my Ralph Lauren sweatpants. I have been indoors for about five days, so I have to adjust to the street noise and the bright light. The city smells wonderful compared with the mental-hospital odor, and I breathe in the smell of hot dogs from the cart on the corner. It's a beautiful day. I shuffle across the streets, not paying attention to red lights and stepping in front of cars. My father pulls me back several times. We go to a gardening store and find a flat, gray, smooth stone with the word *create* engraved in it. It fits into the palm of my hand. Create. I guess I think it will somehow inspire me to write in my journal, or think, or dream, or maybe just recover more quickly. I'm not exactly sure what I think. But it means "do something while you're here." Or maybe it just means "I'll get better soon."

I like the smoothness of the stone. My father buys it for me. It is my good-luck charm for my hospital stay, and I put it on my night table. That night, before I go to sleep, I rub it between my hands and pray that I will get better quickly. The following morning, after I wake up, I realize that the stone's missing. I can't find it anywhere. Since I am horribly confused from yesterday's ECT, I assume that I have misplaced it and begin looking all over the room but can't find it. I am particularly disturbed because my memory is failing me and I'm not even sure that my father left the stone with me and think that he might have taken it home. I call him to check. No, he's sure that he left it on my night table. Maybe I threw it in the garbage by accident. No luck. Finally, at lunch hour, when all of the patients assemble in the dining room, I see Rosie, a black schizophrenic patient in her thirties, carrying the stone around with her, showing it off to other patients as if it were a new diamond ring. She's smiling as she shoves it in front of each patient's face. I approach her and ask her where she found it. On the ward a few days ago. I tell her that, coincidentally, I have the same one and I suggest that the one she has might possibly be mine. She refuses to give it back to me, and I ask the nurse to intervene before I attempt to get her to return my stone by force. After all, this is my good-luck stone from my father and I just want it back. I'm not angry at her. She's sick. This is the stone that is going to get me well and get me out of this mental hospital. Rosie refuses to return the stone and barricades herself in her room. It takes three nurses to get her to come out, and they finally make her return it to me. But this game of cat and mouse goes on for days. No matter where I hide the stone—even underneath my pillow—she steals it, and the nurses have to search her room for it. Even when she is caught with the stone, Rosie claims victory, jumping up and down. It ends up being a fun game to kill time on the ward.

I'm looking forward to my fourth and final treatment, because if all goes well, I'll probably be discharged the following day, and I'm not really enjoying my stay at Gracie Square Spa. I'm also hoping that this will be my last ECT treatment ever and that I can be put on a program of medication that will stabilize the manic depression. In the operating room I thank Dr. Wallenstein and tell him I'll be in touch with him. The final ECT is a breeze. I'm already a pro. I feel great the next day and spend it watching television, and packing up my things, and saying good-bye to my shock buddies and the nurses. At lunch Lena asks me if I feel I am cured. Her question surprises me because she's been ill for so long and it seems as though four electroshock treatments have done the trick for me. I tell her that I am feeling better than when I came into the hospital. "That's how I felt," she tells me. This worries me. Will I be coming back soon, too? I'm feeling guilty for leaving the group behind, but there's no reason to hang around. The next day, when it's time for me to leave Gracie Square and one of the nurses escorts me down in the elevator, Rosie stays behind, watching me as I leave the ward, the stone clutched in my hand

My father brings me home and I reacquaint myself with my apartment. I'm not really sure it's mine. It feels as if I've been away on vacation for a few months, and I have a very vague memory of where I've been and none of the actual ECT. I'm completely exhausted. I unpack my bags and try to make myself comfortable but feel incredibly out of place, as though I've crossed a few time zones and just returned from Tokyo. Ten days in the hospital seems like it was crammed into one afternoon. I spend the entire weekend in bed, unable to move my body. On Monday I drag myself out of bed to go to work, and the crowds of people on the subway overwhelm me. I'm suffocating. Going back to my job at CASES feels like a huge mistake. There's no way that I'm ready for this. When I walk into the office, everybody looks at me kindly, and I just smile. They all know that I've been hospitalized, and the director had no choice but to allow me the time off. I sit down at my desk and just stare at "Page Six" of the New York Post until I'm called into my boss's office. He asks me to have a seat. He looks concerned, and I assume he's going to give me a pep talk, but instead he gently lets me know that he has to let me go because things aren't working out. I'm relieved. I know that I'm barely even capable of sorting paper clips from rubber bands. I stand up, thank him, and walk out. I go back to my office and organize my Rolodex, some files, and my briefcase and say a brief good-bye to the friends I've made in the last couple of months. I go upstairs to Human Resources to take care of the details of my departure. I'm thrilled to be leaving. I get into the subway and head home. When I get into my apartment, I fall onto my bed and drift into a deep sleep until one in the morning.

Fortunately, I qualify for unemployment and disability through my employer, which covers a significant part of my monthly bills. My parents continue to pay my psychiatric and psychotherapy bills. That week we have a family meeting with Dr. Marks to discuss a strategy for my post-ECT and post-firing situation. She recommends that I see a career counselor named Dr. Valerie Pincus, and I set up an appointment for the following week. Continually hopeful that somebody will have the answer for me, I never turn down a suggestion.

Dr. Pincus's office is down in the Village, a brand-new part of town for my mental health care! She is in her midforties, a Bohemian type with long graying hair that she wears pulled back. We spend some time testing my skills and discussing the right job situation for me. "What is it that you like to do?" she asks me. "Well," I say, "I've just had four electroshock treatments. I had to stop five or six people on the street to ask for directions just to get here. What I like to do best is counterfeit paintings, so I think I'm the ideal candidate for just about any job." She laughs. How can anyone imagine that I can return to work now? This is fucking ridiculous. Why didn't the doctor warn me that processing information would be so difficult? Remembering names, numbers, directions, addresses, and details is utterly impossible. I could hardly mop floors at a McDonald's. It's humiliating. What can this woman possibly suggest for me? All I can hear coming from her mouth are terms like "communications," "language skills," "media," "journalism," "creative"—none of this crap means anything to me. They're just words floating in space around her office, around my head, and superimposed across her face. I need to recuperate from this manic-depressive illness. I need bedrest badly. I need to lie underneath my sheets and blankets for weeks. Please just let me sleep this off.

I keep up my doctors' appointments for the next few months and start making a dent in my 250-hour community-service requirement at St. Clare's Hospital. I help plant a roof garden for the patients, an extremely gratifying project that also allows me to be outside; run errands to the deli and the newsstand for them; and do office work for the program director. St. Clare's is a refuge for me, allowing me to escape my home detention for up to eight hours a day. The AIDS ward is very old, and I go from room to room, asking if any patients need any errands done or want any magazines or food from the store. Tanya, a very heavy black woman in her forties with AIDS, with close-cropped bright red hair, is lying on her side in her bed, smiling at me. "Blue eyes, come here," she says. "Could you get me some Doritos or Cheez Doodles, please, okay?" she asks. She reaches into her wallet and takes out $2. "Do you want anything to drink?" I ask her. "No, thanks," she says. She is watching the television, which is six inches from her face, and I tell her she is going to go blind looking at the screen. She motions me out the door. At the corner bodega the Doritos are $1.69. I want to buy her the Cheez Doodles, too, so I chip in the rest. When I return Tanya looks surprised. "I bought one and stole the other," I tell her. Then I sit down in the armchair and tell her I'm a criminal and that's why I'm doing volunteer work here. "Check out my ankle," I say, pointing to my bracelet. When she sees this, she starts laughing. She pushes the television back, props herself up in her bed, and says, "Now you've got to tell me, honey, what a nice boy like you did to get yourself in such a mess." "I'm not quite sure," I say. "C'mon, you can tell Tanya," she says, munching on the Doritos. I explain that a friend and I made copies of original paintings the artist didn't even paint himself and sold them to galleries in Japan for full price. "And can you believe, all he did was sign the paintings?" I say. "Shit, I could do that," Tanya says, and she laughs like she hasn't laughed in years.

Electroshock Addict

May 22, 1995.
This morning I stepped on the scale and was shocked: 245 pounds. I've gained sixty-five pounds in two years. I'm lazy about cooking for myself and rely on ordering in takeout food—Chinese, Mexican, Thai, Indian, pizza, and stuff from the local diner across the street. Luckily I can afford it on my disability payments (I have qualified for monthly support) and help from my family. Having my meals delivered to my front door makes me feel like a prisoner having his food pushed through a slot in his cell. But maybe the scale is wrong.

June 2, 1995.
I'm very comfortable living on the inside and don't even look forward to the four-hour breaks. In fact, I find myself becoming a bit agoraphobic on the streets, preferring the safety of my apartment.

June 14, 1995.
Distance and time run my life. I fight depression by aggressively scheduling activities and allow myself to venture as far as Soho for dinner. Coming back, the cab gets stuck in traffic and I'm thirteen minutes late. The phone rings when I get in the door—the ladies in Boulder nail me. Luckily I only get a warning from my P.O., but after this my fear of being late is transformed into neurotic earliness—I'm constantly looking at my watch and leaving places excessively early to get home in time.

June 30, 1995.
My manic depression rages out of control; I'm staying awake for two or three days straight, having sex with prostitutes (financed by my disability income), drinking heavily, and experiencing para-

noid and suicidal thoughts as well as visual hallucinations—
mostly sharp knives and razor blades slicing my tongue but also
imagining all types of strange objects in the apartment. I watch a
shirt button grow to the size of a tire and roll out of my apartment down Broadway. I see people standing in my bedroom with
perforations around their outlines.

I have been cooped up in the apartment all morning until
noon, when I have my official four-hour period to spend outside.
At twelve on the dot, I rush over to Zabar's for a bagel and lox,
which I wolf down while I stare out and watch the crowd on
Broadway, contemplating how I'm going to spend the rest of my
time out. Nobody seems to be in a particular rush to get anywhere. I thought I had a million things I wanted to do, but now I
can't think of a single one. I'm convinced I've become just as
happy being a prisoner indoors. But I take a walk down to Riverside Park, because everybody tells me it's a good idea to "take a
walk down to Riverside Park." I see all the mothers and nannies
playing with their children and their charges, imagining when my
day will come to have kids. Then I come home. I'm much happier
here. I have my kitchen, my bathroom, my bed, my telephone,
my stereo, and my television. And nobody's watching me. I've
been under house arrest for almost three months, and it's getting
tedious. I'm lonely. And constantly horny. I just want to be
touched and to get off. It's a pretty compulsive urge. I usually can
get away with watching a porn video or looking at a magazine and
jerking off, but today I'm in the mood for something live. It's like
being hungry and captive in the jungle, surviving on plants and
leaves and knowing that you'll be dining on a steak dinner when
you're finally rescued. There is the sense that the urge needs to be
satisfied immediately; it's got to happen within a half hour. Most
of the pleasure is in the mystery and danger of the experience. I
want to hire a masseur/escort to come give me a rubdown. I
check the classified sections of *Next* and *HX*, the local gay magazines, and a few ads with photos look pretty good. A few porn
stars, but that will cost $300 or so, and with disability as my only
income, I'm just looking to spend $150. I see an ad for a guy

named Rex, with a black-and-white photo of a shadowed smooth torso that looks nice and the words "AUSSIE, MASCULINE, HANDSOME, HUNG, BI." He also includes his measurements, height, and weight (six feet one, 190 pounds), and his phone number. I call the number and start leaving a message on his answering machine when I hear him pick up. "Hello, this is Rex," he says with a strong Aussie accent. "Rex, I'm calling about your ad. Are you available today for a massage?" I ask him. "At about five. Were you interested in coming here? I'm in midtown on the West Side," he says. "No, I'd rather you come up here. I'm at 81st and Broadway," I answer, tugging on my ankle bracelet and hoping he makes house calls. "It's a full-hour massage for $150," he says. "I'm very good-looking, well-built, blond, twenty-seven years old, and have been doing massage for five years in Sydney." "Sounds great," I say, then I give him my address and wait. My buzzer rings at exactly 5:00 P.M., and I wait for Rex to come up. I open the door, and he's great-looking. He seems a little out of place in New York—he definitely looks Australian. I take his jacket, show him around the apartment, give him the money, then lead him into the bedroom. Then I deal with the issue of the ankle bracelet. "I should show you this," I say, pointing to the ankle bracelet. "Do you know what it is?" I ask him. "No, can't say I do," he responds. "Well, I'm under house arrest, which means I can't leave this apartment. It's a step up from being in prison. I just didn't want to frighten you, okay? And don't worry, I didn't kill anybody. So just massage around it." I strip naked except for this small black box and strap on my left ankle and lie down on my stomach. I can see him from the corner of my eye; he has a solid body. I feel his hands on my neck and shoulders. He's got a great touch. This is just what I need. "You are my prisoner," he says as he squeezes my shoulder muscles. I don't say anything. "You are my prisoner," he says again. "What are you talking about?" I ask him. "I thought you might want to get into a prisoner fantasy," he says. "I just want a massage," I respond. "I definitely don't want to fantasize about being a prisoner!" I laugh. He goes into the bathroom and comes out wearing a white towel. He is carrying a bottle of baby oil and looks like he's been photographed by Bruce Weber. I'm waiting for him to take off his towel. "Not so quickly," he says. "This is my pool-boy fantasy." He's massaging my lower back and then works his way down my butt to my legs and turns me over. "Now take the towel off your pool boy. That's good," he says. "Do we have to do this fantasy thing?" I ask. "No, not at all," he says. He drops his towel, and standing in front of me is a very hot-looking Aussie. He walks around the bed and lies down next to me, and we jerk off in tandem. And then comes that horrible feeling of guilt and shame because I've paid for this experience with this man who is a complete stranger and totally wasted my money. Quickly, I escort him to the door making small talk, wishing I had never called him.

I'm hanging out with people from my past and coming up with ridiculous ideas to make money. The medication doesn't seem to be doing much good. Dr. Wallenstein believes I should start the ECT again on a weekly outpatient basis—he refers to it as "maintenance," which reminds me of the term "tune-up." At this point I'm ready to believe ECT will bring some balance back into my life, because it did once for a while. In August I have my first maintenance treatment. It's no different from the others. My father brings me to Gracie Square, carrying a bag with a turkey sandwich and a Diet Coke for me to have after my treatment. The sandwich tastes delicious. That evening I host a tenants' meeting in my apartment for twenty people as if nothing had happened that morning, and I feel like I seem totally clear-headed to my neighbors, although it's a struggle to pay attention. I miss a lot of what is said. I have the treatments weekly, on Fridays, for the next four months. After each treatment, it's always the same routine that puts me at ease: I slowly reacquaint myself with my apartment, eat, try to get in a comfortable position (the surfaces always seem so hard), and take a nap. The goal is simply to get my brain functioning again at a normal speed.

Sometimes I think I'm addicted to the Brevital and the ECT

process. I rearrange my schedule so that a treatment falls on my birthday. It feels like a wonderful gift to myself. I start believing that electric current purifies me. I become addicted to the rituals—fasting the night before, driving across Central Park to the hospital in the early morning, connecting to the machines that monitor my vital signs, closing my eyes and counting backward. It's an oddly religious experience. It's my meditation, my yoga, my tai chi.

On the Town

In the middle of August, a while after Jonathan returned to Lauren and Nicole in Denver after a separation, he calls me and tells me he is leaving Lauren. Can he come stay with me in New York? Without asking too many questions or becoming too involved, I tell him that he is more than welcome. I guess I've now officially taken sides, but I will do anything for Jonathan. He's been such a good friend for years, and he really has no other place to go. As a result, Lauren accuses me of ruining her marriage; it's many years before she speaks to me again. Soon the two buddies are finally reunited. When he arrives I send him on a mission to pick up a pizza and some beer for us because I'm still under house arrest and can't go out. Over dinner we both recount what we've been through over the last two years and manage to have a couple of laughs. Jonathan tells me about some of the places he's stayed in and describes the characters he's met along his way: a beautiful Southern blonde who has gashes on her arms starting from her wrists and ending, rather symmetrically, on each bicep; a guy who looks like a movie star who spends hours at a time lying in the sun and takes 60 milligrams of Prozac a day; a sex addict who is forced to surrender his collection of pornography—"a collection which would, I might add, put yours to shame," Jonathan says. Most recently, Jonathan has been living in Boston, working for two lesbians in a flower warehouse. I reminisce about Allison and my Kostabi period: jetting around the world, wads of cash in the freezer, spending recklessly, my trial, and my months at Esmor. On Friday he comes with my father and me to Gracie Square Hospital. After the treatment he covers his mouth with his hand and looks in amazement at my "mummylike" condition. He can barely keep himself from laughing.

Two weeks after Jonathan arrives, 152 days after my house arrest began, I yank the Home Escort out of the wall and return it to Probation. Mr. Henry removes the monitoring device from my ankle. I lift up my pant leg, and he clips the rubber strap with heavy-duty scissors. My ankle feels light. I've been carrying that metal box around for five months. I want to jump up and down and scream, but it's not the appropriate place. I can't wait to get out of his office and onto the street. I've been locked up every single night for five months. I just want to stay out all night. Jonathan, Annike, and I go to Florent at about 3:00 A.M. for dinner and stay until about 6:00 A.M. I'm amazed at how aware I am of the time—I keep checking the clock on the wall. It's the first time in several years that all three of us have been together, and we have quite a few good laughs sharing Kostabi stories from the past. It's like a homecoming reunion.

When in Rome

November 17, 1995.
The mania is still alive and kicking, and tonight I'm looking for subversive fun. I'm out with a couple of friends at Rome, the club of the moment in Chelsea, which is packed, and I'm working on my sixth or seventh vodka tonic and having difficulty standing up. I'm also having a hard time breathing because everyone is blowing smoke in my direction, and I can't hear well because of the cacophony of music and conversation. Some L.A. actor type named Max is keeping me propped up, and I've been successfully freaking him out with tales of electroshock therapy, particularly the parts about the electrodes, the bite block, the 200 volts, and the memory loss. Throughout the conversation, he jokingly asks me

to repeat his name. I think he's just trying to pick me up. I go along with the game and purposely screw up, but I'm actually so drunk, I'm really having a hard time remembering it. Ben? Sam? He's laughing loudly, and we're making lots of noise. He guzzles down his beer, and brings me another vodka tonic, and pulls me by the arm to the back of the bar to check out what's going on. In the back room, someone is dancing on top of the bar, and a lot of guys and girls and even a band of transvestites are crowded around him. A gap opens in the crowd, and I recognize that it's Greg, who attracts a pretty big audience here on the weekends. The room is overheating from the lights and all of the people crammed in it, and I can see the smoke rising to the ceiling and my scalp is sweating and Max is wiping the sweat off his forehead with his T-shirt. He's pointing at Greg and smiling and leans toward me to say something, but I can't hear. Greg is several feet up on the bar, not too far away. He's bare-chested, wearing a baseball cap and a pair of black Versace jeans that are unzipped and hanging loosely on his hips. He has a perfectly sculpted chest, smooth skin, and tousled blond hair. He moves slowly across the bar, carefully stepping around a maze of martini glasses and beer bottles like a kitten, looking at nobody in the audience and kind of half smiling at everyone. He doesn't really dance at all, he just stands and poses, then moves on until he circles around the whole bar. He lets his pants fall to his ankles, revealing a jockstrap and an incredible ass and tan line. His ass is round, hard, and smooth. His cock looks huge in the jock, and he puts his hand inside and gently strokes it. Then he teases the crowd as he gets down on his hands and knees and crawls across the bar like some overgrown toddler. Guys with greedy hands shove dollar bills in his jock. He never flinches; he's like a robotic sex god. I take a $5 bill from my wallet, put it underneath his jockstrap, and stare right into his eagle eyes, expecting some kind of response, but nothing happens. He's from another planet. What does he do in real life anyway? Does he take it from behind or on his back? Does he like tuna and tofu? I want to know, but I'm too frightened to approach him. After he finishes his routine, he jumps down off the bar and walks over to a group of kids in the corner. As Max and I look at each other in awe, he joins them, half naked, for a drink and a cigarette, as if his performance never even took place. We turn our backs and walk over to the bar, and Max gets us both a shot of vodka.

Lox Around the Clock

Sometimes after my ECT treatment I feel like I can just go about my usual daily routine without giving myself any time to recuperate or even rest for an hour or two. I make plans to meet my friend Brian for a 2:00 P.M. lunch at Lox Around the Clock, a diner on 21st Street, after a noon treatment. Feeling a little groggy and light-headed, I hail a cab outside Gracie Square Hospital and direct the driver to Live Bait, a bar on 23rd Street. When I arrive, Brian is nowhere to be found. I'm frightened. Finally, when it dawns on me that I'm in the wrong place, I find my way to Lox Around the Clock, which is right nearby but seems like it's hundreds of miles away. My legs feel heavy, and I'm confused about the time and place and having difficulty remembering where I just came from. When I arrive at Lox Around the Clock, I see Brian waiting at the bar. I shuffle up to him, and he looks frightened. "What the fuck did they do to you?" he asks as politely as possible. "You look like hell," he adds. But I'm feeling pretty happy. His eyes are wide open, and he's covering his face. I don't know how to calm him down. "What's wrong?" I ask. I try to compose myself and pull it together. I'm speeding a bit. I sit down at the bar and order an Amstel Light. I start telling the bartender about my ECT and show him the bruises underneath my bandages from the IV on my right arm. "Look, look at my bruises. I had electroshock therapy this morning," I tell him. "Do they still do that?" he asks me. "Sure," I reply. He keeps pouring drinks and talking to other customers but is fascinated with where I've been this morning, while on the other hand Brian is mortified and embarrassed to be seen with me in this condition and attempts to stop me from talking to the bartender. "Andy, he's busy," Brian says. "He really doesn't care. Please don't do this now." He rushes us through lunch, gets the check, puts me in a cab, and directs the driver to my apartment, in case I attempt to make any crazy detour.

Mutt and Jeff

When our funds begin to dwindle, Jonathan and I finally decide that it's time to pool our talents and resources and resurrect Ivy League Painters. We are an inimitable team, the Mutt and Jeff of the contracting world. We also get a gig working for the "Intelligencer," the gossip column of *New York* magazine. I play snoop and make calls around town, researching items about writers, politicians, actors, and models (we report that a well-known model stuffs his briefs), and Jonathan writes them up. We do this for about six months, scraping together just enough money to live on the Upper West Side. We go out drinking quite a bit with friends and are popular on the dinner-party circuit. Dinner parties are the perfect venue for us because they provide us with what we both need: free food, alcohol, and a good audience. We're invited one evening to the apartment of Suze Yalof, a fashion editor at *Glamour* magazine, who has also invited a group of other people for a dinner party. We both show up a little late, making a loud entrance and announcing ourselves as if we are the guests of honor. Suze gives us both a beer to start our night (she didn't know we had already had two each). Everybody is sitting around drinking cocktails, and we begin telling stories of our day's events—there are absolutely no boundaries. We're a great comedy team, Jonathan playing off my weaknesses and teasing me about all of my medications, electroshock treatments, and prison experiences, me poking fun at him for his great belief in AA and his joblessness. We tell funny stories about some of our painting jobs and our gossip-column experiences. We recount the most irrelevant details of our childhoods. Our speech roams from intelligent to crazy to silly to lewd in seconds. The guests are trying to keep up with the speed of our crazy routine. Our energy is magnetic. We are the two misfits living together, trying to make sense of our lives, and entertaining our audience with our illnesses.

Sometimes I feel as though I've taken on the responsibility of caring for Jonathan as a child or a spouse, and I'm barely able to take care of myself. He takes care of me, too. I take him to an attorney to get advice about his divorce. Our relationship becomes very intense—I've never had such a good friend—and we rely on each other for support as we slowly fall apart together. I'm holding on to him so I don't fade away. Jonathan is also seeing Dr. Fried, and we see Dr. Marks together on one occasion because there's some tension between us. We can't make a move without each other. We share all of our meals, go to the movies together, accompany each other to parties. I fear being separated because now I have somebody to care for me and somebody that I can care for, and the only other people he has any real contact with are his mother in Washington and his daughter, whom he visits in Denver. He also visits Mr. O'Neal, a ninety-year-old drunk who lives upstairs in the building. They drink blackberry brandy together in the middle of the day and talk for hours. I don't know how he even understands Mr. O'Neal's English through his thick brogue. But Jonathan continues to accompany me to the ECT treatments, which become as routine as dental cleanings.

Late one night Jonathan and I are sitting in the kitchen when we begin arguing over a silly issue—money, or rather our lack of it. We've never had a fight before. But this time, for some reason, I provoke him physically until he retaliates by roughing me up and punching me in the face a couple of times. There is plenty of blood, and I am badly bruised. I'm shocked by how violent both of us become. Unfortunately, the next morning I have an appointment with my probation officer and have a lot of covering up to do. I wear a pair of dark sunglasses and I explain that I was mugged at my ATM the night before. She doesn't seem to question the story. Jonathan and I call Dr. Fried to see if she will meet with us that afternoon and serve as a mediator. She's amazed to see us coming in this condition. In a forty-five-minute session she comes to the obvious conclusion that the two of us are not well enough to be living together and need to be taken care of by healthier people. It is probably best that we separate. The next day Jonathan's mother comes to pick him up and take him home to Washington. I never speak to Jonathan again.

Alternative Healing

After Jonathan's departure I feel particularly desperate for an immediate "cure" to my manic depression. I don't think the ECT and medication are working, and I don't have Jonathan to fall back on. I am open to anything, and people suggest just about everything to me. The number-one suggestion is probably exercise. It isn't a bad suggestion, but there are some days that I can't even make it downstairs to check my mailbox, so I don't feel I can count on myself to exercise every day. One friend suggests a meeting with a well-known Kabbalist, one with an acupuncturist, and another with a dominatrix, and I try them all in a period of three weeks. I actually believe that each holds the key to curing my illness. The Kabbalist, a man in his midforties, instructs me to read certain passages of the Scriptures with him and counsels me. He has me convinced that I am somehow possessed by the devil. This does not work for me, and I do not return to see him. The acupuncturist is a tattooed lesbian who lectures me on meridians and sticks needles into my ears until I scream so loud she is forced to take them out. I quickly pay her the $100 fee (minus $10 for my insurance coverage) and never look back. Miss Joanna, the dominatrix, greets me at her door with a small child. Her nanny takes the child to another room, and we talk about a program of wellness. I discuss my illness, and she seems to have a real understanding of manic depression. She suggests nipple piercing and spanking for $150 an hour. I tell her that I don't have time today for a session and that I'll have to schedule something later in the week. I leave her apartment, hail the first cab I see, and throw away her number. But what I really want is a healthy diagnosis. I don't want to be a manic depressive. I call Dr. Heller, a psychiatrist on the Upper West Side, referred to me by a friend. When I sit down in his of-

fice, he asks me for payment up front because of my "legal history." I write him a check for $150. He asks me a battery of ques-
tions; I've heard them all a hundred times. After forty-five minutes
he tells me that I am a manic depressive. The words torture me
still.

Chapter 10

Side Effects

April 7, 1996. New York.

I don't think I've left my apartment more than three times this week—twice to see Dr. Fried and once to pick up my prescriptions. I don't have enough energy to go food shopping, so I order in almost every night. The combination of ECT and adjustments that Dr. Fried has made to my medication has really exhausted me. All I want to do is lie in bed in complete isolation—no television, no music, no telephone, just silence. I crave it. I think this is what best heals me. The thought of putting my face into my pillow is the most pleasant one I can imagine. I am so on edge that the sound of a car horn outside, a noise near my front door, even the ringing of the telephone sends me flying. I can't handle any kind of stimulation. I don't take showers, clean up, cook. I lie around and hope that miraculously I'll feel better the next morning.

April 15, 1996.

I want to start from scratch with a brand-new therapist, while keeping Dr. Fried as my psychiatrist. I don't feel like I'm making any progress with Dr. Marks and I'm motivated to get well, and so I want someone aggressive. Dr. Wallenstein recommends Dr. Carol Sternfeld, a colleague in whom he has a lot of faith. "She's tough and she knows what she's doing," he says, and he tells me I will like her very much.

When I first meet Dr. Sternfeld at her Upper East Side office, I'm greeted by her two dogs, both mutts, who sit in on our session. Immediately I'm drawn to them—Guinness, a mostly black dog who craves attention, and Patch, whose white coat is covered with brown patches. Patch lunges for my hand when I get too close to Dr. Sternfeld. She warns me that he is very protective of her, so I learn to keep my distance from him. I'm quickly struck by Dr. Sternfeld's intense bright blue eyes, which seem to drink in my words. Within five minutes I've decided I want to be her patient. "It's because we both have blue eyes," I tell her. I feel a very strong connection to her. I'm ready to get down to business, and begin talking about my recent experience with ECT and manic depression. "The last year of ECT has sucked every bit of life from me," I tell her. "I feel like my memory's a bit shot and I might be a bit too sedated for this, so I'm not going to be able to give you too much to work with today." "Well, we'll just start slowly from the beginning," she says. Oddly, the past ten years start to unravel effortlessly in the forty-five-minute session with this stranger and the two dogs by her side. It's the first time I ever talk with anyone about my illness with such clarity, which probably comes from the ECT and the medication. Dr. Sternfeld sees me three times a week, and I begin to gain perspective on where I was and where I am now. I still suffer from the manic depression and have problems with medication. I slip into manic episodes for weeks and still find myself in deep depressions that last days. My use of drugs and alcohol isn't helping; it just continues to blur the picture of my mental health. I'm coming to understand the impact the manic depression has had on me over the last ten years, informing nearly every poor choice I made, leading me to risk, danger, and trouble. And I'm coming to understand the reality that my manic depression is a chronic condition. Just last week I was out at 2:00 A.M. on the Upper West Side, searching for a pint of Hershey's chocolate milk at more than five delicatessens. None of them had it. I had to have that brand. I was irritated. How could nobody have Hershey's chocolate milk in the biggest city in the world? I hailed a cab and went thirty blocks to midtown until I found a supermarket that had it. I bought just one and drank it in the cab on the way home. It was so satisfying. But these episodes are less frequent than they've ever been; they're like little blips on the screen, and I've adjusted myself to living with the inconvenience that they cause me.

April 18, 1996.
I call Dr. Wallenstein a few days before a scheduled ECT treatment, which will be my twentieth, an unusually high number. (Most patients are treated in the hospital with four or five rounds over a period of seven to ten days.) I'm feeling particularly lucid. "Dr. Wallenstein, I think I'm done with ECT for now," I tell him. I believe I'm balanced enough that I can work with Dr. Sternfeld, and quite honestly, I know that I'm addicted to the ECT and the premedication. He seems to trust my judgment but tells me to call him if I feel like I'm slipping and want to come back in for maintenance. This strikes me as odd because although I'm rational and capable of making decisions for myself at this stage, if I do slip again I don't think undergoing ECT is a decision I'll actually be able to make by myself.

April 26, 1996.
It frustrates me that I can't just grab the manic depression in my hands and smash it into pieces or burn it or bury it. I've been paralyzed for years, recovering from an intangible illness that cripples my head and now only allows me to function minimally within the confines of my apartment. I'm still more comfortable staying at home, and I hesitate to venture outside a five-block radius in case I have some type of breakdown. I feel only steps away from my mind crumbling and sending me back to the hospital. A year after house arrest, I'm free to come and go as I please now, yet I'm still a prisoner of my apartment. All the trips I take—to my doctors, to the grocery store, to the bank—are scary. They have to be well planned, or else I'm setting myself up for disaster. I'm paranoid about being arrested by cops on the street, attacked by pedestrians, approached by an old acquaintance whom I may not recognize or who may notice changes in my appearance, or being hit by a bus. I want to go outside and see what other people are

doing on the street and what they're buying in the stores, but life is much safer for me inside my apartment.

May 3, 1996.

With the exception of my psychotherapy and psychiatric appointments, I go out only to see friends a few times a week. There are still entire days I don't leave my apartment at all and just go downstairs to check my mailbox. My body—mainly my neck and my limbs—and facial muscles are stiff, I walk with a shuffle, and there's a permanent blank gaze in my eyes, which makes me look like I can stare right through you. I'm like a patient sitting in the lounge of a psychiatric ward watching the doctors and nurses walk by.

May 9, 1996.

I have no idea where the medication regimen is going. Nothing seems to be working again, and the side effects are awful: weight gain, hand tremors, muscle stiffness, dry mouth, diarrhea, and of course the memory loss. These medications are probably going to destroy me. Dr. Fried has me pieced together with thirty-two pills and capsules a day: Wellbutrin, Effexor, Lamictal, Luvox, Neurontin, Zyprexa, and Trazodone. Every week there is something new to mix into the cocktail. I'm utterly hopeless. It's all making me sick. Today I shit in my pants waiting on line for my prescriptions to be filled at the pharmacy. The cashier wouldn't let me use the employee bathroom.

June 8, 1996.

I'm feeling more and more guilty that I can't get myself better. I'm wondering what the ECT actually accomplished and if the medication is really doing anything. Doctors try to treat me through crisis after crisis; my parents watch me stare at them like I'll forever be in this state. I'm their helpless child, only I'm thirty-four years old. We're all confused. When my mania disappears I expect the initial calm of ECT to return, but instead I'm fooled again and thrown into wild depression, an agitated state of melancholy marked with fits of rage. My temper is short, and I argue with everyone who steps in my path. I have an ongoing battle with my landlord over a huge list of problems in my apartment and in the building, and I often become threatening—withholding my rent, calling all of the city housing agencies, starting buildingwide petitions. I beg for the mania to come back because it feels better than this depressive rage. Constantly craving the mania becomes a horrible, frustrating addiction because the price of the euphoria is a bout of depression. This rapid cycling has been going on for years, so I'm accustomed to the frequent mood changes without notice. When I'm in the darkness of the depression I fantasize about my manic memories—getting myself heavily into debt buying clothing, furniture, and paintings, counterfeiting artwork around the world, having sex with anonymous partners, drinking and doing drugs, and even the experience of being a defendant in a criminal case. I am high through all of that and enjoy my crazy lifestyle and put on a show for my friends. Look at me. What would you like to see me do next? Mania isn't nearly as painful as depression, which feels like an awful storm inside my head and leaves me hopeless and despairing.

The Sleeping Dragon

I tell my parents about the lecture I hear by Dr. Frederick Goodwin at Beth Israel Hospital in Manhattan. He's one of the world's foremost authorities on depression and manic-depressive illness, and former director of the National Institute of Mental Health in Washington. Dr. Goodwin talks about manic depression as a chronic illness, but he has a warriorlike approach to treating it that I like. My parents ask me if I want to make an appointment to see him, and I agree to give it a chance. There is a bit of a wait, but in the meantime I complete a case history and take some preliminary psychological tests by mail with one of his social workers. About a month later we head to Washington, in search of the magic cure. Dr. Goodwin is a pensive middle-aged man who meets with me first by myself and later with my parents. He carefully asks me about my psychiatric history and my manic episodes and lows, and I tell him about the current flat, bored, and disconnected feelings inflicted by the medication. "I don't feel like the same person anymore," I complain. "I can't be as funny." I tell him that I don't have the ability to entertain anymore; my jokes don't work. "I'm no longer the life of the party or the center of attention," I say. He scribbles some notes. "Are you drinking alcohol or using drugs now?" he asks me. "Yes, to both," I say. I tell him I'm drinking daily, snorting cocaine and smoking pot on occasion, using inhalants like amyl nitrate, and stepping up my dose of sleeping pills. He tells me that this kind of activity, which is symptomatic of manic depression, is going to get in the way of my recovery. Finally, he calls in my parents and I fear that he'll tell them about the drinking and the drugs. But after the two-hour-long session, he comes to the unsurprising conclusion that I am, in fact, just another statistic—one more manic depressive. He recommends some minor medication changes to Dr. Fried and emphasizes the drug and alcohol issue, which has been ignored for so long because I chose not to make a big deal about it with her, always believing I would just give it up. Now Dr. Fried knows the whole story. I feel like Dr. Goodwin is the last doctor I'll ever need to see, and I'm relieved that he is in general agreement with how Dr. Fried is treating me and that the two have spoken about my future treatment. I leave Washington feeling like I've been given the final diagnosis. There is no reason to search out a fortune-teller, a yogi, a spiritual healer, or a witch doctor. I have manic depression. And the chief expert says so.

With Dr. Sternfeld I start re-creating structure in my life, a life that formerly had no rules, no day, no night. We start by setting a slow and stress-free pace with a schedule that I can follow: a time to go to bed, a time to wake up, a time to shower. During one visit she suggests that perhaps it's time I consider working. I start screaming when she suggests clerking at Barnes & Noble or doing volunteer work. How could she think I'm ready to go back to work? "I'm still sick!" I scream. "You've got to be kidding if you think I'm ready to work!" I have accepted the fact that I'm comfortable doing nothing, that this manic depression has taken control of my mind and body and has every intention of parking itself here for the rest of my life.

A few months later, though, I find myself going through my Rolodex, making some phone calls. I reconnect with former PR contacts and set up appointments with them or people they've referred me to. Soon I'm working on a couple of different PR projects again, even traveling cross-country to meet with clients. It's an entirely different kind of energy this time—rational, sane, healthy. I don't come on like gangbusters—it's a low-key approach to doing PR, but I can still get clients excited. I appear composed, knowledgeable, and determined to get the job done, and, despite my brush with the law in 1993, I still have a good reputation in the business. And I'm helped by the fact that, after trying every possible combination of medications, Dr. Fried has found a cocktail that seems to work well for me for the time being. It consists of 1½ milligrams of Risperdal, an antipsychotic; 750 milligrams of Depakote, a mood stabilizer; 1,200 milligrams of Neurontin, an anticonvulsant; 300 milligrams of Symmetrel, for Parkinsonian syndrome; 30 milligrams of Propranolol, for tremors; 50 milligrams of Benadryl, for muscle stiffness; 2 milligrams of Klonopin, for anxiety; 60 milligrams of BuSpar, also for anxiety; and 10 milligrams of Ambien, a sleeping aid. That's down to a little more than twenty-two pills a day. I can count them out into my hands with my eyes blindfolded. There's an area on my kitchen counter that my friends refer to as my own little pharmacy. The cocktail needs to be tweaked every so often, and I spend a lot of time with Dr. Fried on the phone adjusting dosages, but my moods are starting to stay pretty even.

Throughout this recovery period, I despise manic depression but pretend to be its friend, so as not to set it off. I work with it. I take all the pills at all the right times. I monitor my mood and behavior. I go to sleep on time. I eat well. I avoid stress. I play the good patient. And I don't like any of it. I miss the planes, the trips, the money, the dinners, the alcohol, the drugs, and the sex. My recovery represents a tremendous loss.

When I start feeling like I'm winning the battle and I'm balanced, I get these colossal surges of strength and power, often last-
ing a day or two. I often confuse them with mania. Am I having an
episode, or am I conquering this illness?

The Dragon Awakes

November 27, 1997.
Thanksgiving Day. My parents pick me up at my apartment to
drive to my aunt and uncle's in Connecticut. Dr. Fried has taken
me off Risperdal, the antipsychotic, as an experiment, because of
the severe muscle stiffness, shuffling, and nonblinking. I've gone
four days without it. Before I get into the car I warn my parents
that I'm not feeling well and that my mood isn't going to improve
too much. I don't talk at all during the ride. When we arrive in
Connecticut, I sit by myself in the living room staring at the football game on television. I eat very little. My family is concerned
about me but knows not to make a fuss over my condition, since
that will only upset me. Everybody figures I'm having a bad day,
I'll go home, get some sleep, and be fine in the morning. By the
end of the evening, I've taken so much Klonopin because of my
anxiety (much more than the recommended dose) that I can
barely get into the car. I sleep the entire way back to New York.
That night I'm lying in bed watching television and I look down
and see that my torso, my arms, and my legs are covered with
graffiti—script handwriting, numbers, drawings, nothing I can
quite make out. I realize that as I process thoughts, they get written on my skin, by an invisible hand, until finally there's no room
left. I jump into the shower and start scrubbing my body with a
sponge and Clorox, trying to rub off the hundreds of words, sentences, and drawings covering every inch of my skin. They start
blinking like Christmas lights. After about an hour of scrubbing, I
rinse off my burning skin and I get back into bed, but I'm frightened it's going to return. I don't know what to do next. I call my
friend Bobbie, who lives ten blocks away, and tell her about my
panic. She rushes over at 4:30 A.M. and assures me that there's no

graffiti on my body. She sits with me to try to calm me down, then calls Dr. Fried's pager number, which I know like my Social Security number. While we wait for Dr. Fried to call back, Bobbie stands me in front of the mirror, but I see the intricate designs on my skin. Dr. Fried instructs me to go back on the Risperdal right away. It takes about two days for the medication to take full effect, but I do recover, and Dr. Fried tells me I must stay on it. Plainly, I will never be able to stop taking these medications. Am I more myself on them or less? There's no sense in trying to determine which me is the real me—in the end, I need the medications if I'm to lead a balanced life. I have a chronic illness, and I can't survive without them.

Happy Birthday

January 27, 1998. New York.
It's my thirty-sixth birthday. I meet my friend Jen Copaken for breakfast at the French Roast on Broadway, and over eggs and toast she tells me about a great idea for a screenplay. It's a love story that takes place in Shanghai during World War II; a population of twenty-five thousand European Jews flees the Nazis and resettles there with the help of a courageous Japanese consul in Lithuania. It's 9:30 A.M. and for the first time in years I'm fired up by a creative idea. I'm finding Jen's telling of the story fascinating and her enthusiasm infectious. She's given me something to grab on to. We decide to start researching right away and we work on the screenplay every day for a year. I see Dr. Fried at noon for my monthly appointment, which I had purposely planned for my birthday as a thirty-six-year checkup. It's a playful session; the tone is light. How's your energy? Good. Your sleep? Six to seven hours. Appetite? Normal. She asks me to rate my mood on a scale of one to ten. I tell her eight point five. "Not bad," she says. She checks me for muscle stiffness from the Risperdal. Not great. She examines me for tardive dyskinesia, which can be a side effect of some of the antipsychotics. It usually starts out with a wormlike movement of the tongue, and later it can develop into involuntary

movements of the head, neck, trunk, and extremities. Once it takes hold, it's permanent, even if you stop taking the medication. But I'm fine. I passed the test. Maybe I should increase the Benadryl because of the muscular stiffness from the Risperdal, she thinks. "Yes, take another at bedtime," she tells me. I ask her about dropping the Depakote, the mood stabilizer, to see what happens. The less I'm on the better; it blows me up like a balloon. "Not now," she advises me. She wishes me a happy birthday and reminds me it's been four years since she started seeing me. I'm amazed it's been so long and impressed she's been able to handle me this whole time. So many appointments, crises, and daily phone calls. She sits down and writes me prescriptions and warns me not to stay out too late or do anything crazy. I leave feeling I've had the 25,000-mile tune-up. After making an appointment to see her in February, I spend the rest of the afternoon having a massage and getting a haircut. At home I answer phone calls from family and friends wishing me a happy birthday. I feel like it's a happy birthday for the first time in many years, maybe since I turned thirteen and had my bar mitzvah celebration. My friends Brian and Joe take me to Vong for dinner, and I'm glad to be out. Brian, who enjoys good wine, orders a Pomerol Guillot and a St.-Estèphe Château Haut-Marbuzet; I'm hardly drinking, but I taste both, and they have more richness than any glass of wine I can remember. I remind myself that I'm sober. I leave the restaurant feeling satisfied, get into a cab, and am under the covers by 12:30 A.M., thinking about the twenty-five thousand Jewish refugees in Shanghai.

February 3, 1998.
Today, before she is executed in Huntsville, Texas, pickax murderess Karla Faye Tucker requests a final meal of a salad and a peach. What can she be thinking? The meal I had before my last ECT treatment—and I didn't know for sure it was going to be my last—was two cheeseburgers, onion rings, and a Coke, followed by Entenmann's chocolate-covered donuts and milk before bed. If Dr. Wallenstein electrocuted me I was going to die happy. That treat-

ment was a scary one—I saw myself as a Keith Haring figure, with flashes of energy shooting from my body and the sounds of loud drumming in the O.R. keeping my heart pumping and my oxygen circulating—and I was scared I wasn't going to make it through this one and the image and the sounds wouldn't disappear.

Blind Date

My friends Deb and Paul Kogan are the best matchmakers in Manhattan. They've made three matches that resulted in marriage and brought together a handful of couples who have stayed together for more than six months. Once they were even daring enough to set me up on a blind date with a friend while I was in the middle of electroshock treatment. Now they want to fix me up with Jody, a woman they met at a friend's summer house and think I'll like. Deb gives me all the necessary background: she went to a small school somewhere, worked in the Peace Corps in Uzbekistan for two years, and is pretty and funny. Sounds interesting. This is my first real blind date in a long time. We decide to meet at Henry's on the Upper West Side at 7:30 P.M. I get there fifteen minutes early and drive myself crazy wondering if each woman walking by is Jody. No, too tall. No, too WASPy. No, too young. Maybe that's her. We spot each other looking for an unfamiliar face outside the front door and introduce ourselves. Over Heinekens she asks me about what I do; Deb has only told her I used to be in public relations and in the art business and that now I'm working on a book. Unavoidably, the subject of manic depression and electroshock comes up. She has no negative reaction. Good thing, since it's the only thing I think I know how to talk about after five years, with the exception of my brush with the law. Luckily these stories seem to entertain her. I definitely need another beer at this point but force myself to be strict and have a Diet Coke. But she goes ahead and orders another drink. I really miss how alcohol eases my ability to interact and converse. Jody tells me some great stories from Uzbekistan, like having to drink her neighbor's awful homemade vodka every night to stay warm and being bombarded by snowballs hurled at her by young boys as she walked through town. This is the first time in years I've socialized in such a normal way. When I get home that night, I'm so relieved and energized that I return to an old favorite habit: I make a list of things to do in the morning. The list seems so normal and do-able compared with my old lists. I can walk to the corner instead of hopping on a plane.

1. Toothpaste, toothbrush, shaving cream and deodorant
2. Pick up prescriptions
3. Pick up twelve rolls of color film
4. Leave keys with Deb and Paul
5. Buy new knapsack at Eddie Bauer

I even feel that I'd like to see Jody again, and we have dinner a few more times. But I let things go, I don't call her back. I'm scared entering into a relationship, no matter how tentatively; I'm not ready to be intimate with a stranger. At the same time I realize I'm making a mistake by letting her go. And my biological clock is telling me I want to be married and carrying a kid on my shoulders. But this one will not make Deb and Paul's wedding record list, and I'm a little pissed it didn't work out. But I know that whoever the right woman for me is, she's going to have to be incredibly compassionate, and I'm fully confident that it's just a matter of time and will happen when I'm ready.

Journey to Paradise

May 18, 1997. Galápagos Islands.
I'm snorkeling off the coast of San Cristóbal Island, in the warmest water I've ever swum in, skimming about fifteen feet below the surface. I follow a school of bright red and black fish—there must be three hundred of them—until they dart quickly behind a rock and I can't keep up with them any longer. Then from the corner of my eye a school of neon blue fish, about five hundred of them, come swimming past me, looking like a flag waving in the wind.

It's so quiet and bright down here. I come to the surface and spot my dad floating twenty feet away. His nose and cheeks are getting sunburned, and I warn him for the second time to put on more sunblock. I guess that's my job as the overprotective son on the trip. It feels good to be looking after him for a change. We swim to the beach and crouch down to watch shiny black sea lions huddling on the rocks, thousands of wrinkled iguanas lounging in the sun, and boobies doing their awkward mating dances. These animals have no fear of us. The sea lions lollop right up to us and roll over on the beach, eager to play, covering their slick black coats with grains of sand. Then they swim into the ocean and come back out, glistening with a fresh shine. We're thousands of miles from Manhattan, in the middle of the Pacific, and the beach looks exactly like it must have looked when the HMS *Beagle* landed on San Cristóbal in 1836 with Charles Darwin aboard. This trip to Ecuador to see the Galápagos, the Amazon, and the Andes was a birthday gift I had promised my dad seven years ago, but we had to postpone it, first because my passport was being held by the U.S. government during my legal troubles and then because of my hospitalization and illness. This is the first time I've been out of the country in five years, and although I'm nervous about being away from both of my doctors, I'm also thrilled to be traveling again. And I'm with my dad, so I feel shielded. I'm also armed with a knapsack full of medication, which I keep with me at all times. My dad is having the time of his life, photographing multicolored butterflies in the middle of the Amazon jungle and the crazy Galápagos cacti, which look like wind-twisted sculpture. After exploring the sea and the pure clean beaches, we return by *panga* to the *Parranda,* to sit on deck, have a drink, and wait for the sun to set. It happens too quickly for me each day. Afterward, we eat dinner with two young couples: a poet and a cardiac resident on their honeymoon and a pair of neurologists. Conveniently, there are three psychiatrists on the trip as well, and I feel reassured, like all these doctors are on call for me in this extremely remote place. But I'm also reminded of my illness. I'm dead tired tonight from the sun and snorkeling. My dad looks over at me to see that I'm feeling okay. He's been keeping a close eye on me ever since we left New York, and I've been watching every step he takes, not because of his age—he's in excellent physical shape—but because I'm concerned about him, too. I'm aware that my manic depression has changed my relationship with my father; it's an enemy that we have to battle together. It's brought me closer to my mom and to Nancy, too, but at the same time it's made me more dependent on my family for support at a time in my life when I thought I'd be independent, with a family of my own.

It's about 11:00 P.M., and I go down to our cabin and take out my pills for the evening. I pour them out of their vials into the palm of my hand. Three peach Depakote. One white Risperdal. One brown Symmetrel. Three amber Topamax. Three blue Klonopin. One white BuSpar. One orange Propranolol. One pink Benadryl. One white Ambien. They look like SweeTARTS. I put all fifteen pills on my tongue and take a big gulp of water. The Propranolol, the tiniest pill, the one that keeps me from shaking and trembling and dropping glasses, the one that makes me able to sign checks without slipping off the signature line, gets stuck under my tongue, and I have to maneuver it back onto my tongue and swallow more water to get it to go down. It tastes bitter. I climb into my bed and look out the porthole, and all I can see is ocean and sky. I hear the engines of the ship starting up. As I lie in bed, I'm soothed by the rocking of the ship. I am almost one thousand miles away from the closest continent on my National Geographic map. My father walks in and turns on the bathroom light. The light spills out into the small room.

"Did you remember your medication?" he asks.

"Yeah, thanks for asking, Dad," I say.

"Just checking," he says. "I'm going back up to the deck for a while. See you in the morning." I feel safe in the cabin; it feels like my spaceship has returned from space and is floating in the middle of the Pacific.

A Little Crazy

June 5, 1997. New York.
The return to the city from the pure fantasy of escape in the Galápagos is not as difficult as I had imagined. I still love the smell of
hot tar and bus fumes and enjoy the comforts of air-conditioning,
the telephone, and television. Comparing the beauty of the Galápagos to Manhattan is like comparing a gorgeous naked woman
to one who is wearing layers of clothing in the winter; there is a
certain beauty and mystery to the latter. And both San Cristóbal
and Manhattan seem like such absolute islands to me. Each has
order and structure and is easy to navigate. You can take a boat
around Santa Cruz or the 1/9 downtown to the West Village. I feel
very safe in Manhattan.

July 15, 1997.
Shortly after my return from Ecuador, I feel a bubbling of old
urges and restlessness from the past, and I impulsively fly to Los
Angeles to see if I can put in two full days of appointments and
meetings. It's more of a test than anything else. I get my luggage.
Pick up car at Avis. Check in at Sunset Marquis. Check messages
on answering machine. Meeting with artist interested in represen-
tation at his studio. He's convinced he's Jackson Pollock. His work
is shit and there are so many canvases to go through; I don't know
how to tell him gracefully I'm not interested. So I tell him I have a
dinner appointment and that I'll speak with him soon. I really do
have plans for dinner with my college roommate, his wife, and
their son at their favorite Mexican restaurant. It's odd at first to see
my roommate, whom I met when he was eighteen, with a three-
year-old and his wife, but it makes perfect sense and feels right. Return to Sunset Marquis and hang out at Whiskey Bar for a few
hours. Drink two cranberry spritzers. Smoke two Marlboro
Lights. There are some rowdy girls from Texas at the bar with a
bunch of men, and I'm watching them getting very drunk and
feeling very left out.

July 16, 1997.
I wake up feeling ready for a productive day. Requisite poolside breakfast at hotel: egg-white omelette and fruit salad, $18. Drive to Fred Segal and buy some baby gifts for Annike and her boyfriend, who are living together; she's due in a month. Lunch with former self-help writer/client at the Palm. Drinks at the Mondrian Hotel with a prospective health-industry client who's been referred to me by a former author. Dinner with my father's sister Gloria in the Valley. On the way back, feel like driving past Sunset exit all the way to San Diego (about 130 miles) but only go a few miles past the exit and then turn around and drive back to the hotel. In the past I would have driven all the way to Baja, but I don't need the thrill and just decide to watch television in my luxuriously anonymous hotel room and get to sleep early. Wake up next morning and leave for airport after another egg-white omelette and fruit salad. I've kept myself busy for two days.

When I get back to New York after my two-day L.A. spasm, I wonder if I might be experiencing hypomania, a moderate form of mania in which one exhibits increased energy and rapid speech. Dr. Fried thinks this is probably the case, that I'm definitely not having a manic episode, and she doesn't feel the need to alter my medication. "I feel kind of normal," I say. "Normal, but a little crazy," she says. It's nice to realize that I'm relatively stable and can assess my own condition. After years of trying, I'm able to keep a close watch on my moods.

Group

Group therapy in midtown Manhattan. It feels like a private club meeting every Monday at noon. I'm sitting at a conference table with six other people—men, women, single, married, divorced—with all sorts of common issues—relationship, family, intimacy, work, and communication. At opposite ends of the table sit our two leaders, Dr. Sternfeld and her colleague, who is taking notes. Some of us are drinking bottled water, some are eating salads and yogurts. We all look around the room. Karen starts off the session by talking about her ex-husband, an alcoholic, who continues to call her a year after their divorce. Cheryl talks about her struggle with breast cancer and difficulty as a single mother. Paul is having trouble keeping employees at his company. We ask one another questions as we weave from topic to topic. Tammy, who has a pattern of dating married men, surprises us by announcing that she has finally broken off a long-standing relationship. I talk about my fear of becoming sick again and dependent on my family and how real the possibility seems some days. It's taken me almost a year and a half to figure out that my manic-depressive personality does not define or set me apart in this group. It's a safe place to talk openly about what's on my mind and to get feedback.

A Delicate Balance

This illness requires constant vigilance. After several years of being on medication for my manic depression, I develop an awful cold and sinus condition, so I buy the first over-the-counter medication that I see on the pharmacy shelf and take it every four hours for relief. After four days on the medication, I'm sitting in a diner somewhere on the Upper West Side when I become completely confused about what city I'm in and what day it is. My legs are paralyzed. "Just take deep breaths and drink," my friend Bobbie says. I sip my Diet Coke slowly, but the panic jumps in my veins. I frantically call Dr. Fried on my cell phone, but her message says she's on vacation, so I call her covering doctor, who doesn't respond to my page, infuriating me. Bobbie starts dialing for me because I can't focus on the keypad. My blood pressure is rising and I'm feeling increasingly manic; my thoughts are becoming psychotic. I feel locked inside a globe, like the one I grew up with, showing all of the continents and countries in relief. I'm suffocating underneath South America. I can't hear very well and can't concentrate. I think I'm knocking things over on the table. Bobbie holds my arms trying to calm me down, and I attempt to change my tone and the subject. "How are your parents?" I ask her. "They've been dead for years," she tells me. "Oh, poor Claire and Paul," I say blurrily. I'd forgotten this and apologize to her. Then I leave slurred and hostile messages on Dr. Fried's answering machine. When I try to stand up, energy flows from my torso through my legs and I feel like I'm going to crash through the floor and shoot into the basement. I'm scared enough to feel like I want to be rushed to the hospital, but I don't feel like making a scene. Instead, Bobbie suggests getting some air and returning to my apartment. My legs are stiff, so I shuffle more than ten blocks to my apartment, where we wait for the covering doctor to return my call. He finally calls back three hours later and asks me if I've taken any other type of medication. After lecturing him about his delay in returning my page, I tell him the name of the over-the-counter medication I've taken and he tells me that's the cause of my current condition. He assures me I'm not in any immediate danger and suggests I ride it out for a few more hours until I finally fall asleep. This is just a reminder of how easily I can slip into a manic or psychotic episode because my system has become so sensitive to medication, let alone the interaction between medications. Neither he nor Dr. Fried knows which medication the cold medicine interacted with. I should have been wise enough to ask the pharmacist first. I'm relieved that this isn't going to be a long psychotic episode, but I still have my cold.

Bodega Roses

My niece's birthday is coming up, and I want to find the perfect card for a ten-year-old. She's really grown up so quickly since the day she came home from the hospital, back when I was just getting into trouble selling counterfeit paintings. She knows nothing about that. It's hard to find just the right card for her because she's a very particular kid. I buy her a lava lamp. She'll love it. On my way home I pass a bodega, whose awning shelters row upon row of bright flowers from the February drizzle. I carefully pick out two dozen magnificent white roses for only $8 and carry them home like it's Valentine's Day. But they're just for me. I rummage for the vase that came with the flowers Nancy gave me when I

came home from electroshock treatment at Gracie Square a few
years ago, put my finger under the faucet until the water gets cold,
fill it all the way up, pour in a packet of the magic plant powder,
and then arrange the perfect roses and place them on my cherry-
wood and slate-top desk next to my computer. They no longer
look white against the white walls, but ivory. The stems are bright
green and sturdy, supporting the delicate blooms, which I love to
stroke with my fingers. They feel silky and are almost translucent.
As the days pass, I watch the roses unfold and hear them crackle as
they open. I also notice that the water level is decreasing; they are
thirsty, and I replenish their supply. Is there anything else I can do
for them? I promise to keep them alive until the first day of spring.
The roses open to grand proportions I've never noticed before.
Had I never paid attention? I hear them crackle as I gaze at the
screen and hit the keyboard. I stop what I'm doing and stare at
them to examine them as they expand. Grasping the vase, I turn
the bouquet in a circle and look for the one rose that is really making progress. "There it is," I shout. "That's the culprit." It's standing taller than the rest, and I can actually see it moving in slow
motion. I'm impressed by the beauty of these roses, and all I can
do for them is caress the petals lightly and take care of them.
"Maybe roses need sunlight," I think. The room smells fragrant,
and I am indebted to each of the twenty-four roses.

This morning I wake up early to check my e-mail. When I
look over at the roses, I see that they're no longer ivory—more
beige now, tinged with brown. I try pulling off some of the dis-
colored petals. It helps a little. But they're becoming shapeless
and abstract, no longer the crisp and vital buds I bought a week
ago, and they won't see spring. But I don't need them to stay perfect anymore. They have their own vanishing beauty, and that's
fine with me.

Acknowledgments

I could not have written *Electroboy* or completed my recovery without Jennifer Copaken—a true friend and supporter who inspired me every day for almost two years and continues to do so. I met Jen a year after my last electroshock treatment; I was in a confused state, between memory loss and medications, but she held my hand through the process of writing about my manic depression and ECT. *The New York Times Magazine* published my article about ECT, officially heralding my return after eight long years of retirement. Thank you, Jen.

My deepest gratitude goes to Suzanne Gluck, my überagent at the William Morris Agency, for her belief in *Electroboy* from the first moment she listened to my thirty-second pitch. She was steps ahead of me—in a strange sort of way, she had an overall sense of the book before I did. I was wowed by her speed and enthusiasm. Within two weeks she sold the book to Random House; she wasn't kidding around. A week later, her colleague Alicia Gordon optioned the book for HBO.

Many thanks to Courtney Hodell at Random House for taking the first courageous step in acquiring *Electroboy*. She started from scratch with me and promised that we'd have a book at the end. Courtney allowed me to go where I needed with the manuscript—she made no strict rules—and then started pulling it together and showing me how to make the pieces fit. Her ability to help me tell my story, to make me rethink my experiences and delve into details, was astonishing, and her ongoing patience was enormous. Thanks to her extraordinary assistant, Tim Farrell, for giving the book organization and structure and for his keen editorial insight. He is a true perfectionist. Tim constantly pushed me to rewrite, keeping the pressure on me up until the very last minute.

Jen's work with me didn't stop with that one article on ECT. We spent countless hours in Manhattan coffee shops, where she made lists and drew crazy flow charts for me that took me chapter by chapter. She read and critiqued everything that I wrote, even after she left New York to live in San Francisco with her husband, Todd Yellin, who put up with late-night calls and an emergency visit to the Bay Area.

A very special thank-you to my two primary doctors, for their years of care and concern for me and the time they have invested in helping to keep me as healthy as I am today. I am extremely fortunate to have found both of them. I am also grateful to the six members of my therapy group, who have been together and have supported me for almost three years.

Thank you to my very wise and courageous defense attorney, Stuart Abrams, who fought the toughest battle I'd ever face for me in December of 1993.

Thank you to my sister, Nancy Behrman, who was always there to cry with me and hold my hand and who can always lighten the mood with a good story or some breaking gossip; to Nancy and Nick Davis, my aunt and uncle, who have always shown great interest in and concern for me since I was a small child; and to Ellen Hettinger, a great supporter of me and my family during both the good times and the very difficult ones.

Thank you to Adam Moss for giving me my first writing assignment in New York, at *7 Days,* and the opportunity to write at *The New York Times Magazine.*

Thank you to Hilary Jacobs and Robert Brinkman, two friends who have always shown me great kindness, made me laugh hysterically, and served me great food; to Lucy Lehrer for her friendship and support, especially during my time at Esmor, and for always having the joie de vivre to join me on a bus ride to Atlantic City or a train ride from Paris to Berlin; to Brian Cresto for his friendship, intuition, and great problem-solving advice, and, when it came to *Electroboy*, his gentle criticism; to Christopher Smith for his constant long-distance encouragement, his sense of humor, and his special brand of cynicism; to Jeannette Walls for teaching me to "take it all with a grain of salt" and convincing me on more than one occasion to keep writing; to Melissa Levine and Scott Rosenthal for their nonstop enthusiasm for *Electroboy* and their loyalty; to Deborah Copaken Kogan for showing me the way one year ago and for all of the reinforcement that she and her husband, Paul, provided throughout this process; to Dr. Andrew Elmore for his positive thinking and optimism; to Judy Cramer for her care, interest, and enthusiasm; to Betsy Marino for a lifetime of laughs and for making me feel good about writing about mental illness; to Marilyn Fletcher for keeping close tabs on me and understanding this chronic illness; to Al Lowman, who pushed me to start writing years ago; to Lindley Boegehold, who told me I could write a book; to Elliot Thomson, who told me I should write this book; to Gregory Marro, who understood how difficult this book was to write; to Kenneth Johnson and Garrick, who checked up on me daily; to Robert Adamo, who helped me maintain my positive attitude; and and to Bobbie Freeman, a talented artist and a unique and remarkably giving woman who stuck by me during the darkest hours of my illness.

About the Type

This book was set in Monotype Dante, a typeface designed by Giovanni Mardersteig (1892–1977). Conceived as a private type for the Officina Bodoni in Verona, Italy, Dante was originally cut only for hand composition by Charles Malin, the famous Parisian punch cutter, between 1946 and 1952. Its first use was in an edition of Boccaccio's *Trattatello in laude di Dante* that appeared in 1954. The Monotype Corporation's version of Dante followed in 1957. Though modeled on the Aldine type used for Pietro Cardinal Bembo's treatise *De Aetna* in 1495, Dante is a thoroughly modern interpretation of that venerable face.

BOCA RATON PUBLIC LIBRARY, FLORIDA

3 3656 0366106 8

92 Behrman
Behrman, Andy, 1962-
Electroboy